Praise for *Appealing to Justice*

"Calavita and Jenness provide a subtly texture(
displaying the contradictions of late-modern s(...gal process and
civil rights grow apace alongside an ever-enlarging sphere of punishment and
control. A beautifully written, compelling, and heartbreaking account of the
promise and failure of the rule of law; there is no one better able to tell the
story of these prisoners."

Susan S. Silbey, Leon and Anne Goldberg Professor of Sociology
and Anthropology, Massachusetts Institute of Technology

"*Appealing to Justice* provides unique insight into contemporary 'hyperlegal'
American prisons, analyzing two striking paradoxes: a majority of California
prisoners file formal grievances despite likely staff retaliation and only a
minute chance of success; administrators at all levels offer strong support of
prisoners' rights in general, yet almost invariably deny specific complaints.
The workings of these paradoxes reveal both the deep tensions between legal
rights and carceral control and the profound asymmetry of dispute
processing in this distinctive total institution."

Robert M. Emerson, Professor Emeritus of Sociology,
University of California, Los Angeles

"Jenness and Calavita dispel myths about inmate complaints while capturing
surprisingly candid staff comments regarding their mission, inmate rights,
and the incarcerated. A must-read for those seeking to understand inmate
rights and the need for an independent complaint process. Time for a change?
I think so."

Jeanne Woodford, Former Undersecretary of the California
Department of Corrections and Rehabilitation, and Senior Fellow,
Chief Justice Earl Warren Center, University of California Berkeley
School of Law

"A study of grievance procedures in prisons, *Appealing to Justice* is also much
more. It informs us what it means to be a prison inmate and what it means to
be a correctional officer and administrator. It is at once profoundly
depressing and uplifting. Do not look for simple solutions in this book; it is
filled with complicated truths."

Malcolm M. Feeley, Claire Sanders Clements Dean's
Professor, Jurisprudence and Social Policy Program,
University of California, Berkeley

"Drawing on first-person witness accounts of how legal-rights and carceral logics collide inside the CDCR, this study offers more convincing evidence of the unworkably (con)fused legal, ethical, psychological, social, and institutional cultures of prison—both for incarcerated people and for prison workers—than any number of other studies. Top-rate interdisciplinary scholarship, thoughtful analysis, and smart, sensitive field study make *Appealing to Justice* a powerful exploration of how difficult tough-on-crime legislation has made it to run prisons that are both safe and just."

Doran Larson, Director of the American Prison Writing Archive and the Program in Jurisprudence, Law, and Justice Studies, Hamilton College

"Through engaging prose and evocative evidence, Calavita and Jenness demonstrate how the legal consciousness of prisoners and prison officials reveals and reinforces the incoherence of imprisonment."

Rosemary Gartner, Professor of Criminology, University of Toronto

"This compelling book provides both an illuminating account of life inside twenty-first century American prisons and a pathbreaking analysis of disputing processes in an uncommon place of law. The authors skillfully weave together complex information from interviews and documentary sources to demonstrate powerfully that people in a repressive environment, utilizing a hollow and unresponsive formal process, can nevertheless courageously maintain an insistent rights consciousness."

George Lovell, Harry Bridges Endowed Chair in Labor Studies, Professor and Chair of Political Science, University of Washington

Appealing to Justice

Appealing to Justice

Prisoner Grievances, Rights, and Carceral Logic

Kitty Calavita and
Valerie Jenness

UNIVERSITY OF CALIFORNIA PRESS

University of California Press, one of the most
distinguished university presses in the United States,
enriches lives around the world by advancing scholarship
in the humanities, social sciences, and natural sciences. Its
activities are supported by the UC Press Foundation and
by philanthropic contributions from individuals and
institutions. For more information, visit www.ucpress.edu.

University of California Press
Oakland, California

Library of Congress Cataloging-in-Publication Data

Calavita, Kitty, author.
    Appealing to justice : prisoner grievances, rights, and
carceral logic / Kitty Calavita and Valerie Jenness.
      pages cm
    Includes bibliographical references and index.
    ISBN 978-0-520-28417-3 (cloth : alk. paper)
    ISBN 978-0-520-28418-0 (pbk. : alk. paper)
    ISBN 978-0-520-95983-5 (ebook)
    1. Grievance procedures for prisoners—California. 2.
Prisoners—Civil rights—California. 3. Prisoners—
California—Social conditions. 4. Prisons—Law and
legislation—California. I. Jenness, Valerie, 1963–
author. II. Title.
    HV9475.C2.C295   2015
    365'.64—dc23   2014028928

Manufactured in the United States of America

24 23 22 21 20 19 18 17 16 15
10 9 8 7 6 5 4 3 2 1

In keeping with a commitment to support
environmentally responsible and sustainable printing
practices, UC Press has printed this book on Natures
Natural, a fiber that contains 30% post-consumer waste
and meets the minimum requirements of ANSI/NISO
Z39.48-1992 (R 1997) (Permanence of Paper).

To Nico and Vickie

Contents

Tables

Acknowledgments

This prison research was made possible by many people, both inside and outside prison walls. First and foremost, we would like to thank the many prisoners who agreed to be interviewed, all of whom have been given pseudonyms here for reasons of confidentiality. These men gave freely of their time, recounting their experiences and trusting us in sharing—in sometimes remarkably candid detail—their perceptions, vulnerabilities, and coping strategies related to the inmate grievance system and prison life more generally. Our research obviously would not have been possible without their participation, and we want to acknowledge here our appreciation for their trust in us and for their expressed desire to have their stories told beyond prison walls. We are also grateful to the hundreds of prisoners whose grievance files were part of this research. These prisoners overcame what many told us were external and internal barriers to filing claims, and in doing so they often displayed a profound commitment to rights.

We also thank the many high-ranking officials in the California Department of Corrections and Rehabilitation (CDCR) who allowed us to collect data in California prisons and at CDCR's central administrative offices. This research could not have been launched, much less successfully concluded, without their cooperation and assistance. We would like to thank Steven Chapman, Suzan Hubbard, and Scott Kernan for responding positively to our requests for access to sensitive data. Nola Grannis, Kevin Grassel, Betty Viscuso, and Lori Zamora helped us collect and make sense of official data, while three wardens (who cannot be named to protect the identity of the prisons from which we collected data) played a key role in facilitating data collection by letting us access their prisons for data collection purposes. We also thank the many correctional officers who escorted us into their prisons, brought prisoners to their interviews, and found secure locations where our confidential interviews could be conducted. In the main, these officials worked with our research team in a way that displayed respect and goodwill. We suspect that they (at least sometimes) saw us as busybody researchers, and we appreciate that they nonetheless welcomed us into their world of corrections. Likewise, Lori DiCarlo, Wendy Still, and Jeanne Woodford, longtime employees of the CDCR who were no longer with the department when this research was conducted, provided valuable insights during the early stages of our work.

We thank too the twenty-three CDCR staff members who agreed to be interviewed and who instructed us in the details of grievance administration and the spoken and unspoken rules and practices associated with it. We are grateful for their willingness to listen patiently to our questions—some of which they no doubt considered naïve or worse—and to offer their perspectives and opinions on often sensitive topics related to the inmate appeals process.

At the University of California, a talented and committed team of research assistants deserves considerable credit for helping collect data, and for their assistance in creating and coding multiple data sets. This team includes Ashley Demyan, Danny Gascón, Sonya Goshe, Lynn Pazzani, Krithika Santhanam, Lori Sexton, Sarah Smith, Jennifer Sumner, Sylvia Valenzuela, Samantha Yarman-Patterson, and Monica Williams. Lori Sexton and Sarah Smith in particular played a central role in this research by serving as project managers on the larger project from which this book derives. They worked on data collection and analyses for this project from beginning to end, and throughout they showed a fierce commitment to making sure we collected data and engaged in data analyses in ways that best capture the contours of prison life in general and the structures and dynamics of the inmate appeals system. This work is considerably better because of their contributions. Finally, two other talented research assistants—Alyse Bertenthal and Anjuli Verma—helped us bring the pages of this book into being by securing relevant literature, reviewing and commenting on drafts of chapters, and contributing to the preparation of the manuscript during the project's final phase. Their willingness to attend to substance and details ensured that we could tell a more compelling empirical, analytic, and theoretical story.

Many academic colleagues near and far responded positively to our requests for counsel and our invitations to comment on this work; they did so in ways that significantly shaped and improved the content of the book. In particular, we would like to thank the following for their substantive input at key junctures: Victoria Basolo, Robert Emerson, Philip Goodman, Ryken Grattet, John Hipp, Chrysanthi Leon, Cheryl Maxson, Jodi O'Brien, Joan Petersilia, Keramet Reiter, Lori Sexton, Carroll Seron, Sarah Smith, and Susan Turner. We are grateful also to former California prisoners Carolyn Henry, Curtis Penn, and Malachi Scott, who read a draft of the book and gave us useful feedback and suggestions regarding the details of prison life.

Our editor, Maura Roessner, was wonderful to work with in so many ways. From the first time she expressed interest in the research project to the final few e-mails related to production decisions, we have been impressed with her enthusiasm, attentiveness to detail, and engagement with the substance of the work. We also benefitted from the superb assistance of copyeditor Elizabeth Berg.

Our research was supported by a seed grant from the Center on Inequality and Social Justice at the University of California, Irvine, and thereafter by a federal grant from the Law and Social Science Program and the Sociology Program of the National Science Foundation (SES-0849731). This funding enabled us to engage in massive data collection inside prison, this most invisible and difficult to access of contemporary American institutions. Eric Johnson, our trusted financial analyst in the School of Social Ecology, administered these grants efficiently and effectively, such that we could focus our attention on conducting the research.

Our colleagues at the University of California Irvine and University of California Berkeley (particularly the Center for the Study of Law and Society, where Kitty Calavita has found an intellectual home since her retirement from UCI), have provided us with the intellectual stimulation and friendship that were so critical to the completion of this work. We thank them for the many ways they contributed to this project and, more intangibly, for their generous spirit and collegiality.

These many individuals and institutions deserve acknowledgement for their contributions to this book. That said, the empirical analyses and theoretical claims are ours alone, as are any errors of omission or commission. Prison is an adversarial institution by its very nature, and the subjects of our research often disagreed in their interpretations of events and processes. We have tried mightily to capture accurately the conflicting perspectives presented to us, while incorporating them into a broader theoretical schema. Our appreciation for the voluntary participation of people in this research is perhaps best expressed by our commitment to present the data we gathered from them accurately and fairly. We owe them this and much more.

CHAPTER I

Introduction

Rights, Captivity, and Disputing behind Bars

In 2006, James Williams[1] lodged a grievance with the California Department of Corrections and Rehabilitation (CDCR), citing temperatures of 114 degrees in the overcrowded concrete cells of the desert prison where he was held. It was "cruel and unusual punishment," he wrote, to house people in these overheated cubicles where the only ventilation came from scorching metal vents on the roof. He ended by noting that even the prison dog kennels were air-conditioned. The CDCR denied his appeal.[2] Tens of thousands of prisoners like Williams file grievances in California's thirty-three prisons every year, with the vast majority denied by prison authorities.

The grievance system that Williams used is the legally sanctioned internal mechanism for prisoners to contest the conditions of their confinement, and federal law requires exhaustion of this administrative process before prisoners may gain access to court. In California, the process includes multiple levels of review, all conducted exclusively by the CDCR. Perhaps we should not be surprised that Williams's grievance was denied. After all, the CDCR acts as both defendant and judge in these complaints. More surprising is the fact that despite the odds against success, prisoners' cynicism about the process, and their perception that there are risks to filing, every year thousands of prisoners like Williams do so.

This book began with the hope that the inmate grievance process might provide a window through which to glimpse daily prison life.

Our unprecedented access to prisoners and CDCR officials to interview, and photocopies of hundreds of prisoner grievances, yielded an abundance of descriptive riches. Our interviews and the sample of grievances emerging from this most closed of institutions describe overheated cells but also a range of claims involving food and "chow hall" practices, medical care, staff conduct, physical safety, cell assignments, disciplinary action, visitation procedures, and the chaos of transfers and missing property. Collectively, these data provide a sense of the ordinary punctuated by the exceptional that makes up life inside prison. At a time when the U.S. prison population has increased many times over and far outstrips that of any other nation, empirical research about what happens behind prison walls has dwindled in the United States. Our focus on the prisoner grievance process and what it reveals about prison life more generally is in part driven by the simple need for discovery and description.

These prisoner grievances also shed light on the nature of disputing in an extremely hierarchical setting. They are essentially disputes, and the process they trigger is an exercise in dispute resolution, albeit one that is heavily asymmetrical in design and outcome. For California inmates, prison is a restrictive, overcrowded environment, replete with conditions that are grievable, as documented in the U.S. Supreme Court decision *Brown v. Plata*, 563 U.S. __ (2011). However, as we know from an extensive scholarship on disputing,[3] the presence of grievable conditions—even serious or life-threatening ones—is not in itself sufficient for launching a dispute. Instead, the ability and willingness to name a problem, blame someone for it, and lodge a claim is socially and culturally patterned, with vulnerable or self-blaming populations facing daunting barriers. Williams's grievance and those of so many other prisoners—one of the most stigmatized and vulnerable populations imaginable—are all the more surprising in the context of this previous scholarship on the social and cultural impediments to "naming, blaming, and claiming" (Felstiner, Abel, and Sarat 1980–81).

This enigma is one of the analytical threads of our story, and making sense of it was initially the theoretical driving force of our research. But as we attempted to solve this mystery, our empirical data revealed a cascade of other puzzles. Among the most perplexing were that despite prisoners' cynicism about the appeals process and criminal justice in general, they expressed a profound faith in law and evidence; that CDCR staff praised the grievance process as an important right accorded prisoners yet referred to those who exercised that right as "narcissists" and "whiners"; and that despite a marked degree of consistency in CDCR appeals responses, with most appeals denied at all levels of review, when discussing the process of achieving this consistency, these CDCR staff reported a surprising level of conflict in the ranks.

These disparate findings, like pieces of a jigsaw puzzle with blurry images and jagged edges, only make sense when you look carefully at the bigger picture of which they are part. In broad outline, it is a picture of a late-modern society that has expanded civil and legal rights, yet deprives people of their liberty on an unprecedented scale. This "civil rights society" (Bumiller 1988) embraces the rhetoric of rights, but at the same time has taken a pronounced punitive turn that leaves approximately one in a hundred people in the United States behind bars. The logic of rights and the punitive logic of incarceration are now among the defining ideologies of American society, permeating institutions both large and small despite what appears to be their glaring incongruence.

It is often noted that the increase in incarceration in the United States came on the heels of the civil rights movement and its accompanying advances in legal rights and rights consciousness (Beckett 1997; Hagan 2010; Western 2006). Some scholars have even suggested a causal relationship, with mass incarceration serving to restore social control over racial minorities just as they had secured a measure of equal rights (Loury 2007; Murakawa 2006; Weaver 2007; Western 2006). Whatever the reasons for this sequence of events, they have set in motion a seismic tension that reverberates throughout society and is found in its most primal form in the practices that distinguish the contemporary prison. Indeed, prisons in the United States—overcrowded with prisoners who are savvy about their legal rights, often overseen by activist courts, and guided by thick volumes of regulations—sit at the very fault line of this contradiction. As we argue in the chapters that follow, the prisoner grievance system and the puzzling attitudes and practices that surround it embody these conflicting logics of captivity and rights. What we find is a system fraught with impediments and dilemmas that delivers neither justice, nor efficiency, nor constitutional conditions of confinement. More broadly, our analysis of the prison grievance system and its inherent tensions exposes the conflicting logics underlying the prison system itself and the (post–) civil rights society into which it is inserted.

While the grievance system is a creature of this intersection of mass incarceration and rights consciousness, a close look at its operation reveals not only conflicting logics but, as with all dialectical processes, moments of coproduction and synthesis. As described in the next chapter, the mandate for an internal grievance system was established by the Prison Litigation Reform Act (PLRA) in 1996 as a solution to the growth in inmate litigation associated with the prisoners' rights movement and the increasing prison population; filing grievances is now an institutionalized part of prison life and arguably not only reflects but fuels inmates' rights consciousness. Whether or not the rights revolution of the 1960s triggered the mass incarceration of African Americans and other minorities, as some scholars argue, Congress left little doubt that the PLRA was an effort to suppress the rights litigation of the newly flooded prisons.

However, the PLRA was not only an attempt to quash prisoner litigation; it inevitably incorporated the prevailing logic of rights, requiring states to set up internal mechanisms through which prisoners could challenge the conditions of their confinement. These mechanisms may limit lawsuits and rarely end in victory for the prisoner appellant, but they serve as concrete and daily reminders to prisoners of their right to contest their treatment. In other words, the grievance system that was mandated by Congress to inhibit prisoners' rights mobilization, and which usually leaves prisoners dissatisfied with its outcomes, nonetheless may act as a galvanizing agent for rights consciousness. It is this capacity of the contradictory logics of rights and confinement not only to diverge and conflict but to meet in moments of coproduction that defines its dialectical quality.

This dialectical quality is evident too in our interviews with officials, for they alternately praised the grievance process as an important prisoner right, were openly hostile to those who exercise that right, and touted grievances as a key managerial tool that allows them to maximize safety and security. Thus, while the withdrawal of autonomy in prison and the prisoner agency implied in filing grievances may be at odds, eliciting sarcastic commentary about prisoner appellants from prison officials, these same officials hailed the system for enhancing the most immediate and tangible prison priority—safety and security.

With prison overcrowding endemic in this era of mass incarceration, a central organizing goal is safety. In their survey of mission statements of corrections departments in the United States, the Federal Bureau of Prisons, and the Correctional Service of Canada, Gaes et al. (2004, 9) report that "guaranteeing the safety of the public, staff, and inmates" is the central operating principle. Similarly, Moynihan (2005, 23) finds that the safe warehousing of people is the top priority—and sometimes the sole priority—of the three departments of corrections he examined, "regardless of the goals listed in the strategic plan."

Putting this in the context of our discussion of carceral logic, we can envision three levels of principles at work here, with their related but distinctive dynamics and dialectical relationships to rights. At the cultural level, the so-called punitive turn sits in tension with advancing rights and rights consciousness; and, at the level of the prison, the logic of incarceration includes as defining features loss of autonomy and control of movement, to which a prisoner grievance system appears antithetical (as we hear one official exclaim later, "It's no fun in prison. You came here, get over it"); but at the level of daily prison operation, the core managerial principle is to ensure safe warehousing—a challenge that officials told us is sometimes facilitated by the communication and possibility for venting implied in the grievance system.

Our story, then, is about the clashing logics embodied in the prisoner grievance system and the institutional and individual dilemmas produced by this clash. It is, however, also a story of logics that periodically converge and reproduce each other, as the vehicle with which Congress meant to limit prisoners' legal access—the internal grievance system—contributes to prisoners' rights consciousness, while officials extol inmates' right to grieve conditions as an important tool of carceral control. At the individual human level, it is a story about the lives of prisoners and corrections officials who manage this contradictory system, sometimes with similar points of view and usually with competing interests as captives and captors within the institutional space of prison.

The next sections provide a snapshot of our research context, including the contours of the CDCR as an institution, the challenges of in-prison research, and the methods and data-collection strategies we employed. After that, we trace the outlines of the dialectic of advancing rights consciousness and mass incarceration that is central to our analysis. Finally, we draw a roadmap of the book, including the main findings and arguments of each chapter.

GETTING IN, GETTING STARTED, AND GETTING ALONG: RESEARCH SITES AND DATA SOURCES

When we began this research, California was home to one of the largest correctional systems in the western world, surpassed only by the U.S. federal system. The CDCR is charged with running thirty-three prisons and at the time of this study housed approximately 160,000 people, all but about 12,000 of them in men's prisons. In addition to its mammoth size, the CDCR is by many accounts a dysfunctional organization. In 2006, U.S. District Court Judge Thelton Henderson put the California prison health care system in receivership, having found that its conditions violated the Eighth Amendment's prohibition of cruel and unusual punishment. The receiver in charge, Robert Sillen (2006, E5), described what he found when he toured the facilities at San Quentin State Prison:

> To reach one of San Quentin's medical clinics, you must walk past a row of 20 maximum-security cells with inmates confined behind fine crosshatched wire, barely visible. The floor is strewn with trash, puddles of water and worse from the runoff of inmate showers from the tiers above. Soap and hair drip off the guardrails of the walkways, leaving a slippery mess to dance around as you approach the clinic, which is shoehorned into a converted cell. A mildewed shower curtain hangs in front of the clinic's entrance to keep the water from spraying directly into the medical area. I have run hospitals, clinics and public health facilities for the past 40 years, and medical care in California prisons is unlike anything I have ever seen. Inhumane is the nice term for the conditions. . . . The resulting patient health outcomes tell a gruesome story.

Five years later, the U.S. Supreme Court also concluded that mental and physical health care in California prisons due to overcrowding violated the Eighth Amendment, ordering California to reduce its prison population to 137.5 percent of design capacity (*Brown v. Plata*, 538 U.S. __ [2011]). Reports by journalists, government agencies and academics confirm that grossly substandard health care and other deleterious conditions are common in California prisons.[4] A wide range of special masters, independent review panels, and other experts reported that in fiscal year 2003–2004 one inmate a week died in California due to inadequate medical care (there was a seven-hundred-prisoner backlog for a doctor's appointment), and on average one California prisoner a week committed suicide (cited in *Brown v. Plata*, 538 U.S. __ [2011]).[5]

Contesting their conditions has become more complicated for prisoners since Congress passed the PLRA in 1996. This federal law contains several important provisions, but its centerpiece is a requirement for prisoners to exhaust the administrative appeals process offered by their state's correctional system before gaining access to court (Belbot 2004; Schlanger 2003). In California, inmate grievance procedures are specified in Article 8, Title 15 ("Crime Prevention and Corrections") of the California Code of Regulations. To file a grievance, prisoners are required to complete a form that is officially numbered and colloquially referred to as a "602."

The 602 provides an official venue for prisoners to narrate their complaints, attach evidence in support of their claims, and describe their requested remedies. As we detail in the next chapter, corrections officials then respond to the prisoner's claims and requests with an explanation and official determination. This back-and-forth across multiple levels of adjudication creates a kind of dialogic interaction between prisoners and officials, with the final decision resting with the CDCR's Inmate Appeals Branch in Sacramento. Our research began as an examination of this disputing in California prisons.

Despite the unprecedented growth of the incarcerated population since the early 1970s, there has been a steady decline in scholarly attention to life inside prison walls (Crewe 2005; Fleisher and Krienert 2009; Goodman 2008; Irwin 2005; Jenness 2010; Jenness et al. 2010; Rhodes 2004; Simon 2000; Wacquant 2002).[6] The current paucity of in-prison research contrasts markedly with the era in which Donald Clemmer (1940) and Gresham Sykes (1958) did their work. This dearth of research is certainly not due to a lack of scholarly interest or because the topic has receded in importance. Rather, prison fieldwork is fraught with administrative, bureaucratic, and legal obstacles. To be blunt, prisons are heavily regulated institutional arenas, and officials usually do not welcome researchers. Further, prisoners are considered "special populations" in the language of Institutional Review Boards, making in-prison research all the more difficult. Despite these obstacles, it is critically important to get "inside and around penal facilities" (Wacquant 2002) if we are to accurately portray life inside prison walls.

We undertook this project fully cognizant of the potential challenges of access. One of the coauthors had a track record of research with the CDCR and had good working relations with some key decision makers. Yet even in this best-case scenario, the bureaucratic process of securing research permissions from the CDCR and its research office was fraught with delays, speed bumps, and mind-numbing paperwork (including, at one point, "an application to submit an application" for research). More than two years after we began—years that included multiple trips to secure endorsements from prison wardens, the Inmate Appeals Branch, and the upper echelons of the CDCR in Sacramento—we secured the coveted permissions and prison access.

Parallel to this process of obtaining permission from the CDCR, we obtained the necessary approvals from the Institutional Review Board

(IRB) at the University of California, Irvine, and the California Committee for the Protection of Human Subjects (CPHS) in Sacramento, California. The IRB review process to obtain approval to study populations such as prisoners is particularly daunting. Presumably designed to add an important extra layer of protection when researchers propose to study vulnerable populations, form sometimes trumped substance in an IRB permission process that entailed several rounds of miniscule changes and at least one administrative wild-goose chase.[7] Well over a year after filing with the IRB and the CPHS, and two years after first approaching the CDCR, our study was approved and our research was finally under way.

Interviewing a random sample of all California prisoners would have required accessing thirty-three prisons. Instead, we interviewed random samples of forty men from each of three prisons that together approximate the characteristics of the larger CDCR male population on several important dimensions. These three prisons are scattered around the state and vary by age of facility, custody levels of the population, population size, number of grievances that reach the third level of review,[8] overcrowding levels, and violence rates. Green Valley Prison (GVP)[9] is a modern, maximum-security institution with one of the highest rates of inmate grievances in the state. At the time of our interviews, it housed approximately 5,000 inmates in facilities designed for fewer than half that many. In contrast, California Corrections Facility (CCF) is a minimum- and medium-security prison, with a midrange level of grievance filing. It too is overcrowded, with more than 6,500 inmates in facilities built for slightly fewer than 4,000. Finally, Desert Valley Center (DVC) is a medium-security prison with a relatively low rate of grievance filings. With over 4,000 inmates, it too is severely overcrowded. We chose to collect data in three prisons that vary on a number of important dimensions not in order to compare and contrast findings across them, but rather to secure a diverse sample that is relatively representative of the California prison population as a whole.

Between July and December 2009, we interviewed a random sample of 120 prisoners and 23 CDCR personnel, including wardens, deputy wardens, captains, appeals coordinators, and grievance examiners and supervisors. (For details on our interview protocols and procedures, see appendices A and B.) Our interviews included both closed and open-ended questions, and allowed for follow-up questions and spontaneous exchanges. We not infrequently had to abandon the orderly sequence of questions on our interview instrument when our respondents took discursive detours and side trips, as we balanced the need to be systematic with the desire to keep the tone conversational—a chronic challenge of the semistructured interview.

The research team consisted of five interviewers—the coauthors and three advanced graduate students (including one fluent Spanish speaker). All five interviewers were female, four of the five self-identify as white, one self-identifies as Latino, and all are middle-class. Given the gender, race, and class composition of the research team, we were initially concerned that inordinate bias could be introduced in our interviews with mostly low-income male prisoners, the majority of whom identify as African American or Latino.[10] However, we take some comfort in the findings presented by Jenness et al. (2010, 19), who report on their assessment of interviewer effects when conducting "stranger interviews" (Weinreb 2006) in prison while asking sensitive questions about gang status, as well as sexual assault and other forms of violence: "A series of chi-square tests reveal there is not a statistically significant relationship between interviewer characteristics—younger versus older, White versus non-White, male versus female, professor versus graduate student—and inmate participation rates and usable interview rates. Also, the Spanish-speaking interviewer produced participation and usable interview rates comparable to other interviewers" (Jenness et al. 2010, 21). Furthermore, they found no statistically significant interviewer effects on prisoners' reporting of sexual assaults, nonsexual assaults, or gang status. The only exception to this pattern was that younger and nonwhite interviewers received more reports from prisoners of consensual sex in prison (Jenness et al. 2010).

Because of the complexity surrounding the possibility of interviewer effects as well as the logistical difficulty and potential pitfalls related to matching interviewers and respondents on an array of dimensions, we tried to minimize bias through demeanor and language that signaled acceptance and trustworthiness rather than attempting to eliminate or ignore our considerable differences. We cannot know for sure, but it sometimes seemed to work to our advantage to be perceived (and correctly understood) as different. As Rhodes (1994, 551–52) explains in her eloquent essay on interviewing black applicants in the foster system in England, as a white researcher she "had the advantage of a certain 'stranger value' . . . as 'an outsider.'" Her respondents not only confided things to her that they would not talk to their neighbors or social workers about, but they also "treated me to information which they would have assumed was the taken-for-granted knowledge of an insider. . . . In these discussions, I adopted the equivalent of a pupil role with the informant teacher."

In our interviews with prisoners, we too felt that they were patiently schooling us, in this case in the experiential aspects of prison and the intricacies of the grievance system. We were no doubt correctly perceived by the men we spoke with to be "outsiders," neither prisoners nor corrections personnel, nor people who were likely to have friends or relatives inside prison walls; tellingly, they referred to us as "soft in the hands," "professors," "researchers," "outside people," and "somebody on the outside."[11] Quite apart from how we were perceived, or perhaps because of it, our team was often privy to the kind of tutorials about which Rhodes wrote. Further, it was not unusual for these men to offer apparently candid expressions of anger ("It's like we're on the front lines in Iraq"), remorse ("I was very foolish for what I did"), resentment ("I'm locked in a cage!"), and emotional vulnerability ("I have to deal with my own heartache"), or to admit to behaviors of the sort that Rhodes (1994) and others (Fendrich et al. 1999; Johnson and Parsons 1994) suggest are less likely to emerge when respondents speak to those with possible ties to their circle of peers. While it is difficult to measure empirically, our outsider status may have been an issue for some topics and some men, but at the end of the day it may also have been a research asset.

Despite our initial concerns that prisoners would be reluctant to participate or would hesitate to speak to us in anything but the most guarded fashion, the vast majority readily agreed to participate and with few exceptions agreed to be tape-recorded. In fact, many of these men told us that it meant a lot to them to be able to tell their stories. At one point in the interviewing process, one of the coauthors was scheduled to interview a prisoner during his lunchtime ("feeding" time, in the dehumanizing official slang). When she apologized for the conflict and said he should go to lunch if he preferred, he exclaimed, "Oh, no! This is *way* better than lunch. I get lunch every day!" Word spread in these prisons that we were doing confidential interviews about prison life, and it was not uncommon for us to be approached by a prisoner not on our list asking to be interviewed. To keep a truly random sample, we could not comply with these requests, but they did suggest to us that the research was favorably received by the people we interviewed.

We had initially thought that prisoners might feel vulnerable and be reluctant to speak with us, but staff would be eager to share their perspective. Interestingly, it was some of the lower-level staff who at first seemed the most reticent to be interviewed. But even the most skeptical officials seemed to relax as the interview progressed and evolved into conversation. One incident suggested the sensitive nature of some of our discussions with staff and the unanticipated challenges of such research. During our visit to the Inmate Appeals Branch, one coauthor began her interview with examiner Lucinda Gray and was shortly thereafter joined by the other coauthor. When the second coauthor entered the room, Lucinda suddenly began to ignore the one who was asking her questions. It is not entirely clear what landmine the first coauthor had stepped on,[12] but Lucinda's reaction was abrupt and deliberately obvious, turning her chair away from the interviewer asking her questions and directing her responses to the other coauthor. Despite her apparent anger and the ongoing ice treatment she directed at one of us, Lucinda continued the interview for another hour. It was the most uncomfortable interview we conducted with a staff member, but the team approach no doubt saved it, and this examiner's responses in the end turned out to be some of the richest and most revealing.

The interviews with staff, which were not recorded as per agreement with the CDCR, often lasted three hours or more and ended only when we needed to move on. These officials were so generous with their time that it frequently seemed they were willing to talk with us as long as we would listen. The willingness of these personnel to spend hours discussing their roles in the grievance process, their judgments of its effectiveness and fairness, their opinions about prisoner appellants, and their experiences with other institutional actors—sometimes in remarkably candid terms—suggests that our semistructured-interview balancing act was well worth it.

These interviews with prisoners and staff provide the data for much of what follows, and we quote them extensively. In addition to these interview data, we draw from a sample of the 16,430 written inmate grievances that made it to the final level of review in fiscal year 2005–2006. The CDCR provided us with a comprehensive list of these grievances and the 9,838 prisoners who filed them, and from this list we drew a random sample of 292 appellants from men's prisons and all of the grievances they filed that year. In addition, because fully granted appeals are so rare, we included all granted grievances originating in men's prisons in 2005–2006 (n = 37) in a separate data set.[13] In total, we photocopied and coded 470 inmate grievances and their institutional responses, comprising thousands of pages. These grievance documents—coded for the frames and narrative styles used by inmates and staff—form the basis for our comparative analysis of inmates' and staff's discursive strategies in this relatively formal context, presented in chapter 7. (For details on our grievance coding, see appendix C.)

These unique sources of data provide an empirical window into life in California prisons, revealing its numbing personal and organizational routines, its daily indignities, and its life-altering upheavals. Beyond that, however, the data complicate our understanding of disputing in a total institution of law, and of administrative decision making in a context characterized by the nexus of turbulent cultural currents, paramilitary organizational culture, an ongoing attentiveness to "downstream consequences" (Emerson 1991), and asymmetrical power relations. The following section sketches the sources of the turbulent larger context in which prisons operate and its implications for our study.

CIVIL RIGHTS AND THE CARCERAL STATE

An abstract rhetorical commitment to rights in the United States is evidenced as early as the founders' Bill of Rights. It took more than a century and a half, however, for "rights" to permeate public discourse. A series of important substantive rights evolved in the interim in the form of additional amendments to the Constitution—most notably, ending African American slavery and extending suffrage to African Americans and then to women—but it was not until the second half of the twentieth century that the United States could be referred to as a "civil rights society" (Bumiller 1988), in which both rights talk and rights consciousness were widespread, and explicit opposition to civil rights was culturally delegitimized.

The U.S. Supreme Court decision in *Brown v. Board of Education,* 347 U.S. 483 (1954), is often cited as the opening act of the civil rights era in the United States. There had been grassroots protests against racial discrimination in the 1940s as African American soldiers returned from World War II, but *Brown* was the first official statement of the government's commitment to racial equality in the postwar period. This commitment has been exposed as an integral part of the United States's Cold War strategy, motivated by the self-interest of white policymakers, for whom racial discrimination was seen as an international embarrassment and a propaganda tool for the Soviet Union (Dudziak 2000). And the *Brown* decision has been widely criticized as primarily symbolic and broadly ineffective (Bell 2004; Rosenberg 1991). Nonetheless, as symbolism it resonated and arguably helped rev up the fledgling civil rights movement. By the mid-1960s, a mass movement was well under way, led by charismatic and dedicated leaders and fueled by millions who walked picket lines, desegregated schools, and otherwise risked their lives for the cause (Goldberg 1991; Morris 1984).

As this movement gained momentum, it was joined by social movements to advance the rights of other subjugated groups, most notably the women's movement (Ferree and Hess 1985), the gay and lesbian movement (Adam 1987; Vaid 1995), the disabilities rights movement (Scotch 1984; Shapiro 1993), the crime victim movement (Weed 1995), the hate crime movement (Jenness and Grattet 2001; Maroney 1998), and, as we discuss in chapter 2, the prisoners' rights movement. The 1960s and early 1970s saw judicial decisions that expanded the rights of prisoners,[14] defendants in criminal cases,[15] women's reproductive rights,[16] and in a string of decisions in 1969, the free speech rights of demonstrators and protesters.[17] This is not to say, however, that racial equality and civil rights in general had become an inexorable part of the American creed. It is noteworthy that when the Civil Rights Act passed in 1964—described as "the most sweeping civil rights legislation since the Civil War and Reconstruction era" (Rosenberg 1991, 47)—the country was still conspicuously divided on the issue, with many southern legislators and ordinary Americans viscerally and outspokenly opposed to the concept of "civil rights."

Senator James Eastland of Mississippi blasted the 1964 civil rights bill as "unwise, socialistic, and unconstitutional legislation" (88 Cong. S. 8356 [1964]). Senator Richard Russell of Georgia vowed to obstruct it and argued that passing such a law would further fuel the "militant Negro groups" that he said were behind it (S. 4747). During a filibuster against the original Civil Rights Act, seventeen southern senators rose to speak passionately against it. When a weakened bill was finally brought to a vote, 155 members of Congress voted against it (H.R., June 30, 1964; Sen., June 19, 1964).

By the 1970s, however, rights discourse had become a centerpiece of the American cultural repertoire, so resonant that it was a de rigueur tool of social reformers. A decade after they had bombastically opposed civil rights legislation, many politicians regretted having done so; two decades later, opposition to civil rights was a source of shame and triggered expressions of contrition.[18] Some of this contrition was no doubt politically strategic and less than sincere; what matters here is that opposition to civil rights had become culturally and politically unacceptable over the course of a few years.

The 1970s initiated a period of judicial retrenchments. Among them, the U.S. Supreme Court increasingly required those bringing charges of discrimination to demonstrate intent to discriminate[19]—a "smoking gun" standard that was almost impossible to meet now that discrimination was illegal and expressions of prejudice considered uncouth. Judicial support for affirmative action policies also waned. After their somewhat ambiguous endorsement of affirmative action in *Regents of The University of California v. Bakke,* 438 U.S. 265 (1978), the U.S. Supreme Court issued a series of decisions in the 1980s and 1990s invalidating affirmative action policies unless they were narrowly tailored to compensate for past intentional discrimination.[20] Even in cases in which affirmative action policies were judicially limited, however, it is telling that the challenge was wrapped in the rhetoric of (nonminorities') rights, underscoring once again the cultural power of the rights discourse.

Despite these reversals by an increasingly conservative judiciary, the language of rights remained entrenched, providing legitimacy for ongoing social movements such as those to prohibit discrimination against gays, people with disabilities, and victims of crime. By the turn of the century, these movements had culminated in U.S. Supreme Court landmark gay rights cases *Romer v. Evans,* 517 U.S. 620 (1996), and *Lawrence v. Texas,* 539 U.S. 558 (2003), and congressional legislation such as the Americans with Disabilities Act of 1990[21] and the Crime Victims' Rights Act of 2004.[22] At the time of this writing, the rights revolution in the United States is perhaps most conspicuous in state-by-state extensions of the legal recognition of same-sex marriages and the constitutional demise of the 1996 U.S. Defense of Marriage Act (110 Stat. 2419).

A robust literature critiques the rights revolution, pointing out that many of our formal rights are unenforced or ineffective (Bell 1992, 2004; Freeman 1982; Rosenberg 1991); that even when rights are enforced, they do little to overcome structural inequalities (Bell 1987; Bobo and Smith 1998; Brown et al. 2003; Wilson 1999); that some whose rights have been violated are hesitant to claim the victim status that legal action implicitly requires (Bumiller 1988); and that a focus on rights can be detrimental to social movements by channeling and tamping down their radical energies to accommodate to the legal arena (Bumiller 1988; Scheingold 1974; Smart 1989).

This critique of rights has been countered by those who demonstrate that even unenforced or underused rights can have implications for politics (McCann 1994; Polletta 2000) and for identity (Engel and Munger

2003; Kirkland 2008), and by those who note an elitist bent to the critique (Matsuda 1987; Minow 1987; Williams 1991). Whatever the merits of these critiques and countercritiques, the debate itself underscores the ideological impact of the rights revolution and the prominence of rights talk in contemporary culture. As Bumiller (1988, 5) writes, "The belief in 'rights' may extend far beyond their actualization in statute, case law, and legislation, and their realization in concrete social situations."

As these legal, social, and ideological developments took hold and made *rights* a household word, the criminal justice system began its own transformation, most evident in the frenzied construction of new prisons and the precipitous buildup of the number of people incarcerated. In 1973, Blumstein and Cohen (1973, 198) noted the "stability of punishment" in the United States, with the incarceration rate holding steady for almost half a century. Two years later, incarceration rates began to climb steeply, quadrupling by the turn of the century (Pastore and Maguire 2002). By 2009, despite a persistent and marked drop in crime rates, more than 2.2 million people were imprisoned in America and almost 7.3 million were under the jurisdiction of the criminal justice system—in prison or jail, or on parole or probation (Glaze 2010). In a historically unprecedented shift, the incarcerated population had increased by almost a factor of eight in less than four decades. A prison-building boom accompanied this incarceration surge. California, where only twelve state prisons had been built in the 112 years from 1852 to 1964, constructed twenty-three new prisons from 1984 to 2000, at an average cost of more than $300 million each (Gilmore 2007; Lerman 2013).

This mass incarceration has disproportionately targeted disadvantaged young men, particularly those of color (Alexander 2010; Beckett 1997; Comfort 2008; Gilmore 2007; Hagan 2010; Lerman 2013; Manza and Uggen 2006; Provine 2007; Wacquant 2001; Wakefield and Uggen 2010; Western 2006). Fully two-thirds of the men incarcerated in state prisons are African American or Hispanic. While 1.6 percent of white men between the ages of twenty and forty were incarcerated in 2000, 4.6 percent of Hispanic men and 11.5 percent of black men in that age group were in prison (Western 2006). A similar pattern is apparent among juvenile offenders. The National Council on Crime and Delinquency (2007) reports that African American juveniles with no prior record are incarcerated at six times the rate of whites when charged with the same offence; the rate for Latino youth is three times that of whites. So dramatic are these numbers and the consequences of incarceration for future employment (Pager 2007), voting rights (Manza and Uggen 2006), and access to housing and other such necessities of life (Alexander and Meshelemiah 2010) that this era has been called "the new Jim Crow" (Alexander 2010), in which race discrimination is carried out under cover of felon discrimination. Wacquant (2010, 74) has pointed out that this "mass incarceration" is more accurately the "*hyper*incarceration" of "(sub)proletarian African American men from the imploding ghetto."

While the expansion of imprisonment has its most direct and devastating effects on racial minorities, the "culture of control" (Garland 2001) of which it is one manifestation is felt in virtually every social institution, from the family to schools, churches, the military, the media, and beyond. As Jonathan Simon (2007) shows, the war on crime and the fear associated with it have become such integral aspects of American culture that they threaten the very nature of our democracy. The material effects of this development range from prison buildups to security checks in schools and surveillance cameras in stores, day care centers, and single-family homes. Its ideological impacts are less visible but just as consequential, as carceral logic penetrates our institutions and feeds the very fears and social forces that undergird it.

A number of scholars make a connection between the civil rights movement and the "punitive turn" that followed in its wake. Loury (2007, 3) is convinced that "the punitive turn represented a political response to the success of the civil rights movement." Western (2006, 4) offers a multifactored explanation, but he too links "the punitive sentiment unleashed in the 1970s" to both "rising crime and civil rights activism in the 1960s." Murakawa (2006) details the processes through which conservative politicians tapped the anger of southern whites over judicial decisions such as *Brown v. Board of Education,* 347 U.S. 483 (1954), successfully conflated black civil rights activism and black criminality, threatened judges who were perceived to be soft on crime, and ultimately set off the incarceration surge. Weaver (2007, 230–31) is even more direct, arguing, "Several stinging defeats for opponents of civil rights galvanized a powerful elite countermovement. . . . The same actors who had fought vociferously against civil rights legislation . . . shifted the 'locus of attack' by injecting crime onto the agenda. . . . What the literature usually treats as independent trajectories—liberalizing civil rights and more repressive social control in criminal justice—were part of the same political streams."[23]

The temporal conjunction of civil rights advances with an increasingly punitive criminal justice system is thus well recognized in the literature, with some arguing a causal connection. But it is rarely remarked upon that these two developments and their ideological underpinnings are in some ways fundamentally in tension with each other. While the liberal logic of rights privileges individual autonomy, freedom from discrimination, and protection against repressive state actions, the logic of incarceration prioritizes state control and the suppression of individual autonomy. It is not unusual for the hegemonic components of a given period to be in tension, and just as human beings can effortlessly hold contradictory values and beliefs, this ideological conflict mostly passes unnoticed. But when the tension is cast full-blown into an institutional structure with a mandate to act on both of these conflicting logics—as in the case of the modern prison and its prisoner grievance system—collisions are inevitable.

The courts have wrestled with the question of how the Constitution applies to prisoners and have painstakingly attempted to carve out which rights are preserved in prison and which are truncated or absent altogether.[24] As the majority in *Hudson* (1984, 517) wrote, "While prisoners enjoy many protections of the Constitution that are not fundamentally inconsistent with imprisonment itself or incompatible with the objectives of incarceration, imprisonment carries with it the circumscription or loss of many rights as being necessary to accommodate the institutional needs and objectives of prison facilities, particularly internal security and safety."

The concept of prisons' immunity from some rights mandates, based on their unique "institutional needs," was reiterated three years later in *Turner* (1987, 89): "When a prison regulation impinges on inmates' constitutional rights, the regulation is valid if it is reasonably related to legitimate penological interests." While temporarily resolving the legal issues at hand, such judicial parsing does little to reconcile the tension provoking those issues—a tension that has intensified over the last several decades as both incarceration and rights discourse have advanced. Indeed, the acrobatic complexity of the parsing, its constant revisiting, and the rights exemption accorded prisons when a "legitimate penological interest" (e.g., "internal security and safety") is concerned underscore the stubborn quality of that tension.

Perhaps the most powerful evidence of this tension between rights and carceral control is the endurance of racial segregation in prisons—and periodic, if ambiguous, court mandates to abolish it, followed by prison officials' resistance to its abolition. The ban on racial segregation of public facilities is the hallmark of the U.S. civil rights paradigm advanced in the second half of the twentieth century, and the partial exemption of prisons from this otherwise sacrosanct principle is a testament to the power of the countervailing logic of carceral control. In a law review article evocatively entitled "*Johnson v. California*: A Grayer Shade of *Brown*," Brandon Robinson (2006) briefly summarizes the history of the courts' interpretation of the prohibition on racial segregation imposed by *Brown v. Board of Education*. As Robinson (354) tells it, a 1968 Supreme Court decision (*Lee v. Washington*, 390 U.S. 333 [1968]) relating to racial segregation in Alabama prisons declared that such segregation was unconstitutional, although "a three-Justice concurrence clarified that 'prison authorities have the right, acting in good faith and in particularized circumstances, to take into account racial tensions in maintaining security, discipline, and good order in prisons and jails.'"

Decades later, the California Department of Corrections and Rehabilitation has a de facto policy of racial segregation of prisoners. Arguing that prison gangs engage in interracial violence, officials defend their practice of racial segregation on the grounds that it is essential to prison safety and security. Following diverse lower court opinions, in 2005 the U.S. Supreme Court (*Johnson v. California*, 543 U.S. 499 [2005]) imposed the strict scrutiny standard on prison racial segregation, thereby deviating from the unilateral ban on racial segregation generally imposed in other arenas, and prompting Robinson (2006, 343) to declare the decision "a grayer shade of *Brown*." As of this writing, the racial segregation of California prisons for men remains largely intact.[25] This persistence of explicit racial segregation—the demise of which was the bellwether and signal achievement of the civil rights era—is striking evidence of the power of carceral logic and its head-on collision with the logic of civil rights, a collision that the courts have struggled mightily to mollify.[26]

A preliminary word of caution is in order. We have noted that the logic of rights and the logic of punitive control pull in opposite directions at once. There is an inherent tension here, but we do not mean to imply that empirically they are mutually exclusive. Clearly, prisons vary in the degree to which they constrain autonomy, inflict punishing regimens, and otherwise depress rights and maximize control. Minimum-security prisons and carceral institutions in some other countries—most notably, in Scandinavia (Pratt 2008; Larson 2013)—allow more individual freedoms and impose fewer restrictions than most state prisons in the contemporary United States. Our point instead is that the philosophies and operational logics of rights on one hand and carceral control on the other *tug against* each other; that they intensified in tandem over the last forty years in the United States; and that the resulting socio-ideological turbulence explains much about the attitudes, sociolegal practices, and administrative decision making of prison officials in the United States.

This tension is at the heart of our analysis of the prisoner grievance system in California. As we will see, on the ground level it ensures that a plethora of cognitive and practical problems ensue, both for the institution and for those working and living within it. The fallout of this clash between the logics of rights and incarceration is sometimes predictable but at other times upends conventional understandings, for example about the reluctance of vulnerable people to launch disputes, prisoners' perceptions of fairness, or the lockstep solidarity of prison officials. In the chapters that follow, we present these sometimes surprising findings from our interviews with prisoners and staff and a random sample of grievances through several levels of review.

ROAD MAP OF THE BOOK

The next chapter begins by setting the stage for our empirical analysis with an overview of the Prison Litigation Reform Act of 1996 (PLRA), within the context of the skyrocketing prison population and advances in legal-rights consciousness. We show that the predicted decline in prisoner litigation subsequent to the PLRA was paralleled by a dramatic increase in prisoner grievance filing. Chapter 2 provides a detailed picture of how the grievance system in California works, describes the range of grievances filed, quotes from actual grievances, and presents the best available estimates of outcome numbers. It concludes by pointing out that despite the slim odds of prisoners winning a grievance, this system, which was mandated by Congress to curtail legal mobilization by prisoners, arguably animates their rights consciousness.

In chapter 3, we present findings from our interviews with prisoners, focusing on what they named as problems, what they said they had filed grievances on, and what consequences they anticipated. The extensive list of problems named and grievances claimed provides a valuable empirical window into life inside these total institutions. Beyond that, we note that the frequency of these prisoners' naming and claiming is inconsistent with what one would expect from much of the literature on disputing (Coates and Penrod 1980–81; Felstiner, Abel, and Sarat 1980–81; Hoffmann 2003; Michelson 2007), legal mobilization (Bumiller 1987; Morrill et al. 2010), and "trouble" (Emerson 2008; Emerson and Messinger 1977). Specifically, despite their sometimes significant amounts of self-blame, their stigmatized status, and fears of retaliation and provoking "trouble" for themselves, the vast majority of these prisoners have filed grievances, and many have filed multiple times.

To untangle this paradox, we pay close attention to the repeated references in their interviews to Title 15, the section of the California Code of Regulations that regulates every aspect of prison and prisoners' entitlements—or, to use the prisoners' words, "what we have coming to us." We argue that the institutional context of prison—a total institution in which law is a hypervisible organizing force—enhances this form of legal mobilization by prisoners, trumping the very social and psychological factors that this context otherwise produces and that in other populations tamp down claims making.

Chapter 4 focuses on prisoners' counternarratives, which complicate our analysis of how prisoners make sense of the grievance system and prison more generally. Here we find that despite their cynicism about many aspects of the criminal justice system, nearly half of the men we interviewed expressed a belief in the fairness of the system in general and a surprising faith in law and evidence as the key ingredients in winning an appeal. In addition, many prisoners told us that CDCR officials are human beings who are simply doing a job and spoke of other prisoners as abusers of the grievance system. Not infrequently, they commented that prisoners who abuse the system should be disciplined and subjected to strict controls. As we will see, this apparent ambivalence—cleaving to the fairness of the system that holds them captive, to the solidity of rights that at other points they disdain as a "joke," to the fundamental decency of guards whom they often complained about, and to the carceral logic of control that they mostly chafed at—in some ways parallels disconnects in CDCR staff talk. Above all, it underscores the enduring legitimacy of the law and, more broadly, the cultural power of both rights discourse and carceral logic.

In chapters 5 and 6, we turn our attention to the CDCR staff who routinely handle these prisoners' appeals. Chapter 5 traces the impact of the conflicting logics of rights and carceral control on prison staff. Using data from our sometimes lengthy interviews with them, we focus here on the dilemmas and challenges facing these personnel and their practical, managerial, and cognitive solutions. Almost all of these staff said that filing a grievance is a legitimate prisoner right and that the grievance system is a useful managerial tool. Nonetheless, they ridiculed prisoners who file grievances and trivialized their appeals. We put this incongruence in institutional context, emphasizing staff members' perception of carceral management, or what some officials called the "operational realities" of prison. Drawing on and extending scholarship on administrative decision making, we see that these officials are caught between the perceived practical realities of their carceral institution and attending to its logics, while at the same time acceding to the powerful cultural logic of rights. Impugning the character of prisoners who exercise their right to appeal is a cognitive solution to this tension—and one that is readily available in the broader cultural "tool kit" (Swidler 1986, 273). We argue that this cognitive turn has not-so-subtle racial implications, as the portrayal of the overly pampered prisoner echoes precisely the post–civil rights trope that people of color are entitlement-seeking beneficiaries of special privileges.

In the second half of the chapter, we examine the ways in which an intense focus on rules, process, and paperwork may provide another kind of solution, shoring up certainty in this uncertain terrain and facilitating emotional distance in a field of pain. In a context of messy he said/she said allegations, in which denials can "occasion the imposition of violence upon others" (Cover 1986), staff find cognitive certainty and emotional solace in what they described as "cut-and-dried" procedures. Revealing the depth of the administrative and emotional challenges, however, there were inevitably cracks in this wall of confidence. Officials who repeatedly told us that recourse to rules made their job easy also spoke of "gray areas" that require interpretive leaps, and some who said they had a clear conscience later rued that their job can be, as one person put it, "spooky."

Chapter 6 focuses on CDCR staff as organizational actors who share institutional loyalties and a commitment to carceral logic but hold different positions in the organization and are thus oriented differently vis-à-vis the incarceration/rights tension. Drawing from the scholarship on administrative decision making (Emerson 1991; Hawkins 1992; Mashaw 1983; Sainsbury 2008), we begin by outlining the mechanisms that produce consistent denial decisions at all levels of appeal. Looking beyond this outcome consistency, these staff members' interview responses reveal conflict across ranks that occasionally erupts into name-calling ("knucklehead" being one favorite). We show that these conflicts are patterned and conclude with a discussion of what this pattern can tell us about the dilemmas inherent in an organization that prioritizes the logic of incarceration but also must adhere to a rhetoric of rights, and how these dilemmas are differentially distributed across the organization.

Throughout these chapters, we see the various ways the logics of rights and confinement are entangled in the inmate grievance system and in the legal consciousness of grievance participants. In speaking to inmates and staff about the appeals process, we were at first surprised when we encountered prisoners giving a nod to carceral logic and staff who insisted on the legitimacy of prisoners' right to appeal. Perhaps we should not have been, given that both of these logics are part and parcel of our collective legal consciousness and contemporary culture.

The written grievances in our random sample, analyzed in chapter 7, present a sharp contrast to the flashes of ideological convergence we encountered in our interviews. Tracing frames deployed by prisoners and staff across four levels of review, we reveal that these written documents present in their hardened form the respective logics of rights and confinement. Indeed, the grievance taken as a whole, including prisoners' narratives and officials' responses, offers a dramatic illustration of the broader contradiction. Not only are prisoners' grievances—typically narrated in the language of rights and needs—usually denied by officials, but these officials speak the clipped language of carceral policy and rarely engage directly with the rights and needs issues that dominate inmates' narratives. What is noteworthy, in other words, is not the almost uniform pattern of denial, which is arguably predictable in such an asymmetrical setting. More interesting are the diametrically different languages and logics deployed by the two sides in these formal documents, and the contrast of this rigid opposition with the far more nuanced, not to say conflicted, positions expressed in our interview conversations. The chapter ends with a discussion of the strategic and fluid quality of legal consciousness and the key role played by power inequalities in shaping it.

In the conclusion, we sum up our findings and discuss their implications for our understanding not only of disputing, legal mobilization, and legal consciousness, but of prison life itself. We emphasize that institutional and structural location are critical to making sense of our findings, some of which appear at first glance to be counterintuitive and inconsistent with the prevailing literature. And we reflect on the importance of multiple sources of data across contexts—archived documents as well as spontaneous interview conversations—for complicating our understanding of these processes and advancing theory. Looking beyond the institutional and structural environment and methodological context, our analysis underscores the importance of situating work in its historical setting and the seismic tensions of the larger ideological-cultural landscape. Last but not least, we add our voices to the call for more studies of daily life in prison, this most peculiar yet invisible of American institutions.

CHAPTER 2

"Needles," "Haystacks," and "Dead Watchdogs"

The Prison Litigation Reform Act and the Inmate Grievance System in California

The 1960s and 1970s saw the emergence of an active prisoner rights movement in the United States that focused on improving the conditions of confinement as well as initiating large-scale social change outside of prison. Prisoner rights activism was an integral part of the broader nexus of social movements that gained momentum in the second half of the twentieth century. Indicative of the perceived power of this movement, departments of corrections across the United States set up internal grievance systems to address the threat of politically motivated riots and other prison management problems.[1]

Spearheaded by Black Muslim prisoners, "the radical prison movement insisted that ideas of agency and citizenship be taken seriously" and viewed prisoners not just as the targets for empowerment but as central actors in the transformation of society (Katzenstein 2005, 242). In an early manifestation of this radical movement, striking inmates at Folsom State Prison in Northern California in 1970 drafted a "bill of rights for prisoners" that focused on the rights to organize into unions, to vote, to have access to the media, to receive furloughs, to maintain social ties by allowing members of the community to come into prison, and to be free of mental and physical cruelty (Cuevas 2012).

Muslim prisoners won what has been called "the first modern prisoners' rights case" (Jacobs and Kraft 1978, 36) with *Cooper v. Pate*, 378 U.S. 546 (1964), in which the U.S. Supreme Court upheld their right to use Section 1983 of the Civil Rights Act of 1871 to contest religious discrimination by prison officials. Supported by advocacy groups such as the National Prison Project of the American Civil Liberties Union (ACLU) (founded in 1972) and a network of other local and national organizations, the movement won multiple landmark cases. By the time the radical prison movement died down in the 1980s, the "hands-off" approach that federal courts had traditionally followed with regard to state prisons had been substantially reconfigured, if not abandoned (Feeley and Rubin 1998).

Intensifying the role of the judiciary in prisoners' rights, the Civil Rights of Institutionalized Persons Act (CRIPA) of 1980 allowed the U.S. attorney general to sue officials who operated prisons under conditions that systematically violated inmates' constitutional rights. By the 1990s, almost all of the fifty-three U.S. jurisdictions had had at least one of their penal facilities declared unconstitutional. Perhaps not surprisingly, local officials were becoming increasingly hostile to what they considered federal courts' micromanaging of state prisons.

At the same time, the number of people held in U.S. prisons soared, more than doubling in the 1980s. This explosion in the size of the prison population in conjunction with the prisoner rights' movement flooded court dockets with prisoner lawsuits, and litigation costs swiftly escalated. In 1995 alone, 41,679 civil rights lawsuits were filed in federal court by prisoners contesting the conditions of their confinement, constituting 19 percent of the federal docket of civil cases (Schlanger 2003, 1558). Referring to this period, Adlerstein (2001, 1683) noted an "iron triangle" of imperatives relating to prison management, consisting of local officials' demands for prison autonomy, an emphasis on cost containment, and the advance of prisoners' procedural rights. Adlerstein observed that these imperatives sat in an uneasy tension and ultimately led to passage of the Prison Litigation Reform Act (PLRA) of 1996.

THE PLRA AND "FRIVOLOUS" PRISONER LAWSUITS

When Republicans won Congress in 1994, one plank of their "Contract with America" was tort reform, addressing what they saw as Americans' increasing litigiousness. The effort to rein in what was called the "flood" of prisoner litigation coincided with this endeavor.[2] In 1995, a number of congressional bills attempted to restrict inmate lawsuits—with titles such as Stopping Abusive Prisoner Lawsuits and Control of Abusive Prisoner Litigation Practices—but none was passed. The following year, prisoner litigation restrictions were attached to an appropriations bill and called the Prison Litigation Reform Act (PLRA).

To galvanize support for the restrictions, the National Association of Attorneys General put together a list of what they alleged were the most frivolous prisoner lawsuits, and the short congressional debate surrounding the PLRA consisted primarily of retelling the stories of this egregious litigation. Among them were tales of prisoners suing for the right to chunky peanut butter, a prisoner who complained about a lack of salad bars in his facility, and a New York prisoner who allegedly sued because his towels were white and not beige (141 Cong. Rec. S. 14629 [1995]). Honorable Jon Newman (1996, 522), chief judge of the Second Circuit Court of Appeals, subsequently exposed these accounts as "misleading characterization[s]" of the actual lawsuits.[3] In the meantime, these mischaracterizations had been disseminated in a National Association of Attorneys General news release, cited in the *Congressional Record,* and published in a *New York Times* letter to the editor (see Newman 1996, 520). As they reached the status of folklore, they contributed to a growing disdain for prisoner litigation and a sense of urgency to rein it in.

When the PLRA passed in 1996, its primary intent was to restrict prisoner access to courts, based on the assumption that most inmate litigation was without merit. The fact that only about 1 percent of federal prisoner lawsuits at that time—most of which were filed pro se— were decided in favor of the inmate was used as proof that they were not meritorious. Senator Orin Hatch, a key sponsor of the bill, proclaimed confidently, "The vast majority of these suits are completely without merit. . . . The crushing burden of these frivolous suits makes it difficult for the courts to consider meritorious claims" (141 Cong. Rec. S. 14418 [1995]). Senator Robert Dole introduced the act by quoting then Chief Justice Rehnquist saying that prisoners "litigate at the drop of a hat," and this law would end "inmate litigation fun-and-games" (141 Cong. Rec. S. 4626 [1995]). The examples he gave of allegedly typical issues that inmates litigate involved "insufficient locker space, a defective haircut, the failure of prison officials to invite a prisoner to a pizza party. . . . And, yes, being served chunky peanut butter instead of the creamy variety" (S. 4413). "The bottom line," Dole said, "is that prisons should be prisons, not law firms" (S. 7498). Senator Kyl was equally blunt: "Most inmate lawsuits are meritless. . . . Filing frivolous civil rights lawsuits has become a recreational activity for long-term residents of our prisons" (S. 7515).

Among the PLRA's provisions were several that restricted judicial intervention into prison management, the most significant of which was that consent decrees—court-ordered reforms imposed by means of settlement—were to be terminated unless they were as "narrowly drawn" as possible and used "the least intrusive means necessary to correct the violation" (18 U.S.C. Section 3626[a]). Other provisions restricted the ability of individual prisoners to seek legal recourse. First, the law precluded inmates from suing for mental or emotional suffering in the absence of any physical injury (42 U.S.C. 1997[e]). For example, in *Oses v. Fair,* 739 F. Supp. 707 (D.Mass. 1990), the court confirmed that a prison guard put the barrel of a cocked gun in a prisoner's mouth in retaliation for a rumored affair between the prisoner and the guard's wife. The meager $1,000 in damages imposed by the court would have been prohibited under PLRA because there was no physical injury. Even physical symptoms associated with emotional stress have been disallowed as grounds for a lawsuit. Citing the PLRA, the court in *Todd v. Graves,* 217 F. Supp. 2d. 958, 960 (S.D. Iowa 2002), declared: "Prison itself is a stressful environment. If the symptoms alleged [high blood pressure, hypertension, dizziness, and insomnia] were enough to satisfy the physical injury requirement . . . very few plaintiffs would be barred by the physical injury rule from seeking compensation on the claims of emotional distress. The court has no basis upon which to conclude that result was intended by Congress."

Second, the law eliminated the traditional waiving of the filing fee (at the time $150) for indigent inmates, who constitute the majority of these plaintiffs (28 U.S.C. Section 1915). Instead, inmates who file federal cases have to make a down payment, with monthly installments equaling 20 percent of the money deposited in their prison accounts (28 U.S.C. Section 1915[b]). If an inmate wishes to appeal a court decision, a new filing fee is imposed. Even if a case is dismissed without being heard, inmates must continue to pay installments, with the result that some prisoners are responsible for multiple monthly payments. This filing-fee requirement imposes enormous administrative costs for the processing of these relatively small amounts of money and has been criticized by one judge as "mean-spirited and unnecessary," even while he upheld its substance (*Luedtke v. Gudmanson,* 971 F.Supp. 1263, 1266 [E.D. Wis. 1997]).

Third, the PLRA has a "three-strikes" provision (28 U.S.C. Section 1915[g]). Fueled by the conviction that the alleged flood of meritless lawsuits was the fault of what were derisively called "frequent filers,"

Congress sought to penalize prisoners who file lawsuits that are dismissed. Thus the PLRA requires the full filing fee up front from any inmate who has had three lawsuits dismissed as "frivolous, malicious, or for failing to state a claim for relief"[4]—even though this latter arguably speaks primarily to the legal ineptitude of some pro se filers rather than the merit of their claims.

Most important for our purposes here, the PLRA mandated that "no action shall be brought with respect to prison conditions under section 1983 of this title, or any other Federal law, by a prisoner confined in any jail, prison, or other correctional facility until such administrative remedies *as are available* are exhausted" (42 U.S.C. Section 1997e[a], emphasis added). It thus deleted CRIPA's provision that only internal remedies which are "plain, speedy, and effective" have to be exhausted. As a result, even inmates in states with egregiously faulty internal grievance procedures are required to exhaust those remedies before seeking access to the courts.

Former correctional administrators, activists, academics, and the courts alike have criticized the PRLA. Jeanne Woodford, former acting secretary of the CDCR and former warden at San Quentin State Prison, testified before Congress: "For those prison officials who fear the courts, the PLRA provides an incentive to make the grievance procedures more complicated than necessary. . . . Grievances may be rejected because the prisoner could not clearly articulate his complaint, or for a minor problem such as using handwriting that is too small. I know of at least one state that will screen out appeals if they are not signed in blue ink and yet another state that charges prisoners to file an appeal."[5]

A report on the consequences of the PLRA by Human Rights Watch (2009, 12) concurs: "Some grievance systems include requirements that seem designed to discourage, rather than facilitate, compliance [with the requirements] by prisoners." Likewise, Bordt and Musheno (1988, 7) reveal that even in a state where inmates were once represented on grievance committees, the process was transformed into a "sophisticated social control mechanism serving only bureaucratic interests."

The PLRA has also been criticized as "internally inconsistent," full of typographical errors, and in violation of the Rules of Appellate Procedure (*McGore v. Wrigglesworth*, 114 F.3d 601, 603 [6th Cir. 1997]). Citing Chief Justice Rehnquist, who noted the glaring deficiencies of another piece of legislation by proclaiming that "a watchdog did not bark in the night," Chief Judge Boyce Martin of the U.S. Circuit Court of Appeals, Sixth Circuit, wrote dryly, "When Congress penned the

Prison Litigation Reform Act . . . the watchdog must have been dead" (603). As another federal judge complained, the prison grievance systems can become "a series of stalling tactics, and dead-ends without resolution" (*Campbell v. Chaves*, 402 F. Supp. 2d. 1101, 1106 n. 3 [D. Ariz. 2005]).

Despite these arguably devastating critiques and the many undeniable problems they reveal with the PLRA, the courts have upheld every one of its provisions. For example, the three-strikes provision for "frequent filers" was immediately contested as an unconstitutional violation of the equal protection clause, but has been validated by the courts (*Wilson v. Yaklich*, 148 F. 3d 596 [6th Cir. 1998]; *Abdul-Akbar v. McKelvie*, 239 F. 3d 307 [3d Cir. 2001]; *Higgins v. Carpenter*, 258 F. 3d 797 [8th Cir. 2001]). The courts also have affirmed even the most stringent exhaustion requirements. As one legal scholar notes, "The Supreme Court has made it clear that the PLRA's exhaustion requirement is comprehensive and to be strictly enforced" (Belbot 2004, 296). The U.S. Supreme Court has further decided that prisoners who seek types of relief—such as money damages—for which the internal grievance system is not relevant must still first go through that avenue before accessing the courts (*Booth v. Churner*, 532 U.S. 731 [2001]).

While administrative law doctrine generally requires people to exhaust administrative remedies before filing a lawsuit, exceptions are usually made for minor technical errors or extreme injury. In contrast, the PLRA exhaustion requirement has been interpreted as absolute. For example, in *Woodford v. Ngo,* 548 U.S. 81 (2006), the U.S. Supreme Court decided that inmates who do not initiate their internal complaint within the stipulated timeline, *beginning from the time the contested condition was first experienced even if it is ongoing,* may have their case dismissed on the grounds that they did not appropriately exhaust internal remedies.[6] Schlanger (2003, 1652) observes, "Courts implementing the PLRA seem . . . to be looking to the extraordinarily harsh doctrinal framework of habeas 'procedural default,' which gives federal courts almost no discretion to excuse even the most technical of procedural errors."[7]

The courts have also endorsed the broad discretion the PLRA gives states in the formulation and implementation of grievance procedures. In this regard, Schlanger (2003, 1650) notes, "Essentially, then, the sky's the limit for the procedural complexity or difficulty of the exhaustion requirement." Jeanne Woodford, former acting secretary of the CDCR, acknowledged this complexity and the problematic nature of the exhaustion requirement when testifying before Congress in 2008 and asking for "necessary fixes" to the Prison Litigation Reform Act. As she explained, "The exhaustion requirement of the PLRA, which was made even more stringent by a Supreme Court decision in a notorious case with my name on it, presents prisoners with often-insurmountable obstacles to overcome in order to file complaints in federal court."[8] She went further: "Because of the PLRA, that prisoner may be forced to suffer for over a year while he completes the exceedingly complex, and forever delayed California CDCR grievance process before he can even file a lawsuit. I do not think that the PLRA was intended to cause such harm, but it undoubtedly has, and needs to be fixed" (4).

There are only a few deviations from the pattern of strict court deference to the PLRA guidelines, and the extremity of these cases reveals just how high the threshold is for such deviations. In one such case, an inmate's grievance was heard by the courts despite the fact that he had missed New York State's fourteen-day deadline for internal appeals. The case involved a prisoner who was unconscious and disabled during those fourteen days due to the negligent medical care his suit was challenging. The prison had dismissed the plaintiff's grievance for failure to comply with the timeline despite his incapacitated state. The court in *Cruz v. Jordan* (80 F. Supp. 2d 109 [S.D.N.Y. 1999]) found in the prisoner's favor, declaring that remedies were effectively not "available" to him in his unconscious state, but the decision was overturned on appeal for other reasons (Neal v. Goord, 267 F.3d 116 [2d Cir. 2001]).

In another (partial) deviation from the pattern, in 2007 the U.S. Supreme Court decided unanimously in favor of Michigan inmates whose cases were dismissed because, even though they satisfied the PLRA's exhaustion requirement, they did not specifically plead (or state) that they had done so in their complaints. While Chief Justice Roberts decided for the inmates, he nonetheless used the occasion to decry prisoner lawsuits: "Most of these cases have no merit; many are frivolous.... We are not insensitive to the challenges faced by the lower federal courts in managing their dockets and attempting to separate, when it comes to prisoner suits, not so much wheat from chaff as needles from haystacks" (Jones v. Bock, 549 U.S. 199 [2007]).

These few extreme cases aside, the courts have overwhelmingly deferred to the congressional intent behind the PLRA to limit prisoners' lawsuits. And indeed, subsequent to enactment of the PLRA, the rate of prisoner lawsuits fell substantially. The number of prisoners' federal civil rights cases declined by 33 percent from 1995 to 1997, even as

prison populations continued to increase. By 2010, the per-prisoner filing rate had fallen by more than 60 percent (from twenty-six federal
cases for every thousand prisoners in 1995 to eleven per thousand in
2010)—a decline most experts attribute to the exhaustion requirement
as well as the new filing fees the PLRA imposed and the legislation's ban
on emotional damage awards (Belbot 2004; Schlanger 2003; Schlanger
and Shay 2008).

MECHANICS OF THE CALIFORNIA PRISONER GRIEVANCE SYSTEM

The PLRA left it to the individual states to design and implement their
own grievance systems, and as we have seen, courts have given them
wide leeway to do so. Despite this flexibility, the broad outlines of most
states' systems are remarkably similar. They generally require that an
inmate who wishes to file a grievance first appeal informally to the official with the most immediate jurisdiction over the condition being contested. Subsequent to that, there are usually three levels of formal review,
with the appellant able to contest the official response until the third
and final level.

Many state systems are riddled with difficulties for prisoners attempting to have a grievance heard. In Mississippi, the prisoner handbook
that outlines grievance procedures conspicuously neglects to mention
any deadline for filing, meaning prisoners may easily miss the narrow
five-day window of opportunity. In addition, Mississippi prisoners have
their grievances dismissed if they do not include the "magic words, 'This
is a request for administrative remedy,'"[9] The Mississippi policy includes
no timeline for officials to respond to inmate grievances, and it is not
uncommon for inmates to wait years before hearing anything about
their grievance. In the meantime, they are precluded from filing another
grievance (unless they are willing to withdraw the pending one), which
the ACLU and others argue creates an incentive for official inaction and
pressure on inmates to drop appeals that may no longer be relevant and
which act as a barrier to further complaints (42).

Other states' grievance systems are also problematic. An evaluation
of the Ohio inmate grievance system in 2001 found multiple problems,
including frequent retaliation against inmates who file and policies that
are so intricate and spread across so many different sources that few can
make sense of them (Nathan 2001). The same study reported that Ohio
fails to inform prisoners about the filing deadlines and the possibility of

appeal. Washington State's procedures are scattered across various sources and "difficult to find," and Hawaii's procedures are "difficult to follow" (quoted in *Brief of Amici Curiae* 2006, 43–44). Michigan has a so-called modified access policy that bars some prisoners from filing for ninety days unless they get permission from officials. Lengthy response times are widespread, with official responses sometimes taking years, long after the issue being complained about has become moot (43).

The Inmate Grievance Task Evaluation Report conducted by the Missouri Department of Corrections surveyed thirty-nine states and the District of Columbia and found that problems with prison grievance systems are pervasive (cited in *Brief of Amici Curiae* 2006, 43–44). Officially presented evidence suggests that California is no exception. In 2011, the State of California's inspector general, Robert A. Barton, submitted a special report to Governor Brown tellingly titled "CDCR's Revised Appeals Process Leaves Problems Unaddressed." In it, the inspector general revealed the findings of his review and identified three broad areas of concern that required action by the CDCR, including the lack of a way to verify receipt and processing of appeals, the need to provide information to inmates that would enable them to resubmit rejected appeals, and confusion resulting from the rapid implementation of changes in the appeals process (Barton 2011). In their report on the California correctional system's exposure to litigation, Feeley and Swearingen (2008, 11) faulted the internal grievance system: "It shifts focus from an inquiry concerned primarily with the declaration of rights and wrongdoings to one focused on the prison's own institutional goals of resolving disputes quickly and to their own advantage."[10] To understand these concerns, it is necessary to review the history and the nuts and bolts of the California grievance process.

California instituted an inmate grievance system in 1973 at the height of the prisoners' rights movement, well before the PLRA required such procedures. That same year, the California Senate commissioned a study of the newly established grievance system. In their 1973 report, the study's authors made three central recommendations. First, they urged the appointment of a deputy director of legal affairs to manage the grievance system, "with the power to order action . . . to correct errors and injustices"; second, they recommended that "appeals officers" with legal training be appointed at each prison; and finally, they stated that there should be an "external ombudsman" with independence from the corrections department to provide oversight.[11]

None of these recommendations was put into effect, but the external ombudsman raised the most hackles. The superintendent of one prison[12] wrote to the deputy director of corrections, "I am against an external ombudsman. I feel that the entire grievance procedure can best be handled by people within the system." The warden at San Quentin State Prison wrote, "An ombudsman should *not* have the authority to overrule the administrator, as this would lead to chaos [emphasis in original]."[13] The director of corrections, R.K. Procunier[14] summarized the department's reaction, writing to the chair of the Select Committee on Penal Institutions: "I remain firmly opposed to the concept [of an external ombudsman]. It is our obligation to develop an effective internal review system, and the existence of a parallel outside review system would operate to reduce the feeling of responsibility and duty which is necessary to make the departmental system work effectively. Additionally, if the department does the job the way it should be done, there will be no need for external supervision of the same questions."

The 1973 procedures resembled in broad outline those of the current system. The most striking difference is the relatively miniscule number of grievances that prisoners filed in those early years. In the year following the system's establishment, only about 500 prisoner appeals made their way through the system, as compared to more than 16,000 thirty years later.[15] Even considering that the prison population in California by 2006 reached approximately 160,000—as compared to only 20,000 incarcerated in the early 1970s—the rate for these final appeals had risen by 400 percent.

Today, California inmate grievance procedures are specified in Article 8, Title 15 ("Crime Prevention and Corrections") of the California Code of Regulations (CCR). The article begins, "Any inmate or parolee under the department's jurisdiction may appeal any departmental decision, action, condition, or policy which they can demonstrate as having an adverse effect upon their welfare." To file a grievance, prisoners are required to complete an Inmate/Parolee Appeal Form—officially numbered and colloquially referred to as a "602." These forms codify the prisoner's complaint and requested remedy as well as the CDCR's response to that request, creating a dialogue of sorts between prisoners and CDCR officials.

When we began this research, inmates were required to attempt to resolve their grievances informally with the relevant staff as the first step in filing a 602. This "informal" characterization was in some ways misleading, as it was the first official, written step in the 602 process. It was informal only in that it was not logged into the tracking system. At this level, the inmate wrote his complaint in the first section of the 602 form ("A. Describe Problem"), followed by his requested remedy ("B. Action Requested"). The official to whom he presented his 602 then filled in his response ("C. INFORMAL LEVEL Staff Response").

In some cases—such as an allegation of staff misconduct, contestation by the inmate of a serious disciplinary violation charged against him/her, or an inmate complaint about his/her classification—this informal step was waived. In such cases, the inmate still filled in the 602 form, but it bypassed informal-level responders. If the informal effort was unsuccessful, or if it was bypassed, three levels of formal review were available. The informal level of review was eliminated in 2011, but the subsequent three formal levels were largely unchanged.

At the first formal level, the inmate's description of his/her complaint is limited to one paragraph on the 602 form, plus an additional page, front and back, if the inmate wants to expand on his/her concern—an addition that most appellants avail themselves of; supporting documentation may be attached too, and often is. The inmate forwards this to the inmate appeals coordinator (IAC) at the prison, a position commonly held by a CDCR correctional officer II (CO II, a middle rank, below that of captain). The IAC screens each grievance to determine if it is complete and in compliance with CDCR regulations, and returns to the appellant those that do not conform to strict requirements. Among the most important of these requirements is that the 602 be filed within fifteen days of the incident being contested.

Other reasons for screening out a grievance include such things as "unclear appeal issue" or "not within the jurisdiction of the department" (CCR, Title 15 §3084.3). If the stated reason for screening out an appeal can be corrected (for example, the inmate did not submit the proper documentation), the appeal can be revised and resubmitted. The IAC then usually routes the grievance to the correctional authority most relevant for the complaint (for example, the captain of the yard where the prisoner resides) for a first formal response. The response takes one of three forms: granting the requested remedy in full, granting the requested remedy in part, or denying the requested remedy. The official response and justification are entered on the 602 form beneath the inmate's narrative. If dissatisfied with this outcome, the prisoner may explain his/her dissatisfaction beneath the official's response and submit the grievance for a second formal review, conducted by the warden or—more commonly—his/her designee, such as the deputy warden or the IAC. Once again, the grievance may be granted, partially granted, or denied. These responses too are entered on the 602 form, directly beneath the inmate's second-level narrative.

If the appeal is not fully granted at the second formal level, or is partially granted but leaves the prisoner dissatisfied, the prisoner may request a third review by the CDCR director of adult institutions, who in turn delegates the review to the Office of Inmate Appeals in Sacramento ("Inmate Appeals Branch" [IAB]) under the direction of the chief of inmate appeals. There, each grievance is read and responded to by an examiner who may or may not conduct further investigation. Investigations sometimes involve telephone calls to officials at the prison where the complaint originated or document retrieval, but they rarely involve a trip to the prison.[16] In the final section of the 602, the Inmate Appeals Branch informs the appellant of its decision, including a written statement that makes it clear the appellant has exhausted all internal remedies.

There are a few general exceptions to this process. After the CDCR medical system was put in receivership by the courts in 2006, medical appeals were given their own track (this did not affect our data since the grievance sample we collected was from 2005–2006). A separate form, 602-HC (Health Care), is used when the complaint involves medical, dental, or mental health care, and specialized staff evaluate and respond to them at each level. Another exception involves allegations of staff misconduct. The procedure for these allegations is carefully constructed to preserve the privacy of the implicated staff according to the California Peace Officers' Bill of Rights.

The official process for handling staff complaints was specified in a CDCR administrative bulletin sent to all supervisory personnel in 2003. The bulletin consisted of a seven-page "training module" followed by several attachments and a multiple-choice test. It began: "Staff complaints raise important issues with respect to how we manage our core responsibilities. Information developed through staff complaint inquiries can provide the Department critical information regarding its effectiveness at managing the inmate population. . . . Since institutions are environments where allegations of misconduct may reflect attempts by inmates to manipulate or retaliate against staff, the right of staff to due process is critical to preserve the integrity of the system" (CDCR 2003, 2).

Because of concern for the rights of staff and possible repercussions for their careers, and because it is assumed that inmates may "manipulate or retaliate," the focus of the procedures specified in the bulletin is on guarding against false charges. For example, inmate grievances alleging staff misconduct must be accompanied by a "Rights and Responsibility" form signed by the inmate. The form states in part: "It is against the law to make a complaint that you know to be false. If you make a complaint against an officer knowing it is false, you can be prosecuted on a misdemeanor charge. (An inmate/parolee who makes a complaint against a departmental peace officer, knowing it is false may be issued a serious disciplinary rule violation in addition to being prosecuted on a misdemeanor charge.)"

While these official parameters of the prisoner grievance system are spelled out in the California Code of Regulations, Title 15 ("Crime Prevention and Corrections"), and in various administrative bulletins and memoranda, the details of its operation vary from prison to prison. For example, in one of the prisons we visited, the IAC is primarily a screening and routing agent; in another, the IAC specializes in responding to disciplinary appeals for the chief deputy warden; and at the third prison in our sample, the IAC answers all appeals at the second level, except those that deal with contestations of disciplinary infractions, disability issues, and complaints about missing or damaged property. Staffing for appeals also varies, with some prisons including several IACs and assisting clerks, while others are equipped with a sole IAC who does everything from physically collecting 602s from boxes in the cell blocks to investigating prisoners' allegations.

Despite such variations, many constants characterize the operation of the system, and in subsequent chapters we focus on the most important recurring patterns. Several constants are worth noting here for introductory purposes. First, the wardens are not typically involved in the grievance process except to sign off on them at the second formal level before they leave the institution for final review in Sacramento. Warden Donald Brown[17] told us he delegates the signing of grievances to his deputy warden, who signs his own name. "I never touch them," he said. "I never see them. I don't have anything to do with appeals . . . unless it comes up as part of a lawsuit." There is one exception to this hands-off approach. When a complaint against staff is involved, these wardens take note. Warden Sandy Reyes explained, "I wanna see everything on staff complaints. Everything else goes to the chief [deputy warden]. . . . The inspector general has the authority to come in here whenever, so I'm gonna cover my ass [on staff complaints]."

A second constant is the emphasis on efficiency and speed of processing. As we see in more detail in chapter 5, the paper-chase aspect of the 602 process was emphasized by all the CDCR officials we interviewed, from IACs, to captains, wardens, and associate wardens, to examiners and managers at the Inmate Appeals Branch. One IAC showed us her process, completing her initial review of an appeal in less than sixty seconds as we watched. With up to thirty appeals arriving at their desks every day, these IACs work under enormous pressure and have devised assembly-line routines to enable them to keep the pace. This is not to say that inmates' grievances are always answered in a timely manner. As many prisoners told us and official CDCR data confirm, appellants may wait months for responses and sometimes never hear anything at all. But the pressure of moving paperwork forward and not falling behind in the face of the steady stream of incoming 602s was palpable throughout our conversations with these staff. When we first visited the Inmate Appeals Branch in Sacramento and were shown cabinet after cabinet of inmate appeals tucked in files lining the walls of a cavernous room, we were overwhelmed by the sheer volume of grievances being processed at any given moment and historically.

As we see below and throughout the book, a third constant is the low positive response rate.

DIVERSE GRIEVANCES, UNIFORM OUTCOMES: GRANTS, PARTIAL GRANTS, AND (MOSTLY) DENIALS

The substance of these grievances—the issues these prisoners file on—varies more than the mechanics of the process. The CDCR categorizes grievances according to "nature of complaint." These official classifications are generally straightforward, with the exception of "staff complaints." Indicative of the contentious nature of complaints against staff, several administrative bulletins have been issued instructing officials how to classify them. For example, Administrative Bulletin 98/100 reads: "When an appeal alleges staff misconduct and other issues . . . the inmate/parolee shall be notified that the staff complaint is being handled and that the other issue(s) must be appealed separately." In spite of this instruction, several grievances in our sample in which prisoners complained about officials who had interfered with their visiting privileges, damaged their property, or withheld medical care were classified not as staff complaints but rather "visiting," "property," or "medical." In one case, a prisoner who had been given a disciplinary infraction said he had been "humiliated and intimidated by 4 female officers" and that the infraction they gave him was uncalled for. Angry that his appeal had been classified and responded to as "disciplinary," the appellant protested, "Failure to process this staff complaint as such is clear case of covering up staff misconduct." In a similar case in which a staff complaint was processed as "disciplinary," the prisoner appellant declared, "The Department becomes complicit in the code of silence . . . covering up corruption."

There are no doubt institutional and administrative-political reasons why the prisons would want to underclassify complaints against staff— and hence why an administrative bulletin would be necessary and why it is nonetheless periodically contravened. However, other categories of complaints are less complicated and generally align with our independent classification.

As reported in table 1, according to CDCR classifications, the most common complaint raised in the written grievances in our random sample related to medical needs, followed closely by contestations of disciplinary actions. Together, medical and disciplinary complaints comprised approximately 37 percent of the grievances in our sample. Testifying to the diversity of these grievances, the six most frequent categories of complaint (medical, disciplinary, property, disability accommodations, programming and work issues, and complaints against staff) together accounted for only about two-thirds (66.1 percent) of the total. Other complaints referred to living conditions related to the physical facilities; custody and classification issues, such as whether a prisoner was classified as gang-affiliated or what custody level he/she was assigned to; case information/records, such as whether an inmate's earned credits had been accurately recorded; legal issues, including whether the prisoner had access to the law library and legal materials; transfers to other prisons, sometimes far from family; funds, such as disputes over deposits and withdrawals from trust accounts; visiting privileges, including disagreements about who may visit; segregation, including, but not limited to, solitary confinement; problems with mail delivery; and other issues.

Medical complaints accounted for almost 20 percent (19.9 percent) of the appeals in our random sample (see table 1). They come from prisoners requesting mental health care, pain relief, specialist referrals, and surgery, as well as from those contesting the quality of care they have received. Alfonso Lopez reported experiencing chronic trouble breathing and pain in his lungs. He wrote in his grievance that when he finally saw a doctor, "he recommended pepto-bismal and said they'd call me back in the morning. They never called me back and I continued to have severe pains in my lung and I was getting a fever almost every day." Thereafter, another doctor diagnosed him with pneumonia, and Lopez wrote: "They gave me anti-biotics for a week and shots, but still

TABLE 1 TYPES OF GRIEVANCES AS CATEGORIZED
BY THE CDCR, 2005–2006

Medical	58 (19.9)
Disciplinary	51 (17.5)
Property	24 (8.2)
ADA	22 (7.5)
Program/work incentive*	20 (6.8)
Complaints against staff	18 (6.2)
Mail	17 (5.8)
Custody/classification	15 (5.1)
Case information/record	15 (5.1)
Living conditions	14 (4.8)
Transfers	13 (4.5)
Funds	8 (2.7)
Visiting	7 (2.4)
Legal	5 (1.7)
Segregation	4 (1.4)
Reentry	1 (0.3)
Total	292 (100%)

SOURCE: Inmate Appeals Office, California Department of Corrections and Rehabilitation.

* The CDCR recognizes "program" and "work incentive" as separate classifications. However, they are combined here for presentation purposes and because they are combined in the classification scheme used in this research, as presented in chapter 3.

I was sick. Then they switched anti-biotics and I took them 'til they finished and still I was sick. . . . Now this is May, approximately 5 months later and still I have pain in my lungs. . . . They've taken way too long to follow up on the Valley Fever test that came up positive back in [date] and I feel my lungs is just getting more and more damaged."[18] Lopez requested to see a specialist "that is compitant and capable of determining what the problem is." His appeal was denied at the final level of review because, according to the CDCR, Mr. Lopez had received adequate treatment. Further, the Inmate Appeals Branch stated, the grievance "did not reveal a specific date related to the appellant's allegations of inappropriate medical treatment." This omission constituted a problem because "any issues related to his allegations should have been submitted within 15 days of the incident."

Another appellant, Anthony Thompkins, pleaded for the state to provide him with dentures. He wrote on the 602 form, "I've got major dental problems. I just had 3 teeth removed from the top here at [prison]. I have no teeth on top now. . . . I would like for the dentist to start the process for dentures. I need attention. . . . Thank you very much." When he was denied at the second formal level, Thompkins responded simply, "I must note that I'm in serious or dire need of dental care, soon." He was once again denied, with the Inmate Appeals Branch explaining that "Reception Center[19] inmates are provided limited dental services. . . . Although he may disagree, the appellant is receiving the appropriate dental intervention according to departmental policy."

Grievances that contest disciplinary infractions made up 17.5 percent of the appeals in our sample. It is perhaps not surprising that these appeals are second only to medical care in frequency, as disciplinary infractions on one's record can increase prison time and sometimes result in the denial of important privileges, such as yard time and visiting. They often involve several intertwined issues, and because the imposition of a "115" (the official number of the CDCR form used to report disciplinary infractions deemed serious) requires a hearing and grants certain due process rights, these grievance files are often the longest and most complicated.[20] In one such case, Donald Jones was in solitary confinement, where he reported spending twenty-three hours a day with a cell toilet that had been "turned off" for three days. According to his grievance, Jones had received a 115 disciplinary infraction because he refused to relinquish his food tray to the solitary confinement officer after eating, in protest against his backed-up toilet. Jones's handwritten appeal read: "Inmate [Jones] ask that attached 115 be dismissed and removed from his C. File. Yes inmate [Jones] did in fact hold his tray . . . inmate [Jones] held his tray in protest trying to get his cell toilet turned back on. . . . Because he had been in his cell 24 *hours smelling his own wastes* from when he used the toilet." The CDCR denied Jones's appeal at the final level of review, writing a short paragraph beginning, "The appellant was afforded all due process rights in the adjudication of the RVR [Rules Violation Report] and all procedural guidelines were met."

According to the CDCR classification scheme, property complaints comprise 8.2 percent of the grievances in our sample, making them the third-most-frequent category of appeal. Property is often missing or damaged as a result of, among other things, prisoners' transfers between prisons, administrative segregation, and cell searches. Norman Conrad began his grievance by describing his cell search: "I was told to exit my assigned cell, after being strip searched and wait in the dayroom until officers had finished searching. I was told that a receipt would be left for any confiscated items. Which brings me to the first problem. I cannot read the receipt, nor could my housing unit officers. I therefore had to take an inventory and determine what was missing. The following items I have looked for and know they are not here." Conrad attached an additional page, listing eleven missing items beginning with "organizer address/phone book, pad folder w/calculator, one pair prescription glasses and case."

Conrad's appeal was "granted in part" at the final level of review. The director of the IAB wrote that the address book and the pad folder with calculator were "confiscated" because they had hard covers that were considered contraband, as were the brown slippers, which "had an unknown language sewn on them," and the glasses because "the frames were made of wood and did not conform to custody regulations and the appellant already had in his possession two other pair of prescription glasses." The grievance was "granted in part" because, the IAB wrote, the prison "shall allow the appellant to choose one of the methods listed within CCR 3191 for disposing of personal property which is unauthorized."

Grievances filed under the Americans with Disabilities Act (ADA) are classified separately because of the particular legal issues they might raise. ADA appeals comprise 7.5 percent of our sample and run the gamut from requests for equipment such as canes and leg braces to accessible housing and, in several cases, softer shoes than the standard state-issue footwear. In his grievance, Harold Baker reported suffering from diabetic neuropathy. He wrote: "There are times—like right now—when my feet has cuts/sores on them and I don't even know where they came from. I have almost no feeling sensation in them, except when I get those pins and needle pains. Last night, there was blood on my socks. . . . [I request] that I receive some softer soled shoes." Baker's appeal was denied. In a short explanation, the IAB wrote that the doctors who examined him, although not denying his diagnosis of diabetic neuropathy, did not think he needed soft-soled shoes, and that the appellant "must realize that he cannot dictate what type of medical appliance or shoes he should be provided."

Many inmates in California have work assignments, and some attend programs, such as for drug addiction, alcohol dependency, or anger management. Almost 7 percent (6.8 percent) of appeals involve complaints about work and other programs, primarily complaints about their chronic inaccessibility and long waiting lists, which make it hard for prisoners to earn the credit given for participation in work or programs. Martin Garza wrote that he had been "disciplinary-free for three years" and that he was classified as eligible for a work assignment.

"However," he wrote, "having waited patiently . . . it has now become very evident that instead of progressing towards the top [of the waiting list], I've constantly been lowered. . . . Whether it be favoritism in the form of inmates being given jobs for the services in helping IGI [institutional gang investigator] or being yard informants, it is not proper as it continues pushing those of us that are equally entitled to the back of the line (list) and meanwhile are not able to earn our credits for good time and work." Garza's appeal was denied at the third level because, according to the IAB, "the appellant has not submitted any evidence to show that he was being treated with any form of discrimination or prejudice."

Complaints against staff, as officially classified, comprise 6.2 percent of the sample. While they include allegations of disrespect and actual physical battery, they often refer secondarily to property damage and disciplinary action. In one fairly typical case, Wayne Smith wrote that a correctional officer had entered his cell when he was not there to do a cell search, "tearing up his property bedding throwing clothes sheets blankets and other personal property all over the cell." Smith argued, "This cell search was conducted as a sole purpose as to harass prisoner [Smith] and taunt, target, and as a course of retaliation and reprisal for other staff misconduct [that] prisoner [Smith] has filed on this officer."[21] The IAB denied his appeal, writing, "An inquiry has been completed" and "[the officer] was exonerated of the appellant's allegations."

Prisoners' grievances vary not only by category or topic but by the apparent severity of the problems contested. A handful of the grievances in our sample raise arguably minor complaints, such as that of the inmate who filed a grievance because he was not allowed to receive an issue of *Black Men Magazine* because officials said it contained "explicit images that depict frontal nudity." He asked that the pages in question be sent to him so he could attach them to his 602 as proof that they were not contraband. While his appeal was "granted" at the second level, and the appellant was told the magazine would be issued to him, he did not receive it and appealed to the final level of review. Curiously, the IAB denied the appeal and wrote simply, "The appellant has failed to present compelling evidence and convincing argument to warrant modification of the decision reached by the institution."

Some apparently minor cases are nonetheless poignant. In one such case, Ramon Gutierrez wrote on a 602 that his sister had sent him a letter and enclosed "A Small Book of Stamps." He said the mailroom had removed the stamps and had not inventoried them as required by noting on the back of the envelope that something had been enclosed and

removed. He appealed to the CDCR for $3.70 to reimbur:
stamps. Gutierrez alleged that the mailroom "has been r
mistakes" and urged them to take "responsibility," conclud
the Book of Stamps does not cost much. But it is the princip
reviewer at the IAB denied him, stating categorically: "All r   . ...at
contains money orders, stamps . . . are inventoried and the contents are
written on the outside of the envelope. The envelope had no inventory
listings; [therefore] there was nothing enclosed but the letter."

Other claims are about very serious issues, quite apart from how
persuasive the grievance might be to any given reader. For example,
John Gardner, who allegedly wanted to target a sex offender, did
research in the law library to single out his victim and was said to have
conspired with fellow inmates to beat and slash the target in the prison
yard with a toothbrush outfitted with razors. He was placed in administrative segregation as a result. It is impossible to tell from this very
large file whether the "charges are based on false and unsubstantiated
information," as Gardner alleges, or how to evaluate his claim that "I
am not lie'n or making false claims."

In many cases, claims asserted in written grievances are both arguably
serious and credible, especially in light of the documentation on conditions of confinement in California's overcrowded prisons. Indeed, one
group grievance[22] cited many of the same conditions that the U.S. Supreme
Court found to be unconstitutional in *Brown v. Plata,* 563 U.S. __ (2011).
The prisoners alleged "eight contentions of deprivations of procedural
due process and of the minimum necessities of life in violation of USCA
Constitutional Amendments 8 and 14." Many of these directly related to
overcrowding. The prisoners wrote, "[This prison] is designed for 2,320
and houses 7,062. . . . The increase . . . has caused indecent and inhumane
conditions of confinement that is affecting Shelter, Ventilation, Plumbing,
Sanitation, Fire Safety, Medicine and Noise [each detailed in separate sec-
tions]. These conditions are totally without penological justification and
are barbarous and contrary to conditions of civilized decency." When the
prison replied that "triple bunking . . . was mandated by the CDCR due
to an increase in the inmate population," the prisoners noted, "The Eighth
Amendment is not a maybe or sometimes proposition." The CDCR
responded at the final level of review that the appellants had not presented
"any evidence or documentation" that they had "suffered adversely."

Despite this vast range in complaints, their seriousness, and the per-
suasiveness of the appellants' arguments, the evidence suggests that
these grievances are almost always denied. It is not our goal to track the

success of grievances or to determine what factors influence whether a grievance is screened out, granted, partially granted, denied, or lost in the process of being adjudicated—a goal that in any case would be stymied by the absence of data on the fate of grievances at the informal level and by what appears to be a very small number of fully granted appeals. Still, it is useful to estimate the grant rate not as a goal in itself, but as the backdrop for our analysis of legal mobilization and institutional disputing processes.

Not surprisingly given the asymmetrical nature of the process, the grant rate for grievances appears to be low at every level of formal review. It is impossible to estimate grant rates at the informal level because when we were collecting data, the CDCR did not log in informal grievances.[23] To complicate matters further, calculating grant rates for the formal levels of review is problematic because the CDCR's annual reports classify as "granted" any grievance that is either "granted in part" or "granted in full," effectively combining two distinct rulings into a single categorical outcome. Thus, in the Annual Report of the Inmate Appeals Branch for 2005–2006, the agency classified 55 percent of grievances as "granted" at the first level of review, 44 percent as "granted" at the second level, and 5.8 percent as "granted" at the final level.

Our research reveals that the real grant rate is far lower than these statistics suggest (see table 2). The 15,836 written grievances that reached the third level of review in 2005–2006 and for which an outcome is known provide the basis for our best empirically derived estimate of full grant rates and the ratio between full grants and partial grants. Of these grievances, only 0.2 percent were granted in full, 4.7 percent were granted in part, and 93.6 percent were denied. If we assume that this 1 to 23.5 ratio of full grants to partial grants roughly applies to earlier levels of review, we can calculate that of the 55 percent of "grants" reported by the CDCR at the first formal level, only an estimated 2.3 percent were granted in full; at the second formal level, of the 44 percent reported as "granted," an estimated 1.9 percent were granted in full.[24]

This extraordinarily low rate of grants was affirmed in our interviews with CDCR staff. When asked to estimate how many appeals they had dealt with over the course of their careers, the modal response of these CDCR personnel was "thousands," yet 95 percent of them estimated they had fully granted thirty or fewer.[25] Sonya Thurman, an Inmate Appeals Branch (IAB) examiner who described herself as "liberal" and expressed genuine concern for the welfare of prisoners, could recall fully granting only one grievance over the course of ten years.

TABLE 2   FINAL ADJUDICATION OF GRIEVANCES FOR POPULATION AND SAMPLE
DATA, 2005–2006

	Population (%)	Sample (%)
Denied	14,815 (93.6)	269 (92.1)
Granted in part	738 (4.7)	15 (5.1)
Granted	37 (0.2)	0 (0.0)
Canceled	243 (1.5)	8 (2.7)
Withdrawn	3 (0.0)	0 (0.0)
Total	15,836 (100)*	292 (100)

SOURCE: Inmate Appeals Office, California Department of Corrections and Rehabilitation.

* The total number of grievances submitted in 2005–2006 that made it to the third level of review was 16,430. The adjudication of 594 cases was not known; the total reported here reflects the total number of cases for which an outcome was known.

Several other personnel drew a blank when we asked them to describe an appeal they had granted. IAC Danielle Garcon told us, "I can't think of one offhand because it's so rare." Lucinda Gray, an examiner in the IAB, said categorically, "I *never* grant in full. I only grant in part."

Further, our random sample of grievances reveals that some "partial grants" are more symbolic than real. For example, in several of these partially granted grievances, officials wrote as the basis of the partial grant, "An inquiry into your allegation has been conducted" or "The appellant has been provided with a thorough response." In one case, an inmate alleged that being denied his Afrikan Swahili dictionary constituted "racial/cultural discrimination"; the first-level response was a "partial grant" on the grounds that—while his dictionary remained on the list of contraband—"staff will not discriminate against prisoners regardless of race, ethnicity, or culture." (The prisoner subsequently called this a "spurious partial grant.") At least one partial grant was listed as such simply because the CDCR had reclassified the type of grievance—which had not been requested by the appellant, nor did it have any bearing on the substance of what the inmate had asked for.

Leanna White, an experienced IAC, told us of a prisoner who filed a grievance alleging staff misconduct and requested that the staff member be disciplined, writing parenthetically that staff should be properly trained. His grievance was "granted in part"—the granted part being the statement "All our staff receive training." Later Leanna added, "Often we do a partial grant if there is an inquiry, even if the inmate didn't ask for that." Summing up the symbolic nature of partial grants, IAB official Dave Manning told us, "Almost every partial grant is pro forma."

While many of these partial grants are pro forma, on occasion the opposite is the case. In a few grievances that received a "partial grant" at the final level, the substance of the inmate's requested remedy appeared to be granted in *full*. In such cases, it is difficult to escape the conclusion that officials are reluctant to give prisoners the satisfaction of a full grant. As examiner Lucinda Gray told us, she does not grant in full because if she did, "He [the appellant] runs down to his cellies and says, '*See! I told you I was right!*'"

It is impossible to decipher from our sample of grievances and interviews precisely how many of these grievances *should* be granted. However, the extremely low rate of granted grievances across the board—for all categories and for arguably minor, serious, and convincing appeals alike—suggests an inability or unwillingness on the part of the institution to validate these appellants or take their charges seriously. These low odds of success, however, do not deter prisoners from filing, nor do the inherent limitations and asymmetries of the process, topics to which we now turn as we again widen the analytical lens.

THE PRISON LITIGATION REFORM ACT, INTERNAL DISPUTE RESOLUTION, AND THE RIGHTS DIALECTIC

Congress passed the PLRA to stem the tide of prisoner lawsuits in the wake of heightened rights consciousness and skyrocketing incarceration rates. Looked at more broadly, the PLRA ushered in the latest phase of a transition from the radical prisoner rights movement, which emphasized collective rights and wide social change, to the prisoner litigation focus of the 1980s and early 1990s, to the dominance of the individualized grievance process. This devolution of avenues for prisoner mobilization, from the broadest and most collective to the most narrow and individualized, has dramatic consequences for prisoners and the institutions that hold them, and is consistent with similar developments in other arenas.[26]

Scholarship on alternative dispute resolution (ADR) reveals the limitations of internal grievance handling in a variety of venues and counterposes it to the advantages of the formal legal arena. Edelman, Erlanger, and Lande (1993, 504) argue, "Claims based on rights are generalizable whereas claims based on interests and needs [emphasized in ADR] are more often individual in nature. . . . To the extent that dispute resolution forums transform disputes from rights claims to individual problems, they depoliticize those claims and preclude future claimants from grounding their claims in precedent. . . . By determining

the discourse applied to a problem, those in control of the dispute resolution process narrow the set of possible solutions."

Scholars of internal dispute resolution (IDR)—that is, disputing handled through processes internal to an organization—suggest that these
limitations are particularly pronounced when the disputing occurs in
the workplace, where "complaint handlers" are primarily concerned
with "maintaining the smooth functioning of the organization" and
avoiding litigation. In the process, "allegations of rights violations are
often recast as typical managerial problems" (Edelman, Erlanger, and
Lande 1993, 511).

To the extent that complaints are increasingly handled through these
internal disputing procedures and not by courts, they are decollectivized. Edwards (1979, 109) warns, "Disputes ... [focus] attention on
individual cases rather than collective concerns and on exceptions
within established policy rather than policy itself." Edelman, Erlanger,
and Lande (1993, 530) concur: "Individual complaints are rarely linked
to public rights and ideals, and the complaint resolution process does
not involve public recognition of those rights or public articulation of a
standard to which other employees may appeal."

More tangibly, the odds of appellants winning in such internal systems are extremely low. As scholarship on IDR in the workplace reveals,
worker complainants are severely hampered in environments where
structural inequality is the norm and employers are primarily responsible for shaping the process (Edelman, Erlanger, and Lande 1993; Edelman, Uggen, and Erlanger 1999; Edwards 1979; Hoffmann 2001,
2005). Such limitations are all the more pronounced in prison, where
those who handle complaints have full control over both the process
and the outcome, and where "exit" (Hoffmann 2005) is not an option.

Further, just as internal disputing compared to litigation focuses on
the individual case and does not establish visible precedents, thereby
narrowing its social impact, so the prisoner litigation of the 1980s had
shrunk the agenda of the preceding radical prisoners' rights movement
(Katzenstein, 2005). The decrease in prisoner lawsuits and the rise in
prisoner grievances following passage of the PLRA thus marks the latest
stage in a thirty-year move away from a broad vision of change and
collective benefits to an individualized and constricted bureaucratic
process.

Yet neither Congress's efforts to curb prisoners' right to go to court,
nor the inherent limitations of informal and decollectivized grievances
as a vehicle for dispute resolution, nor the low odds of winning have

extinguished the rights consciousness that has played a lead role in driving this trajectory and that continues to animate grievance filing. Indeed, as we will see throughout these chapters, the grievance system—mandated by Congress as a solution to mounting inmate litigation and now institutionalized as an integral part of prison life—may itself be one of the central pivots that keeps rights consciousness alive. For, as we argue in the next chapter, prison is a unique kind of institution, in which law is a hypervisible presence, formal rules ostensibly regulate every aspect of behavior of both the captives and the captors, and otherwise disempowered inmates school themselves in the policies that govern them, including how to contest violations of those policies.

Much like the letter writers from a bygone era that Lovell (2012) studied, these prisoners are not defeated by their encounters with the grievance system. Lovell writes eloquently of the complaint letters that ordinary Americans sent to the federal government between 1939 and 1941. Triggered by the establishment of the first Civil Liberties Unit (later, the Civil Rights Section) in the Department of Justice, these letters complained of violations of civil rights in an era in which civil rights had not yet become a household word. The nature of the complaints in the letters varied, but they had in common that the letter writers rarely received any relief from the government in response. Nonetheless, Lovell (32; emphasis in original) writes, "There is . . . little to suggest that writers' sense of entitlement was dampened by their engagement with law. To the contrary, writers more often seemed *emboldened* by the choice of a legalized rhetoric of rights," with many persisting for several rounds in their contestation.

Just so, our sample of prisoner grievances and our conversations with prisoners suggest that the grievance process, while unlikely to yield positive responses, by no means diminishes appellants' self-identity as rights-bearing subjects or their desire for redress. Indeed, as we see in the next chapter, in this institution in which law is the master text, the grievance system is prisoners' concrete and daily reminder that they have the right to contest. As one prisoner told us, when officials violate a rule, "We go get that book [the Title 15] and we write it up."

CHAPTER 3

Naming, Blaming, and Claiming in an Uncommon Place of Law

Tens of thousands of California prisoners file grievances annually, and as we saw in the last chapter, they file on a wide range of issues. In this chapter, we draw on our interviews with prisoners to explore how they talk about their problems and the grievances they file, as well as their overall perceptions of the appeals system. A central focus is on the relationship between what they tell us their problems are on one hand, and what they report their grievances are about on the other. In other words, we look here not only at their grievances but at the rarely examined front end of disputes and the connection between the two. Our exploration of these naming and claiming processes—processes that are only accessible through intensive interviews—reveals a great deal about disputing but also about the institutional context within which it takes place and the contradictory forces that permeate it.

Lovell (2012, 24–25) has written persuasively about the advantage of letters and other written documents as sources of data, for they provide a considered and deliberate historical record. It is particularly advantageous to be able to examine the historical record in the form of written prisoner grievances (analyzed in more detail in chapter 7) side by side with these interactive interviews. Interviews can fill in the gaps that inevitably characterize formal documents and offer insights not available from less spontaneous written sources. Our interviews with these California prisoners about their problems and grievances, described in this chapter and the next, not only inform us about how and why some problems become official grievances but reveal surprising aspects of disputing in this most asymmetrical setting. In later chapters, we extend the analysis by incorporating findings from our interviews with staff.

The prisoners we interviewed ranged in age from twenty to sixty-seven, with a mean age of 38.3 years. According to official CDCR data, they are a diverse group in terms of race/ethnicity, with 40 percent classified as Hispanic, 24.2 percent as white, 30.8 percent as black, and 5 percent as "other." They vary, too, according to the nature of their offense, custody level, sex offender status, gang validation, and mental health status. In general, our sample closely resembles the total California male prison population (see table 3).

The nature of the grievances these men discussed generally parallel our sample of written grievance documents described in the last chapter. They told us they had made formal allegations of inadequate medical care, property damage, erroneous disciplinary infractions, staff misconduct, and many other issues, and as in the written documents, they frequently mentioned the possibility of reprisals for filing. Interestingly, however, the pattern of the grievances they described does not map on exactly to the pattern of the problems they initially named. Specifically, as we will see, concern about reprisals appeared to suppress somewhat complaints against staff, relative to the frequency with which they discussed staff misconduct as a problem. Despite this relative hesitancy to file grievances against staff, among the most striking initial findings to emerge from these interviews is the high rate of both naming and claiming. Indeed, consistent with the high volume of formal grievances warehoused in Sacramento, virtually all of these prisoners named multiple problems, and most said they had filed at least one grievance, with many saying they had filed dozens of times.

CLIMBING THE DISPUTE PYRAMID

An extensive scholarship examines the processes through which people come to recognize a circumstance they confront as a problem, assign responsibility or blame for that circumstance, and lodge a grievance or mobilize action over it (Albiston 1999, 2005; Blackstone, Uggen, and McLaughlin 2009; Earl 2009; Edelman, Erlanger, and Lande 1993; Edelman and Cahill 1998; Edelman, Uggen, and Erlanger 1999; Emerson and Messinger 1977; Engel and Munger 2003; Felstiner, Abel, and Sarat 1980–81; Hendley 2010; Hoffmann 2001, 2003, 2005; Major

TABLE 3   A COMPARISON OF SELECT CHARACTERISTICS OF THE STUDY SAMPLE
AND THE TOTAL POPULATION IN CDCR PRISONS FOR MEN*

	Total Study Sample		Total Adult Population in CDCR Prisons for Men**	
	No.	%	No.	%
Total	120	100	146,360***	100
Age				
sample mean=38.3				
population mean=37.4				
18–25	16	13.3	22,968	15.7
26–35	40	33.3	46,738	31.9
36–45	30	25.0	40,884	27.9
46+	34	28.3	35,770	24.4
Race/ethnicity				
Hispanic	48	40.0	56,880	39.2
White	29	24.2	37,954	26.2
Black	37	30.8	43,451	30.0
Other	6	5.0	6,738	4.6
Offense				
Crimes against persons	69	60.5	80,202	54.8
Property	19	16.7	26,892	18.4
Drug	21	18.4	26,418	18.1
Other	5	4.4	12,841	8.8
Custody level				
1	18	15.7	25,226	19.6
2	47	40.9	43,288	33.6
3	17	14.8	31,037	24.1
4	33	28.7	29,405	22.8
Sex offender registration				
Yes	20	16.7	21,381	14.6
Gang				
Yes	20	16.7	22,070	15.1
Mental health classification****				
Yes	34	28.3	29,606	20.2

SOURCE: CDCR's Offender-Based Information System, March 2009.

* Based on official CDCR records and attendant classification schemes.

** Figures exclude inmates in fire camps.

*** The total used to compute percentages varies depending on missing data. For example, the percentages for custody level are based on a total of 128,956 prisoners with official classification scores.

**** Correctional Clinical Case Management System (CCCMS) and Enhanced Out-Patient Program (EOP) inmates, referring to those with chronic or acute mental health disorders.

and Kaiser 2005; Marshall 2003; Morrill et al. 2010; Nielsen 2004; Nielsen and Nelson 2005). A basic premise of this literature is that "trouble, problems, personal and social dislocation are everyday occurrences" (Felstiner, Abel, and Sarat 1980–81, 633), but for disputes to emerge they have to be perceived as injurious. Once an individual perceives and names a problem, it may climb the "pyramid of disputes" (Felstiner, Abel, and Sarat 1980–81; Michelson 2007), with someone being blamed and, in relatively rare cases, claims asserted. Studies of this "naming, blaming, claiming" (Felstiner, Abel, and Sarat 1980–81) find that if, when, and how the process unfolds depend on a wide range of social-psychological, cultural, political, institutional, and structural variables (Coates and Penrod 1980–81; Felstiner, Abel, and Sarat 1980–81; Hoffmann 2003; Kaiser and Major and Kaiser 2005; Michelson 2007; Miller 2001; Morrill et al. 2010; Sandefur 2008).

This disputing literature sets the stage for our discussion of prisoners' reported problems and grievances, for in some ways our findings stand in stark contrast to it. Among the factors often said to inhibit both naming and claiming is self-blame. Attribution theory posits that those who blame themselves for a circumstance or event are less likely to identify the situation as injurious, much less feel entitled to a remedy (Coates and Penrod 1980–81; Felstiner, Abel, and Sarat 1980–81; Hendley 2010). Studies also reveal that self-blame is structurally patterned such that those with fewer resources or in vulnerable social locations are predisposed to both self-blame and a feeling of disentitlement (Michelson 2007; Morrill et al. 2010).

It is argued, too, that people often do not launch claims because they fear that doing so may stigmatize them as troublemakers or target them for retaliation (Bumiller 1987, 1988; Michelson 2007; Miller and Sarat 1981, 541). As with self-blame, the anticipated repercussions of complaining are generally patterned by social location, with those in less powerful social positions more susceptible to fears of retaliation and consequently less likely to contest wrongdoing and attendant injuries (Kanter 1979; Michelson 2007; Miller and Sarat 1981, 541; Morrill et al. 2010; Sandefur 2008). For example, in their study of youths' legal mobilization, Morrill et al. (2010) found that African American youths had a higher rate of perceived rights violations than white youths but were no more likely to have taken action, suggesting that African Americans "lumped it" more often than whites.

The effect of power and vulnerability on the ability and willingness to file claims is well documented in studies of the workplace. Some of

Bumiller's (1987, 1988) African American respondents said they were reluctant to file a discrimination complaint against their employer because they feared retaliation, and some tried to deflect blame from the employer ("He didn't really mean to be unfair") or otherwise rationalize the problem away ("It's not that big a deal"). Other research that examines the effect of gender in workplace disputes confirms the importance of such power asymmetries, as women face not only the usual imbalance of power between worker and employer but also gender-based inequalities; as a result, they confront greater subjective and objective barriers to making claims than their male counterparts (Calhoun and Smith 1999; Fletcher 1999; Gwartney-Gibbs and Lach 1992, 1994; Hoffmann 2005; Lind, Huo, and Tyler 1994).

Studies of legal consciousness also examine how people understand and perceive law and act on those perceptions in both legal and extralegal arenas (Engel and Munger 2003; Ewick and Silbey 1998; Kirkland 2008; Marshall 2003; Merry 1979, 1990; Nielsen 2004).[1] These studies complicate the picture presented above, as they reveal that disempowered people across the world and in settings as varied as welfare offices, the workplace, housing projects, and the realm of marriage and the family actively engage law as a tool of resistance and a "weapon of the weak" (Cowan 2004; Lazarus-Black and Hirsch 1994; Lovell 2012; Sarat 1990; Scott 1985; White 1990; Yngvesson 1993). Ewick and Silbey (1998) point out that while attitudes about law and legal practices are replete with contingencies and contradictions, they are nonetheless rooted in social and cultural structures, institutions, and ideology. To affirm complexity, in other words, does not negate the social pattern. Gilliom (2001, 91) summarizes the stacked deck against the marginalized and socially disempowered: "The institutional, structural, and social pressures push against the assertion of rights."

Engel and Munger's (2003) study of legal consciousness among Americans with disabilities further complicates the picture of disputing, particularly the notion of a unidirectional disputing "pyramid," by revealing the recursive quality of rights consciousness, its interactions with identity, and its fluidity across time and social/institutional location. Their data, derived from life histories of eight individuals, challenge the linear assumptions of the naming, blaming, claiming model of disputing and suggest that shifts in self-identity can and do interrupt, reverse, and upend that process. Not only does self-identity shape their subjects' perception of whether they are treated fairly, but, Engel and Munger argue, the rights consciousness of those with disabilities may impact their sense of social inclusion even in the absence of formal rights mobilization. Despite Engel and Munger's challenges to the "disputing pyramid" literature, they too find that one's institutional location, social position, and resources are critical variables in shaping rights mobilization.

Several scholars note that cultural forces make Americans "slow to perceive injury" (Felstiner, Abel, and Sarat 1980–81, 652) because of a "cult of competence" that discourages them from seeing themselves as victims of mistreatment. In her study of American blacks' perceptions of and responses to racial discrimination, Bumiller (1987, 430; 1988, 78) found an "ethic of survival," one dimension of which is a denial of injury in the interest of preserving self-respect. Not only may claiming the status of victim have negative implications for self-image, but endurance is positively valued. Several of Bumiller's (1987) respondents expressed pride in their ability to, as one man put it, "mak[e] it through the rain" (431) and "weather the storm" (432). This is arguably particularly pronounced in men's prisons—institutions defined by constructions of masculinity anchored in self-sufficiency, where "be tough and strong" is a common refrain articulated by prisoners.

In the context of this literature, the extensive naming of problems and use of the grievance system by prisoners—among the most vulnerable and stigmatized of populations—is at first glance paradoxical. Many of the men we interviewed expressed self-blame for their incarceration, and most of them reported that corrections officials retaliate against those who file grievances. We explore here this paradox of prisoners' extensive naming and claiming despite powerful internal and external obstacles. Clearly, prisoners confront a plethora of conditions that are ripe for contestation—for instance, the 114-degree heat that Williams described, with which we opened this book, or the overcrowded conditions detailed by a group grievance and condemned in *Brown v. Plata*, 563 U.S. __ (2011)—and this must be part of any explanation for why so many of them file grievances. But as decades of literature on disputing and legal mobilization have documented, the presence of grievable problems— even serious ones—is not in itself sufficient to explain the recognition of injury, much less the launching of a grievance, particularly in a context of vulnerability, self-blame, stigma, and a commitment to "hanging tough."

To untangle this paradox of extensive naming and claiming by prisoners, it is useful to consider the words of Justice Stewart, who once said, "What for a private citizen would be a dispute with his landlord, with his employer, with his tailor, with his neighbor, or with his banker becomes, for the prisoner, a dispute with the State" (*Preiser v. Rodriguez*, 411 U.S. 475, 492 [1973]). He was implicitly noting that prisoners inhabit what Goffman called a "total institution" (1961), where virtually all of one's daily activities are organized and overseen by the authorities. Goffman was writing of life inside a mental hospital when he coined this term, but as indicated in the subtitle of his landmark book, he also applied it to "other inmates," as did Cressey (1961), Foucault (1977), and others (Inciardi 1990; Kaminski 2003) who have described prison as a total institution (cf. Farrington 1992).

We argue here that in addition to being a total institution, prison is above all a place of *law*. Surrounded by gun towers and armed guards, with passage from one part of the facility to another governed by "ducats,"[2] with ubiquitous "out of bounds" signs[3] informing prisoners of the lines they may not cross and the penalties for violation, and with everyday practices such as disciplinary actions referred to colloquially by their legal form numbers (e.g., in California, "115s" and "128s"), prison is what you might call an "*un*common place of law" (revisiting Ewick and Silbey 1998). In contrast to the pervasive yet submerged and subtextual quality of law in everyday life, there is nothing *sub*textual about law in prison. Prisoners' willingness and ability to name problems and file grievances must be seen within this context of prison not only as a total institution but as a conspicuously legal one where explicit rules govern every aspect of behavior. As we will see, this legal-institutional context enhances prisoners' mobilization of law, in some cases overriding the very stigma and vulnerability that the context otherwise produces.

Law in prison is not only ubiquitous and hypervisible; it is also unique in that its primary purposes include securing captivity, suppressing many ordinary rights, and rationing amenities that most Americans take for granted. But it also provides prisoners with a mechanism of redress. Rights consciousness may be enhanced in this context, as prisoners are acutely aware of what they are deprived of and what they are entitled to. In our interviews, prisoner after prisoner made it clear he understood that "this is jail, not Yale," "if you can't do the time, then don't do the crime," and some version of "I get it. I'm in prison." At the same time, again and again we heard the refrain "I only want what I got coming to me," followed by articulations of what prisoners are entitled to by virtue of being a prisoner in California.

Before looking in more detail at these men's mobilization of grievances and their orientation to law and rights, we turn now to the myriad conditions these prisoners talked about as problems.

NAMING PROBLEMS

The 120 prisoners we interviewed spoke of a wide range of problems. Contrary to what one might expect from the literature, neither the stigma and vulnerability of prisoners, nor the self-blame that many of our respondents expressed, nor the "hang tough" ethic of prison seemed to inhibit them from identifying what they perceived as problems.

Our interviews began with conversational questions about where they were housed and how it was going for them. A surprising number of these prisoners (44.2 percent) told us at first that they were doing well (e.g., "I get along just fine," "Goin' cool," "All right," "It's goin' good," "It goes well for me"); some (17.4 percent) even said they were doing very well ("Can't get no better"). Early in the interview, we asked them if there were things in prison that were particularly bothersome to them. This may seem like a peculiar question to ask of people who are deprived of their liberty in conditions that courts have declared to be cruel and unusual, but some of these men (17.6 percent) initially told us they had "no problems" and nothing was bothersome.

Over the course of our conversations, however, virtually all of them (96.2 percent) talked of problems, with over sixty specific issues mentioned. Even those who originally reported no problems eventually raised multiple complaints about prison life. Most men (55.7 percent) cited some aspect of living conditions, such as dilapidated facilities, bug infestations, excessive heat, and broken plumbing (table 4). Beyond this multifarious category of living conditions, the most frequently mentioned problems had to do with inadequate medical care (39.6 percent), disrespect from staff (38.7 percent), property missing or damaged by the CDCR (33 percent), and lack of or problems related to rehabilitative programs or jobs (27.4 percent). Previous literature on California prisons (e.g., Hunt at al. 1993) has singled out gangs, race relations, and the havoc they wreak for inmate interaction as the focal concerns of prisoners. While some of the prisoners we interviewed talked about these things, the issues they talked about most often—decent living conditions, medical care, and respect for both person and property—reflect universal human needs.

A wide range of problems associated with living conditions figured most prominently in these prisoners' interviews. James Little, a black[4] man in his forties who is housed in one of the older prisons, said: "You have the way they feed you, the cleanliness of the place, how it looks. Look at the ceiling. . . . It's like living outside. You've got ants and

TABLE 4   TOP FIVE PROBLEMS NAMED, OVERALL AND EXCLUSIVE OF GRIEVANCES
FILED

Problems Named in Entire Interview*			Problems Named, Exclusive of Grievances**		
Rank	Problem	Percent	Rank	Problem	Percent
1	Living conditions	55.7	1	Living conditions	42.5
2	Medical care	39.6	2	Staff respect	37.7
3	Staff respect	38.7	3	Programming/jobs	25.5
4	Property	33.0	4	Medical care	18.9
5	Programming/jobs	27.4	4	Overcrowding	18.9

* Includes problems named anywhere in the interview, including in the context of a specific grievance.
** Includes problems named outside the context of a specific grievance.

roaches and stuff you can't get rid of." Several spoke of the relentless heat in some desert prisons. Adolfo Flores, who was interviewed in handcuffs and started out by saying it was awkward to speak to "somebody on the outside," soon spoke of many problems, beginning, "It's *hot* over here! My goodness it's hot. . . . Once the summer came we had a record heat of 115 degrees. No air coming through the vents [of the cell]. None. . . . We were *cooking*. There was no air."

Sometimes conditions relating to concrete daily needs came up. Another black inmate, Edward Packer, when asked about the most common problem people face, told us, "It's hard to get laundry . . . and you gotta go through all kind of drama to get it . . . They come up with a fine reason you ain't gonna get it." Steve Lopez, a Mexican American who has been in prison for over a decade on a two-strikes drug charge and who lives with one hundred other men in what used to be a gym and is now outfitted with triple bunks, described the conditions: "You're sharing six toilets with a hundred dudes."

Food was mentioned frequently in these conversations. Several spoke of a dish they referred to as "SOS." David Miller, a white prisoner who was raised in group homes and had been in prison for twenty years, said: "A few months ago we had this really bad, really just horrible, bad . . . SOS. You know, SOS is, is uh, crap on a shingle, Shit On a Shingle. Have you heard of that? . . . It's just hamburger meat, it's gravy on toast type of thing. But it was vegetarian. Instead of regular hamburger meat, it was vegetarian, soy, blah. It was just horribly bad. You couldn't eat it. We all threw it away." Complaints about the quality and quantity of food may seem minor compared to more life-threatening concerns, but as Thomas Jenkins told us poignantly, "It's not a minor problem. Food's almost everything in here." Michael Johnson had a similar take on what some people might consider minor. "What's small to one man might be great to another," he said. "This guy [an officer] goes home every day to his wife, to his mistress, to his boyfriend, to whatever. So, what he might think might be small might be major to a guy who's bein' told when to eat, when to go to sleep, when to boo-boo, when not to boo-boo. So . . ."

Complaints about medical and dental care included some gruesome stories. Ali Smith, a black prisoner serving a two-strikes mandatory sentence for burglary, told us of the aftermath of an accident during his transfer to the prison by state bus:

> A mobile home ran into the state bus and the bus flipped over. I fractured my collarbone, injured my spine, broke two of my teeth right here. . . . They were supposed to take me to the hospital. Instead they cut us out of the bus and just transported us on another bus. And then we came here and then still didn't get seen by medical for like another two weeks. . . . They had me sitting here for like a whole two weeks after knowing that I was injured. You could see my bone up here, my collarbone. I couldn't bend over. My lip was slit right here.

Others also spoke of problems seeing a doctor or getting medicine. Harold Steele, a white Vietnam War veteran with posttraumatic stress disorder who is doing a life sentence for murder, said he pulled his own decayed teeth because the backlog to see a dentist was so long. David Cummings, a white prisoner in his mid-forties who is serving time at Desert Valley Center and is housed in a "Sensitive Needs Yard" (SNY),[5] told us of his experience trying to see a doctor: "I don't think a person should have to go man down [*man down* is the term used to inform correctional staff that a prisoner has impaired mobility and cannot respond to commands] if you got a serious medical need. . . . I lost my hearing and my eye was drooping almost closed, and it took them four days to see me. . . . When they finally did see me the doctor thought I had Bell's palsy." It turned out that he had an advanced ear infection and had temporarily lost his hearing. Later he recounted how difficult it was to get painkillers because officials assumed he was an addict when he complained of his pain.

Other telling examples include Donald Scott, a white prisoner at California Corrections Facility who had open heart surgery before coming to prison and said he had gone two weeks without his medication.

Donald reported, "They left me without my medication for two weeks. I take blood thinners. I have hardening of my heart and . . . I told them I need my medication or I was going to have a stroke." Martin Pedigrew, a white man with a history of mental health problems serving time at Desert Valley Center, told us he had a skin infection for a year and a half before getting care. He said, "I was trying to get antibiotics. I was having an itch that was like unbearable, man. It went on for, like I said, a year and a half. They were telling me, 'It's in your mind.' I'm like, 'Yeah, if it was in your mind and you were itching every day . . . you could at least try antibiotics.' And I finally seen the dermatologist and he goes, 'Yeah, you've got a skin infection.' Gave me antibiotics. It just knocked it out." Roberto Menendez also talked about the challenges of getting medical attention: "[One] guy wasn't getting medical treatment and [so he] overdosed on water. That dude almost died. He wasn't getting no treatment so he had to go another route. You gotta go through different routes, you know, to finally get their attention."

Missing or damaged property takes on added meaning in prison, where personal possessions may be one's only link to the outside world. Tyrone Jones, a black prisoner and former gang member/turned Christian (who, when asked his racial identification, said he was "black, or Afro American, or whatever they're calling us now"), said his property was lost while he was in administrative segregation: "My pictures and stuff was in there. . . . That was real important to me. . . . That's the only way I see my son was through those pictures." A Samoan prisoner, Hemana Amataga, explained the emotional importance of pictures to prisoners: "Some people, pictures that's all they got."

Edward Packer described his transfer to a different prison, when guards on the bus told the prisoners not to talk to each other and that if they talked their property would disappear. Two men started talking anyway, and none of the prisoners' property was waiting for them at the other end. Edward said, "So when we get to [the name of the specific prison] I wait for my property and my property never showed up. . . . I'm like, man, now I don't have my watch, I'm really stressed out, my watch is gone . . . my personal pictures and everything. Pictures and stuff like that of my mom, my girlfriends back in the day. . . . I'm thinkin' a guy might be walking around with my pictures and you know I really don't like that, that somebody get ahold of my personal stuff like that." Several others mentioned the importance of personal pictures and their traumatic loss. David Miller, the white prisoner who had grown up in group homes, said he had recently been sent to the "SHU" (Security Housing

Unit)[6] and all his belongings had been lost or taken: "I've got five kids, and that was my babies' pictures. My sister's dead, my aunt, my grandmother, my uncle—all my people that I loved and all my kids growin' up, for like twelve, twelve and a half years of pictures. That's all I got in the world. That's my whole, my whole, um, that's my furniture, that's my everything. And it's all gone. They threw it away cuz they're mad at me."

Steve Lopez, who spoke of sharing six toilets with a hundred men, discussed the humiliations of prison and staff disrespect, telling us what happened after tobacco was found in a cell. After that, he said, everyone had to be strip-searched on a daily basis: "Every time we go out [to the yard] and come in, we gotta get strip-searched. Every day. . . . You know, it's humiliating. You feel harassed." Min Kim, who identifies as Korean and black, also talked about the humiliations of strip searches:

> They would have us come out of our cells . . . and they would have female officers in the tower . . . and in the yards, and they would strip-search us. All our clothes, everything. . . . And then they'll have us lined up, like ten guys in a row. They'll strip us out, buck naked, and say, 'Bend over and cough.' This was a policy. . . . Every day, if you wanted to go to the yard, you had to be strip-searched, bend over, and cough, in front of female officers and everything.[7]

James Little, the black prisoner in his forties who spoke at length about living conditions, said the most common problem prisoners face is "prison, period." He has spent much of his life in prison and referred to people like himself as "convicts" who have done what he called "hardcore time" and who "demand respect," as opposed to people who are just in prison briefly, who, he said, will "lick [the officers'] boots" and "jump through the hoops." He covered almost all of the bases in terms of complaints, emphasizing what he called "asshole cops":

> The officers here are . . . on some kind of power trip most of them. Because you're over somebody doesn't mean you can just treat them any kind of way or talk to them any kind of way, or look down at you. We're human beings just like you are. . . . They got their way of doing what they wanna do. And they get away with it. . . . Say like I'm a cop and I don't like you. I'm going to get this big rapist dude and put him in a cell with you . . . or I'm going to pay him some lunches or give him something to get you. . . . Or . . . I'm going to tell the blacks the whites are whoop-de-whoops or [stuff like] this. Oh, *man,* all that type of stuff really happens like they say on TV, it really happens.

Later in the interview, James said, "This place is a joke. . . . They give these people too much power over you, over your life, your freedom.

They got these power-tripping people [guards] that need psychological evaluations . . . because they're the guys that got their lunch money taken in elementary school and now they're getting back on people."

Min Kim, who talked about daily strip searches, reported that he had seen "COs that pulled [a] guy out of the cell, handcuffed him, and just started beating him. . . . They had handcuffs on him, knocked him out cold on the ground." He concluded this story with a statement punctuated by nervous laughter: "It's like we're on the front lines in Iraq, you know?" Min later told us about the burns that can come from having to lie down on hot concrete in the yard: "What they have us do if something happens on the yard, they tell us to . . . we have to lay flat on the ground with our hands out like that [gesturing]. However, it's 115 degrees down there, and that's concrete out there. And so you got guys that have burned their arms on the concrete, you know, and they have us lying there for hours. Sometimes an hour, two hours . . . and the guys are literally burnt, out on the ground."

David Miller, the white man who had been raised in group homes and had been in prison for twenty years, spoke of the time officials told the prisoners they were going to confiscate all their books and magazines. David said the guards told them, "And fuck you punks. If you don't like it, do something about it." The prisoners went on a hunger strike, and David reported, "they [the guards] came in and sprayed us really bad with big canisters of this 5.0 [pepper spray], which I don't think is even legal. . . . And you're in this little cell that's about this big [gesturing]. . . . And they sprayed you until you, you die or give up, pass out or give up. I passed out, and they came in and handcuffed me."

Manuel Gonzalez, a Hispanic man in his twenties serving time in maximum security, put it this way: "They treat us like . . . we're a bird in a cage. You know? And, they just get to open us up, or do whatever they want with us. Tell us when to do this and when to do that . . . there's no reason you should be treated like this, you know?" David Miller said simply, "I'm locked in a cage."

Many others also focused on staff disrespect. Peter Owen, a young white man in a minimum security unit, reported, "We call this like PC [protective custody] for cops here. Because they get away with stuff here that they wouldn't get away with at a level 3 or a level 4. . . . There are no lifers here at all. Everyone here has a release date, so police officers think that it's okay to use obscene gestures, put us on the spot in front of other inmates, and they can get away with it here because they know most people won't do anything because . . . they don't want to do extra time." Tyrone Jones, who talked about his son's pictures among his missing property, said, "The COs tend to think we're not human. We're not people, we're just criminals. . . . COs get to mess with you . . . you know what I'm sayin'? They get to pick at you, and this is people's lives versus a game to a CO. . . . It has nothin' to do with their life. But it has somethin' to do with *our* lives. Because they have the power to take away time. And that's something God gave us, is time."

The emotional fallout of threats to one's sense of self, such as those evoked by strip searches and staff disrespect, is intensified in the prison environment. In her description of a maximum security prison, Rhodes (2004, 56) notes, "A sense of exposure and shame—the threat of being 'broken'— . . . becomes a pervasive pattern of feeling, apart from any particular incident of overt humiliation." She continues, quoting Michael Ignatieff: "In the best of our prisons . . . inmates are fed, clothed, and housed in adequate fashion. . . . Yet every waking hour . . . [prisoners] still feel the contempt of authority in a glance, gesture or procedure. . . . Needs are met, but souls are dishonoured" (57). The prisoners we talked to spoke at length about a wide range of problems. Some were related to the *in*adequacies of how they are "fed, clothed, and housed." And others were about the threats to dignity and "dishonoured souls" that Ignatieff and Rhodes chronicle so eloquently and that are expressed in these raw firsthand accounts.

SELF-BLAME AMONG PRISONERS

Contrary to what one would expect from the scholarship on self-blame and its tendency to suppress the ability to name injurious conditions, the men we interviewed identified prison conditions as problematic even when they expressed significant levels of self-blame. Almost 35 percent (34.7 percent) volunteered the sentiment that they blamed themselves for their incarceration. They expressed self-blame in very clear terms. Jesus Avena, a Hispanic prisoner in a level 2 prison, said simply, "Whose fault is it? We brought ourselves here." Malik Jackson revealed, "It's pretty much my fault for being in here. . . . I smoked a lot of marijuana . . . got into it with the mother of my child. . . . All the basic faults of prison men." Martin Tate was matter-of-fact: "I broke the law, and this is the price I have to pay." José Pena said philosophically, "I'm a narcotics offender. . . . I know my mistakes . . . so I'm at peace." Steve Lopez, who had spoken movingly of the humiliation and disrespect in prison, leaned in to confide, "You know what? And this is a secret, so don't tell nobody. I've actually asked for this, because what I was doin' on the streets . . ."

Occasionally, too, an "ethic of survival" (Bumiller 1987, 1988) and a "cult of competence" (Felstiner, Abel, and Sarat 1980–81) were revealed. For example, the term *convict*, which some prisoners used to refer to themselves, connotes a sense of pride in the ability to do "hardcore time." Relatedly, prisoners speak of "doing time rather than letting time do you" as both an imperative for survival and a badge of honor.

Yet these same men were fully capable of identifying the problems of prison. James Little, who insisted he was a "convict" capable of doing "hardcore time," spoke at length of the problems in prison. In one of the most self-blaming interviews, Darryl White, a black prisoner serving a two-year sentence for a sex offense, said he had to "take responsibility" for being in prison but went on to say, "If you were to stay here a month, I guarantee you would see things that [you'd say] '*This* can't be right.'" And Steve Lopez, who revealed the "secret" that it was his fault for being in prison, began the interview eager to talk about the problems: "Well, sure, where do you want me to begin?" José Pena, who said, "I know what I did so I'm at peace," did not let others—in this quote, guards—off the hook: "We messed up, so what? You're no better than me [just] because you're in a green suit."[8]

Self-blame may muddy the perception of a situation as injurious, as suggested in the literature. However, almost without exception the men we spoke to—including those with significant levels of self-blame, as well as those expressing some version of an "ethic of survival"—pointed to problematic conditions both large and small, dramatic and seemingly mundane. Further, as we see in the next section, they not infrequently filed claims about those conditions, often overcoming daunting obstacles to do so.

GRIEVANCE FILING: "YOU KNOW THAT SOMETIME YOU JUST GOTTA GET UP"

Almost three-quarters of the men in this study (73.3 percent) said they had filed grievances with the CDCR. More than three-quarters (76 percent) of these had filed more than once; some said they had filed dozens of claims; a handful reported filing more than fifty; and two said they had filed about a hundred times. Even among those who blamed themselves for being in prison, most have used the grievance system at least once.

As revealed in table 5, a majority of prisoners within virtually every official demographic or status group—age, race/ethnicity, offense category, custody level, registered sex offender category, gang status, and mental health status—had filed a grievance. While the likelihood of filing increases with prisoners' age (probably reflecting length of time in prison, and therefore increased opportunity),[9] even in the youngest age group (eighteen to twenty-five years) more than half (56.3 percent) had filed an appeal. Our random sample included few noncitizens, but of the nine permanent legal residents and seven people "currently without papers," 56.3 percent and 57.1 percent, respectively, had filed at least one grievance. Likewise, over three-quarters of those sentenced for a crime against persons, of those housed in custody levels 3 and 4, of registered sex offenders, and of those with mental health problems reported filing at least one grievance. Men who identified as African American or black were most likely to have submitted a 602 (86.5 percent), but the majority of whites (79.3 percent) and Hispanics (58.3 percent)[10] also reported using the 602 at least once.[11]

The fact that African American inmates file more than those who identify with other races/ethnicities is contrary to what one would expect in light of existing literature (Anderson 1999; Bumiller 1988; Morrill et al. 2010). One possible explanation is that the prison environment, consisting disproportionately of people of color, upends the usual racial hierarchy and relative empowerment, as others have found in women's prisons (Kruttschnitt and Gartner 2005), with corresponding shifts in rates of legal mobilization. If so, this explanation underscores the extraordinary power of institutional context.

Beyond these individual-level demographics, most of our respondents from each of the prisons and custody levels have filed grievances. While a majority in each prison have filed, the size of that majority varies. At maximum-security Green Valley Prison, 87.5 percent of our interviewees reported filing a grievance while in a California prison; at California Correctional Facility, 70 percent reported doing so; and at Desert Valley Center, 65 percent said they had filed. This variation parallels custody levels. Of the men we interviewed in custody level 4 (maximum security), almost 88 percent reported having filed a grievance; 82.4 percent of those in custody level 3 have filed; 66 percent in level 2; and 61.1 percent in level 1 (minimum security)[12]—a pattern we will revisit when considering the impact of prison as a total legal institution on grievance filing.

These men are well aware that the odds are against them in the grievance process. In describing their experiences with appeals, inmates were

TABLE 5   PROPORTION OF PRISONERS WHO REPORT FILING A GRIEVANCE WHILE
INCARCERATED IN A CALIFORNIA PRISON*

	Number of Participants in the Study	Number of Participants Who Reported Filing a Grievance (%)
Total	120	88 (73.3)
Age		
18–25	16	9 (56.3)
26–35	40	31 (77.5)
36–45	30	20 (66.7)
46+	34	28 (82.4)
Race/ethnicity		
Hispanic	48	28 (58.3)
White	29	23 (79.3)
Black	37	32 (86.5)
Other	6	2 (33.3)
Offense		
Crimes against persons	69	53 (76.8)
Property	19	14 (73.7)
Drug	21	12 (57.1)
Other	5	3 (60.0)
Custody level		
1	18	11 (61.1)
2	47	31 (66.0)
3	17	14 (82.4)
4	33	29 (87.9)
Sex offender registration		
Yes	20	16 (80.0)
Gang		
Yes	20	12 (60.0)
Mental health**		
Yes	34	28 (82.4)

SOURCE: CDCR's Offender-Based Information System, March 2009.

* Based on official CDCR records and attendant classification schemes.

** Correctional Clinical Case Management System (CCCMS) and Enhanced Out-Patient Program (EOP) inmates, referring to those with chronic or acute mental health disorders.

often adamant in their critiques. David Cummings, serving time in a level 1 prison, was derisive of the process:

> Prisoner: It's a hassle, a bunch of rhetoric, and you don't normally get anywhere. . . . It's laughable.
>
> Interviewer: It's laughable?
>
> Prisoner *(deadpan)*: Hilarious.

Even more emphatic, Robert Nasau, a black prisoner serving a five-year sentence for possession of a controlled substance, reported, "Of course they can basically do to us what they want and, you know, your word doesn't mean crap." James Little, also serving time for drug possession, commented on the informal level of review, which by policy was not logged in: "Me writing my grievance out and giving it to [the correctional officer], all you got to do is tear it up and say you never got it." He also commented on how hard it is to get "justice" with a 602 even when it *is* processed: "They use these back doors and loopholes." Summarizing his frustration with the asymmetrical quality of the process, Nathaniel Forest, an American Indian in a level 2 prison who had filed twice, said, "They decide. You just complain." Asked whether they agreed, strongly agreed, disagreed, or strongly disagreed (or none of the above) with the statement "602s work pretty well," only one of our respondents strongly agreed (twenty-nine others agreed).[13] In contrast, forty-three either agreed or strongly agreed (twenty-eight and fifteen, respectively) that "inmates think the appeals process is a joke because nothing ever comes of it."[14]

As we explained in the last chapter, the grant rate for grievances at every level of formal review appears to be very low. In addition to the remote likelihood of prevailing and prisoners' related cynicism, several other features of the prison landscape present potential disincentives or barriers to filing. As we saw above, many of these men blame themselves for their imprisonment, and the literature suggests that people who blame themselves for a situation are unlikely to launch a claim (Bumiller 1987, 1988; Coates and Penrod 1980–81; Felstiner, Abel, and Sarat 1980–81; Hendley 2010; Hoffmann 2003; Michelson 2007). Indeed, among the men we interviewed, those who expressed self-blame for imprisonment were somewhat less likely to have filed a grievance (although the correlation is not statistically significant). Surprisingly though, even among those who blame themselves, a clear majority had filed at least one grievance. Further, there is a statistically significant negative correlation between the belief that one has been treated fairly by the criminal justice system and filing. Once again, however, even among those who said they had been treated fairly, the majority had filed a 602 (58.1 percent, compared to 81 percent of those who said they had been treated unfairly).

Prisoners are a highly stigmatized population, and by virtue of their imprisonment, they have been officially labeled troublemakers. Staying out of trouble was a persistent theme in their narratives about managing prison life. Almost half of our sample (47.2 percent) spontaneously mentioned "staying out of trouble," "keeping to myself," or "minding my own business" as their operating principles in prison. Marcus Greeley, a white man who has been in prison on and off for close to two decades and has become a Buddhist, told us he deals with potential problems or things that are bothersome by staying out of trouble: "I don't . . . get involved with anything I perceive [to be] negative. So, I, I'm trouble free." Min Kim, who had said that prison was "like the front lines in Iraq," started his interview by saying, "I don't personally have a problem. . . . I know how to conduct myself to where I'm not, uh, stickin' out like a sore thumb. . . . [I] just stay out of the way." Former Louisiana State Penitentiary prisoner and author Wilbert Rideau (2013, A21) explained in his autobiographical book that this is why most prisoners do not engage in even "peaceful protest": "The typical inmate does not want trouble. He has little to gain and too much to lose: his job, his visits, his recreation time, his phone privileges, his right to buy tuna, ramen, and stale bread at inflated prices in the commissary."

Staying out of trouble and *perceiving* trouble were often conflated in the comments of men who have been labeled troublemakers. When asked if there were problems for inmates, Edward Packer, whose property and personal pictures disappeared after a transfer, said, "Ya know . . . you can get in trouble if you want to, if you want to get in trouble, but you know, other than that it's easy." Asked again if there was anything bothersome, he answered, "No, cuz you can stay out of all that." Later in the interview, in response to being asked if he had ever used the law on the outside to solve problems, Edward said, "No, because [I don't want to] put myself in a sticky situation. I see them other guys get caught up in sticky stuff, you know, but me, I try not to get caught up with that kind of stuff." Mark Crenshaw told us he had never filed a grievance in prison because "I've never wanted to draw any more attention to me than absolutely necessary." Likewise, Simone Menton, a young Hispanic man who had never filed a 602, said he had never filed a lawsuit either: "Nope. Stay as far away from the law out there as I can."

This population has *known* trouble.[15] They have suffered troubles (such as abuse, homelessness, and drug addictions) and been in trouble—often simultaneously and in ways difficult to untangle. One would think that this complicated relationship to trouble—both in itself and compounded by self-blame—would be a powerful inhibitor of naming, blaming, and claiming. Yet even among this group who spoke of the importance of avoiding trouble, the majority had at some point filed a grievance.

Potential barriers to filing go well beyond subjective factors such as self-blame, stigma, and the related concern about "trouble." A central aspect of the trouble these men spoke of was retaliation by officials against prisoners who file grievances. More than 61 percent of inmates raised the issue of retaliation in their interviews, sometimes in response to a question and sometimes impromptu. Further, in the last section of the interview, when we asked whether they agreed or disagreed with the statement "COs retaliate against people who file 602s," 70.5 percent either strongly agreed or agreed (in contrast to 17.9 percent who disagreed, and only one person who strongly disagreed).

Prisoners often elaborated on their fear of retaliation. Roberto Menendez, in maximum security at Green Valley Prison on a twenty-four-year sentence, had filed five grievances in just under five years in prison. He said he had not filed more "cuz it don't work. And if it does work, then they're gonna take it out on you one way or another. . . . They'll get real vindictive . . . they'll get back at you. . . . It's just too much, you know." Armando Martin, a Mexican prisoner serving a life sentence at California Correctional Facility, estimated he had filed twenty times and said he hadn't filed more "because I know there's always consequences."

Many men were specific about what might happen when they file a grievance, and their descriptions closely matched the substance of some of the written grievances reviewed in the last chapter. Frank Boutin, who identifies as both Hispanic and white, had served almost fifteen years in maximum security Green Valley Prison, and had filed twenty appeals, reported he had seen retaliation:

> Because they file a 602, all of a sudden all their stuff, they transfer them somewhere and all of a sudden, their property's missing. Gone. . . . Ya, and they never see it again. And they put them on a bus and they transfer them up and down the state, and they never get off the bus. [Q: "What do you mean they never get off the bus?"] They give them the bus treatment. [Q: "But they've got to get off eventually."] You get off for like one day and you're back on the bus in the morning. . . . And I've seen that happen.

Evan Worsham, in prison for two years on a DUI conviction, had filed twice; he echoed an observation made by many others in our interviews and in the written grievances we analyzed: a prisoner who files grievances may get his locker searched, or his property taken, or be transferred. As Evan said, "You better be ready to deal with the repercussions that go with it, and sometimes staff does retaliate, and you get your locker searched more, or you're moved from where you're at to someplace else, you know . . . it can be a hassle for you." Jorge Bermudez, who had been in prison for over a decade and had filed three times, was succinct: "They might roll you up. Send you somewhere else. Or they might come over here and just take whatever you have."

By far the greatest fear of retaliation has to do with release dates. Sometimes this was expressed in the context of discussing daily prison life. Paul Sutro, in prison on a drug charge, explained that prisoners often endure abuse by guards in order not to jeopardize their release date: "I've seen somebody get roughed up [by a guard] over something really stupid . . . like picking up a tray that wasn't his in chow. The cop brought him in the other room, slammed him up against one of the file cabinets and said, 'You got a fucking problem?' And gets all up in his face. He wants to go home like the next guy, so he looks down at the ground and says, 'No.'" James Little was characteristically eloquent:

> You got to remember that they ["cops"] will act like they're cool like a snake. They'll act like they're cool with you and then they'll bite you . . . that's why I don't get into much of anything. I try not to see a problem. I don't let them see that I have attitude. Because that's what they do, they test people, they see what you're workin' with and see if they can get under your skin. If they can, they're goin' to be on you. So you can't let them see you sweat. . . . Then you think, 'I'm really trying to go home,' but this dude is just pushing, pushing, pushing, and they do that, and they know they can get away with that. . . . And that really tears you up because you get to thinking about 'okay, I want to see my granddaughter who I haven't seen.' . . . Oh, man, they can get under your skin.

When discussion of release dates came up, it was almost always in this context of filing grievances and the potential for retaliation. Frederick Mason, an African American in his mid-twenties serving a three-year sentence for possession of a controlled substance, said he had never filed a grievance. He told us, "I'm too close to the house, so most of the issues is not worth me filing a 602 and then . . . being a target by the COs." Martin Pedigrew, who said prison was like *Groundhog Day,* was matter-of-fact: "I just want to do my time and get out of here. I don't need no extra time. They gave me quite enough, thank you." Hemana Amataga, who had earlier said that "some people, pictures that's all they got," also explained to us why some people do not file grievances: "Everybody at this prison is pretty much close to going home, so we don't want to mess up our date." Richard Hawkins, a white man serving time for burglary who had only filed once, said, "The more you push paperwork towards officials in these facilities, the harder they can make it on you. Oh, they can make it extremely hard on you. They can actually take your date away." Robert Nasau said he had filed about fifteen times and reported that he was punished for it: "I had a good job in the program office; it took me three years to work up to that position . . . and they just snatched it away from me, and they moved me here . . . scrubbing toilets." He continued, "Yes, there was retaliation and . . . that's why I'm not going home August 2nd."

In this context of self-blame, stigma, cynicism, and vulnerability, it is all the more remarkable that the vast majority of these prisoners have filed grievances. When we asked them why they used the grievance process despite its limitations and the repercussions for them, we often heard some version of "it's all we got" or "what else can I do?"[16] But even considering how serious the problems of prison life can be, how high the stakes for prisoners are, and the absence of any other official mechanism for redress,[17] it is unclear why this particular institutional population often overcomes the significant barriers to making claims that suppress it among other vulnerable and stigmatized people.

It might be argued that prisoners have a high rate of filing grievances simply because the PLRA requires them to exhaust internal remedies before gaining access to court. While this explanation is plausible, our data do not support it. When asked whether they had ever filed a lawsuit while in prison, only 14.3 percent of our respondents said they had—with many of these lawsuits appealing trial-related processes, competence of legal representation, prison sentences, and other matters unrelated to inmate grievances. Further, of the 217 inmate grievances these respondents described in detail, only 11 had been taken to court. It is possible that some prisoners file grievances with the intention of getting access to court but later change their minds or find that accessing the courts is close to impossible. Again, however, our data suggest otherwise. During the interviews, prisoners very rarely mentioned utilizing the inmate appeals system to get to court, despite the fact that the interview schedule allowed ample opportunity for them to provide their views on the appeals system, the function of the system, their motivations for filing, their experiences with the system, and the overall performance of the system. When asked if they had ever filed a grievance "to get to court," 93 percent said they had never done so. In short, there is very little evidence to suggest that prisoners use the inmate appeals system primarily to get to court.[18]

It might alternatively be argued that these men file grievances primarily to exercise agency within the disempowering context of prison. Milovanovic and Thomas (1989, 56) suggest that the litigation of jailhouse lawyers has symbolic meanings even when unsuccessful in court. They argue that this constitutes "an existential response to repression." It is an interesting argument but difficult to test empirically. The data we have do not suggest that such symbolic functions account for the bulk of these grievance filings. Over the course of sometimes lengthy and meandering conversations, our respondents rarely touched on the psychological rewards of appealing conditions of confinement; they were more likely to note the demoralization of losing an appeal (for example, David Miller told us the grievance process is a frustrating "mind game") than the subjective satisfaction of filing one.

The next section turns to a more institutional analysis of extensive grievance filing, focusing on what we call the "rule of law" in prison. Clues about the importance of institutional factors in an explanation of prisoners' legal mobilization are found in what these men told us about the power of Title 15 and the Department Operations Manual (DOM).

IN PRISON, LAW RULES

Leshone Powers, a black inmate in a level 1 prison who has filed two appeals, explained that he does it despite his fear of retaliation, because "right is right and wrong is wrong." Other prisoners referred not only to "right" and "wrong," but more specifically to *law and policy*. Indeed, the narratives of these men were replete with references to Title 15— copies of which are given to every prisoner who enters the system—and the DOM. These published documents are generally understood by prisoners and CDCR personnel alike to contain the official rules of prison life (as opposed to the informal rules created and sustained by prisoners and officials). They indicate rights, obligations, and privileges under California law, as well as describing legally mandated processes and procedures.

Carlos Nagarro, a Hispanic man serving a three-year term for forgery, quoted chapter and verse of Title 15. Asked about the problems of prison, he did not hesitate: "Our Title 15 says that we're supposed to get three hours a week of yard time. We don't get that, you know, so that's a problem. . . . That's stated by the State of California, saying that's our exercise time." Similarly, Edgardo Cameron, a Mexican inmate interviewed while he was in a cage in administrative segregation,[19] cited Title 15 in explaining a grievance he had written: "The problem was the visiting. I had no visiting. . . . For Title 15, whenever an inmate gets transferred from prison to prison, his visiting file is still good." Later Edgardo said everything prisoners have coming to them is spelled out in Title 15: "It's written in the Title 15—inmates got this coming, these proportions, this much food, so when we on our tray don't get that same amount of food, [it's a violation]."[20] Luis Ramirez, a Mexican prisoner in his sixties who has served almost thirty years of a life sentence, summed it up at the end of his interview. He said he wanted people to understand that prisoners file 602s because "it's a right that is being violated. We have a right to get certain things because the DOM says that we have a right to this and that."[21]

Many of our interviewees emphasized that if they have to abide by the myriad rules and regulations that apply to them, staff should comply with their departmental policies too. Darnell Williams, a black prisoner with a disability, said he was told by a correctional officer that he could not have the "boots and braces" he was supposed to get for his disability and asked us rhetorically, "Who is *he* to overshadow the guidelines?" When asked what was the most important 602 he had filed, Leshone Powers said it was one in which staff had falsified documents relating to his classification status. He explained, "There's rules and regulations for *us* to follow . . . and in this DOM *they* have rules and regulations to follow. So *they* just can't come and do as they please and *we* can't just do as we please because there's rules set for both sides. . . . And when *they* break their rules, they should be penalized. . . . So if *we* break a rule, they punish us by a 128 or 115. If *they* break a rule, *they* should be punished."

Michael Johnson was eloquent, stretching out his words slowly: "I'm incarcerated. They take my freedom. Now, until a man can show me that he could walk on water, float in the air, touch a child and heal 'em, get rid of disease and whatever, until a man can show me that he's at the next stage of existence, I don't see no difference in humans. So, if you break a law, I think you should be punished for it, just like I'm sitting here now, cuz I'm punished for breakin' the law. I think you [an official] should be punished too."[22] Tyrone Jones, whose picture of his son was lost when he was in Ad Seg, filed a citizen's complaint and a 602 for staff harassment and disrespect. He explained, "Cause they has their rules too. So you can't call me out a name [just like] I wouldn't call you out a name." Edward Packer, the prisoner whose property disappeared after his transfer, similarly explained that he consults the Title 15 when he files: "Yes, they break a rule, we go get that book [Title 15] and we write it up. . . . They can't break the rules, cuz that's the rules." Adolfo Flores explained that when prisoners file appeals, "if the Title 15 says that's what we got coming, then they [the officials] can't go against it. And when they do, that's when, you know, they [prisoners] start filing appeals. Your Title 15 says this. Those are your own rules and regulations. Why are you goin' against them?" Trevon Moore joined the chorus: "They [officials] not goin' by their rules. . . . They supposed to be told that this is the rules, and if the rule says this, then they supposed to abide by the rules." Javier Ortiz, a Mexican American prisoner first arrested when he was fourteen, had spent much of his life homeless and had never filed a grievance because, he said, "I can't read or write." The first thing he told us when we asked him if there were problems in prison was, "Just the way they have some of the rules that they—we obey the rules, but at the same time they don't apply to them, to the rules. The COs don't."

Law and society scholars have noted that law permeates everyday life but often seems "remote," "sit[ting] on a distant horizon of our lives" (Ewick and Silbey 1998, 15). In contrast, law in prison is rarely invisible, taken for granted, or submerged. Instead, its presence and its relevance for all things is relentlessly apparent. Not only are minute aspects of life inside prison shaped by legal officials and exit not an option—as in many other total institutions—but here the levers of law are conspicuously on display. We do not mean to imply that all legal rules are actually implemented in prison, nor that the gap between the law-in-the-books and the law-in-action is any less pronounced in prison than elsewhere. The point instead is that while law in everyday life is salient but largely subterranean, in prison it is emblazoned across the landscape.[23]

It is not surprising that prisoners mobilize law—or the proxy that is immediately available to them, the administrative appeals process—in this context, where law governs every aspect of their behavior and scrupulously rations the goods that supply their daily needs. It is consistent with this interpretation that the maximum security prison—the total carceral institution that is most tightly governed by rigid strictures and explicit mandates—produces the most inmate grievances per capita. Recalling Kruttschnitt and Gartner's (2005) and Lerman's (2013) comparative work, we know that the microtrajectories of a prison affect inmates' experiences, even as prison itself is the master text. Just so, prisons vary according to the rigidity and palpability of their legal constraints—with the maximum security prison being the prototype of the total legal institution—but it is a defining feature of all prisons that they are in essence places of *law*-full captivity.

In "After Legal Consciousness," Silbey (2005, 338) observes, "Th[e] sense of the self [as rights-bearing] and these . . . perceptions [of the utility of the legal system in demanding rights] are cultural products learned, shaped, and framed by interactions in specific locations." Later she adds, "In institutions cultural meaning, social inequality, and legal consciousness are forged. In institutions law both promises and fails to live up to its promises" (360). We see here that the perceptions and legal mobilization practices of prisoners in total carceral environments—their legal consciousnesses—are formed in ways that are distinct from that of vulnerable people in other contexts, attesting to the importance of institutional location.

We can take this one step further, because the foregrounding of law and policy in prison inevitably centers attention on rights. In a context in which prisoners are deprived by law of most of their autonomy and many basic amenities, they focus like a laser on what they "have coming to them." Nor do violations of these rights dilute that focus or undermine rights consciousness. Instead, these prisoners mobilize the grievance system despite their slim chances of winning, asserting as Luis Ramirez did, "It's a right that is being violated. We have a right to get certain things."

Yngvesson (1993) studied the working-class people of Turner Falls, Massachusetts, who bring their troubles to the county court. Although the court staff often constructed their legal mobilization as an indicator of the working class's lack of self-control, the action had an altogether different meaning for the complainants themselves. Yngvesson explains, "For Turner Falls complainants . . . complaining (to the court, as well as to numerous other state and government agencies) was a way of *establishing* control, however transitory, in lives that were clearly not self-fashioned. Living in the constant shadow of these agencies, the spaces for self-assertion were constricted, dependent on relationships with others, and typically contingent on creative use of the very institutions that dominated their lives" (96, emphasis in original). For these prisoners, whose every move is "constricted," not only does filing grievances deploy the laws of the "very institution that dominate[s]" them, but it galvanizes a consciousness of rights in a context in which rights are severely limited.

In a culture that extols human autonomy and individual agency, those held in an institution such as prison, which by its very logic suppresses both, are caught in a powerful cross-current. It may be that in the context of this cultural-institutional turbulence, the "ethic of survival" dictates not that they ignore their injuries and "weather the storm" silently (as Bumiller's respondents said they did), but that they stand up and confront the wind's blows head-on. One of the coauthors was discussing with a group of prisoners Bumiller's article and the desire of her respondents not to put themselves in the role of victim by claiming discrimination. During this conversation, which happened outside the research setting, the group nodded assent when one prisoner declared, "I'd feel like a victim if I *didn't* stand up for my rights."

To summarize our argument thus far, despite a heavy dose of self-blame, cynicism, and concerns about retaliation, it makes sense that inmates in total institutions that foreground law, engage with it.[24] Not infrequently contesting what they see as violations of their rights and of the policies that are meant to govern the prison, they—like the welfare poor described by Sarat (1990, 374)—harness law to try "to get [the institution] to live up to its own *raison d'etre*."

REVISITING RETALIATION, DECONSTRUCTING THE DISPUTING PYRAMID

This is not to say that internal and external impediments have no effect on grievance filing. As we have seen, even though a majority of those who blame themselves for their imprisonment have filed, there is a negative correlation in our sample between self-blame and the likelihood of filing. Further, more than one-third (36.4 percent) of the men who had never filed reported that they had at some point considered filing a grievance but did not, and 60 percent of those who had filed at least one appeal said they had considered filing other times and decided not to.

Concern for retaliation permeated the narratives of many of our respondents, and a closer look at what they said provides a clue as to how that concern plays out in grievance filing. These narratives suggest that the retaliation prisoners fear most is triggered by one type of grievance: complaints against staff. We heard again and again that grievances against staff (as opposed to, for example, dilapidated living conditions, inadequate medical care, or missing property) are the most likely to result in retaliation. Malik Jackson, a black man serving a three-year sentence who had never filed an appeal, said, "If you 602 somebody, or a staff or something like that, there's gonna be retaliation. . . . And there's retaliation around here. . . . It won't be physical . . . and it might not be mental, but something's gonna happen and you know some-body's not gonna like you, so you're just causing yourself to make an enemy." Evan Worsham, who had filed two grievances, explained, "Sometimes they [grievances] blow up in your face. The staff retaliates, especially if you write them on staff. . . . They're in a position where unless you feel strongly about it, it's a good idea just to . . . do what you have to do, but you have to be willing to go and take the extra crap that goes with it. . . . So you better make sure you want to mess with that. That's how I feel. Or what I've seen." Leshone Powers, who also had filed two grievances, said he should file more: "I think about it each week, I should do it, I should do it, but I have to remember if I start a 602 [against a CO] . . . my house would be tipped upside down. It's like opening up a can of worms."

Cesar Perez, who was interviewed in Spanish and said he had never filed a grievance in more than a decade of incarceration, explained, "If you do a 602, the officers will send you to the hole. Once a new officer . . . he slammed the door on me and smashed my finger. And he broke it. And this part was dislocated . . . and there was a lot of blood. And they told me if I wanted to do a 602 I'd have to go to the hole."

Martin Pedigrew, housed in a Sensitive Needs Yard on a sex offense, said he had filed only once in six years, and explained why he did not file more:

> You know sometimes you don't want to [file]. You're thinking you can become a troublemaker by doing 602s, they retaliate to that. Like when I finally filed it, it was a medical issue that was like going on two years and wasn't resolved. I was like, man, I've got to do it. . . . But like I said, the more you do it, the more the cops hassle you. If you're writing a 602, *especially if you're writing on officers*—they say they're not allowed to retaliate but they do. They come tear up your locker or take your TV, whatever they do [emphasis added].

Armando Martin, in prison on a life sentence, said, "One thing . . . that I've learned in prison is that you try your best—after so many years of bein' in the system—never to 602 an officer. Medical or certain items . . . you know, up to a point, but when it comes to staff . . . you try not to because there's *always* consequences." Several people reported that when an inmate files a complaint against staff, the retaliation may come from another staff member. For example, James Little said, "I've seen a person file a 602 on an officer. . . . He [the officer] will have another officer or friend just go through your stuff and take what they can."

The formal process for staff complaints is slightly different than for other types of grievances, and the details of this process arguably compound prisoners' perceptions of vulnerability. As discussed in chapter 2, when alleging staff misconduct, prisoners are required to sign a form acknowledging that they understand they may be prosecuted for a misdemeanor and sustain a disciplinary violation if they file a false complaint. This requirement and the not-so-implicit assumption of prisoner prevarication raise the stakes on staff complaints and, in combination with prisoners' concerns about other forms of retaliation, may be definitive barriers to filing in these cases.

A close look at the types of grievances the 120 prisoners we interviewed reported filing bears this out. Remember that the problems most frequently mentioned by these prisoners had to do with living conditions, medical care, staff disrespect, property, and programming/jobs, in that order (table 4). The 217 grievances these men reported to us diverged from this pattern in two important ways. First, staff complaints took a distant fifth place in grievances filed—with only 8 percent of these grievances concerned with staff misconduct.[25] When we asked these men what their most *recent* grievance was about, only 7.2 percent reported that it was a staff complaint.[26] Second, and related to this, missing or damaged property—a less contentious issue with fewer potential repercussions[27]—was less often named as a *problem* but became a much more common focus of *grievances* than staff misconduct, which was more rarely claimed.

Some of these men filed grievances against staff despite the potential repercussions, but they often left staff complaints on the ground floor of the disputing pyramid—naming them but not claiming them.[28] There is never a one-to-one equivalence between naming problems and claiming remedies, with people often simply "lumping it." Our interviews with these men reveal not only that there is a significant amount of both naming and claiming, but that there is a pattern to prisoners' "lumping"—a pattern produced in part by a widespread perception of reprisals against those who file staff complaints.

THE DIALECTICS OF GRIEVANCES AND RIGHTS

As we have seen, despite significant self-blame and fears of staff reprisals, California prisoners file tens of thousands of grievances every year, with lumping it occurring disproportionately in cases of staff complaints. Prison is an institutional context that center-stages explicit rules, rigid procedures, and "law-full" restraints, helping explain prisoners' intense engagement with law through the grievance process. However, law in prison is unique beyond its mere hypervisibility. It is designed above all to secure prisoners' captivity and spell out the details of, and limits to, their rights. In this context, rights consciousness is paradoxically enhanced, as prisoners focus on how to preserve the rights they retain and defiantly contest perceived violations. Nor does the slim chance of a victory seem to deter them when, as Luis Ramirez put it, "it's a right that is being violated."[29]

Several decades ago, Stuart Scheingold (1974) coined the term "the myth of rights" to refer to the misplaced faith in rights discourse to empower the subordinated, arguing that rights are a blunt weapon with a tendency to boomerang. Since then, many law and society scholars have critiqued rights discourse as ineffective, pointing to the failures of rights talk in areas as diverse as women's reproductive rights, desegregation, and racial economic justice (Bell 1992; Bobo 1998; Rosenberg 1991; Smart 1989). As usual, things are not so simple, though, for even unenforced or ineffective rights can have powerful consequences (Lovell 2012; McCann 1994; Milner 1989; Polletta 2000; Schneider 1986). McCann (1994) demonstrates that while the movement to legislate a right to pay equity for women failed to achieve the desired legislation, it politicized its participants. Lovell (2012, 32) reports that letter writers to the U.S. Justice Department complaining about perceived civil rights violations in 1939–1941 "often seemed emboldened" by their action, even when (as was usually the case) it did not secure any concrete results. And Polletta (2000) documents the positive political consequences of African American mobilization during the civil rights movement even when concrete legislative and social goals of the movement failed. As she describes the power of that mobilization, "Standing up for one's rights was the goal, not merely [a] means" (390).

"Standing up for one's rights" in prison through filing grievances is usually an individual act not connected to a larger social movement like that of the civil rights era. Nonetheless, like the civil rights participants whom Polletta studied, these prisoner appellants rarely achieve tangible victories, but they persist anyway in their "standing up," filing thousands of grievances every year. Engaging the legally prescribed mechanism available to them, they contest conditions both life threatening and seemingly mundane. The act of filing may enhance prisoners' rights consciousness, as McCann and Polletta would predict; at the very least it serves as an indicator—a touchstone—of that consciousness. It is ironic indeed that this system conceived by Congress as a bastion against prisoner legal mobilization serves as a tangible reminder to prisoners of their rights and an institutional invitation to invoke them.

In the next chapter, we look again at this dialectical relationship between rights and incarceration as we listen carefully to some of the surprising turns these prisoners' narratives take.

CHAPTER 4

Prisoners' Counternarratives

"This Is a Prison and It's Not Disneyland"

As we have seen, these prisoners name many problems, and most have filed grievances about issues ranging from the prison facilities, medical care, and staff disrespect to the appeals process itself. Some of what they told us about their problems and grievances aligns with what is found in the academic literature as well as government reports that provide critiques of the prison system in California and elsewhere. They are consistent too with an adversarial relationship between prisoners and those who imprison them in what the courts have deemed overcrowded and unconstitutional conditions. In some sense, then, the tenor of their complaints about prison life is not unpredictable.

Surprisingly, however, interspersed with these complaints about the CDCR and prison conditions and prisoners' insistence that the appeals process is "rigged up" against them were a number of counternarratives. In particular, these men's observations about the fairness of the criminal justice system, the humanity of CDCR staff, and the role of truth and evidence in the appeals process, as well as their implied respect for carceral logic, offer an apparently competing perspective on prison as an institution and on the people who staff it and the laws that govern it.

PERSPECTIVES ON FAIRNESS: "FAIR IS FAIR"—OR NOT

These prisoners often complained vigorously about many things, but many *also* told us unambiguously that the criminal justice system had been fair to them. When we asked toward the end of the interview, "Looking back over your experiences in life and things you've done, do you think you've been treated fairly by the criminal justice system?" almost half of the men in our study (43 percent) said they had. Furthermore, they provided a variety of reasons for this conclusion, revealing the complicated ways prisoners think about criminal justice in general and the courts and sentencing in particular.

Many men focused on the slack the system had cut them prior to the event that resulted in their current incarceration. Orlando Martinez explained his thinking this way:

> [I base] that on a lot of stuff that I've done [and] the criminal justice system . . . gave me opportunities and . . . like, for example, I got possession of a controlled substance for sale while armed . . . and instead of sending me to prison right away, they give me opportunities, [an] occupation, Prop 36, drug programs that are actually helping my addiction and, yeah dude, that's how . . . they give me chances and opportunities. They suspended me instead of probation, giving me another chance. . . . Yeah, I've had a lot of chances, a lot of chances.

Edgardo Cameron, the Mexican inmate who was in a cage during the interview, also spoke of second chances: "I think I got a second chance, a second chance at life. I had just paroled. . . . I was only out for thirteen days. I get busted again for carjacking. They dropped the carjacking down to second-degree robbery and they only gave me twelve years. It was with a gun and yet the judge or the DA still showed me leniency and only gave me twelve years when he could easy have given me twenty-five to life." Terrell Davis concurred: "My attitude is I did the crime. I committed a crime, and, uh, everybody has a job to do so I feel that, I feel like they treated me just. I coulda got a lot more time, but I feel like I was treated fairly. For the crime that I committed, they gave me eight years. I think I was treated fairly." Several prisoners, including Leshone Powers, told us they had committed crimes that went undetected and therefore on balance things were fair: "Because I've done a lot of bad things in my life and for the things I haven't been caught for, I believe . . . that I'm paying for what I've done . . . all the other stuff I've done [and didn't get caught for]. . . . I believe that it evens out."

Others explained their assessment of fairness as a product of the law in more absolute terms. Reginald Thompson, in and out of prison since he was eighteen, simply noted that "the law is the law": "They go by the law. These people have been doing this [harsh drug laws] for years, before I was even born. Their laws are laws that we have to abide by. They use the same laws on me they use on anybody else out there."

Tellingly, others used the law as a point of departure for assessments of fairness *and* unfairness. For example, after Reginald Thompson said the system had treated him fairly, the interviewer sought a kind of routine affirmation of his statement before going on, posing the rhetorical question, "So the criminal justice system's pretty fair?" At that point, the prisoner began vigorously criticizing the repeat offender laws that had put him in prison, saying: "Yeah, they're fair, but I still have problems with how they've added all these other laws to enhance a person; like, for instance, how they take my past, prior convictions, and use them against me. . . . They do these things for a reason, to keep the prisons full. I'm not perfect, but fair is fair. . . . Convict me on the crime that I come here for. Don't convict me again on my past. . . . *It's not fair at all"* (emphasis added). This 180-degree turn in less than a minute dramatically underscores the fluidity of legal consciousness, a quality we will see throughout this chapter and again in later chapters when we discuss staff talk.

Expressions such as these were not confined to descriptions of the criminal justice system as a whole. Many prisoners periodically affirmed the legitimacy of, and extended the benefit of the doubt to, the institution that holds them captive, offering up empathy for correctional officers about whom they otherwise complained and speaking with reverence about the role of truth and evidence in a grievance system they called "a joke."

IDENTIFICATION AND EMPATHY: "I SEE THEIR SIDE
AND THIS SIDE"

Among the most conspicuous of the counternarratives that emerged in these prisoner interviews was one that underscored the humanity of guards and other CDCR personnel. Raymond Sterling, a white inmate in a minimum-security yard who was one of the few who asked not to be recorded, said of correctional officers: "There are some bad apples, but they are just people like the rest of us. You know, when you are with people eight hours a day, you see them as people. . . . It's inevitable, because they *are* people and you have to see them that way."

Others made sharper distinctions between good officers and bad ones. As Martin Tate put it, "You can tell which guards are cool." Orlando Martinez was one of many prisoners who had filed a claim about lost property, but unlike most, his property was recovered. He praised the officer who got it back for him, noting, "The CO didn't give me no attitude, you know. It wasn't like someone was *making* him give me my stuff back.... The respect was there, and he apologized. He apologized like, you know, 'I'm sorry,' you know what I mean?" Orlando concluded, "Sometimes you run into good officers." Jamal Williams spontaneously interjected in the midst of his interview: "You know, you have some guards, they cool, you know. They [say] like 'I'll see what I can do for you.' I've seen that happen."

Adolfo Flores, the Central American who was on "lockdown" and was handcuffed and shackled to his chair when we interviewed him, provided a particularly dramatic account of officers. In one exchange, he described incidents of officer misconduct he said he had seen, including a guard kicking a prisoner when he was on the floor. He began by quoting the prisoner imploring the guard: "Dude, you asked me to get on the floor. I on the floor. Why you still kickin' me? I not resisting, you know?" Adolfo continued, "So, that happens.... I guess the officers sometimes feel they want to push their authority." He went on without missing a beat, "You know, there are some good officers and then there's some ones that's bad, take it a little too far." This man, whose handcuffs were visibly chafing and who complained of pain in his hands not from the cuffs but from an earlier workplace injury, concluded, "Most of 'em leave me alone, you know?"

Roland Castro, also on lockdown and in handcuffs, agreed: "If you don't mess with them, they don't mess with you. It's like if they get respect, they give respect back. Every once in a while you'll meet a few that are, you know what I mean, that are disrespectful. But other than that ... the majority of them are [pretty respectful]." A number of these men noted that guards and other officers are simply "doing their job" and are "okay" people. Jesus Avena, who earlier had complained about an officer "who has no respect and ... talks to people like they're animals," told us, "To be honest with you, you know you hear a lot of people talking a lot of crap about officers ... but in general they're okay. They're just doing their job.... They're doing their job and they're not out to bother anybody. You know, they got their family to go home to and they're trying to get along. You know, in general I'd say they're okay."

Malik Jackson also said, "You know, there are certain guards here that, you know, are just like me.... I feel like they're just doing their job, you know, they're getting paid, taking care of their families." Even when advancing scathing critiques of conditions of confinement, some prisoners observed that officers are just "doing their job." David Miller had been in administrative segregation for three years. He began his interview by describing his cell with no windows and barely enough room to turn around. David complained about a range of things, including "evil" prison administrators who "break down your family unity" by putting inmates in prisons far from their relatives. He called the 602 process "nothing more than a mind game" and spoke of "super cops" and guard "antagonists" who "poke you with a stick" when you are having a bad day. But then he added, "Some try to do their eight hours and go home. . . . Most of 'em are pretty decent people. . . . A lot of them are really decent people just doin' their job." Later, David waxed philosophical: "They gotta do their job, and we gotta do our time."

Others went out of their way to grasp officials' points of view, not always completely successfully. Simone Menton explained why he had never filed a grievance: "I'm pretty sure they [officials] try their best to do what they can, you know what I mean? I'm not on their side or anything. But I mean, I can't tell what they're thinking." Armando Martin, who had many medical problems, had filed multiple grievances, and complained about conditions throughout the interview, also expressed a commitment to understanding CDCR staff's point of view, to make sense of it. After telling us a staff member had mistreated him, he added, "I also try to look at it from the other person's point of view. Sometimes when the staff will see an inmate . . . it could remind them of somebody they've dealt with in the past. . . . They're thinking, 'Oh, this guy's, you know, I remember somebody like that. They did that wrong' or whatever. . . . That's why it's important for the inmate to have respect, have patience."

Marcus Greeley, a self-identified Buddhist, reported that trying to understand officials' perspectives was his strategy for coping. When asked how he dealt with problems, he told us, "Being . . . neutral. I mean, I see their side and this side." When he described an officer's misconduct and reported that he had not filed an appeal about it, Marcus explained somewhat cryptically, "I'm on their side."

PERSPECTIVES ON FILING GRIEVANCES: "SOME OF THESE GUYS REALLY ABUSE THE 602S"

Occasionally, prisoners' views of staff were informed by their opinions of other inmates' behavior. Armando Martin complained that he sometimes does not get responses to his appeals but continued, "After seeing so many [frivolous] 602s, I can understand why a staff member would not want to respond to all of them. . . . I understand it from the staff's point of view, that probably they've had bogus 602s where people [have been] playin' the part for years." Roland Castro[1] also brought up frivolous filing impromptu, telling us, "People file for a lot of things, for stupid reasons. I think that's why they don't, uh, look seriously when people file 602s." In a similar vein, Mark Crenshaw, a white man convicted of a sex offense and serving time on a Sensitive Needs Yard, had never filed a grievance and spent most of his interview talking about frivolous filing. He told us, "I've known quite a few guys . . . if the CO looks at them different, they'll say it's derogatory. . . . They'll drop a 602 on it." He said he "lay[s] low" so as to "not bring attention [to myself]." He continued, "I've seen an officer turn from a really normal caring guy to he's got these 602s and they get more short-tempered with you. . . . They're just trying to do their job, and some of these guys really abuse the 602s."

Our quantitative data suggest that prisoners distinguish between their own filing behavior and that of "other inmates" whom they see as sometimes filing unnecessarily. Because we had imagined that prisoners might file grievances for symbolic or expressive purposes—especially in light of the knowledge that their grievances are not likely to get the desired results—we asked a series of questions designed to probe this possibility. Specifically, we asked whether they had ever filed a grievance "for reasons other than what is written on the form; for example, to get to court; to get back at an official or guard; just to tell the story of what happened to you; or to get something off your chest." Perhaps not surprisingly in retrospect, these respondents seemed to interpret the possibility that they might use the 602 "for reasons other than what is written on the form" in a negative light, suggesting frivolous or manipulative filing. The responses are interesting in this context. While only 14.8 percent of respondents initially said they had used the 602 for reasons other than or in addition to securing the remedy they requested, 71.3 percent said "other inmates" did so. Seven percent said they themselves had sometimes filed to get to court, but 60.7 percent attributed that motive to other inmates. Fewer than 6 percent of respondents said they had ever used the form to get back at a guard, while more than 72 percent said other inmates did. And 35.7 percent[2] and 10 percent, respectively, said they had used the form to tell the story of what happened or to get something off their chest, while 69.1 percent and 62.1 percent, respectively, said other inmates used it in these ways.[3]

When we asked at the end of the interview whether they "strongly agreed; agreed; neither agreed nor disagreed; disagreed; or, strongly disagreed" with the statement "Some inmates file too many 602s," 63.6 percent of these prisoners[4] either agreed or strongly agreed. Forty-two percent agreed or strongly agreed with the statement "I sometimes think inmates feel too entitled," and 46.8 percent agreed or strongly agreed that "most inmates file 602s for minor or non-existent issues."[5] When asked what he would do about the frivolous filing he described, Malik Jackson said, "If I was the warden, I'd have to read over it and look it over and see if it's really serious . . . and if it has something to do with a life-threatening situation, [I'd take action] . . . but [not] if it's something that's really petty as in you can live the next day." Similarly, Martin Pedigrew, who had filed only once in six years and complained about retaliation, derided others for filing too much: "They [prisoners] complain about everything. I mean, in the wintertime it's too cold. In the summertime it's too hot. It's one complaint after another. . . . They complain about the meals, not enough food, too much food, cold. . . . Mainly it's just petty stuff in my opinion." He continued, "A lot of people just, they didn't go to dinner until six-thirty and they expected to go at six. There's a lot that write just trivial [stuff]."

Related to the issue of other inmates' frivolous filing was the notion that if you do not give officers trouble, they will leave you alone. Jesus Avena, who reported that other people "talk a lot of crap about officers," also said, "I personally never had any problems with officers. . . . In all these years I never had, but then again, I mind my own business and I never get in their face or anything." And Martin Tate, a white prisoner who has never filed a grievance and reported that the criminal justice system had treated him fairly, told us, "As far as the guards go, some of them take it a little far. They've been good to me. If you do what you're supposed to do, you just stand here and do as you're told, you won't have any problems. . . . Bottom line here is you do what you're supposed to do, you'll be all right." Edward Packer said matter-of-factly: "The food and stuff here is cool and the staff here is all right. Me, I never had no problem with staff but I stay out of their way." Orlando Martinez struck the same chord: "A lot of COs, they give us our space. . . . As long as we do what we got to do, then they'll leave us alone. You follow the rules and you don't make pruno,[6] [and they say] 'Don't abuse this, don't do nothing wrong, and we won't mess with you'."

Others gave staff in general a pass. One of the most extreme versions of this was expressed by Malik Jackson, who had never filed an appeal (although he had considered it on occasion) because, he said, "if you're right, you're hurting someone's job maybe. You never know if that's their twentieth 602 or their hundredth 602 and that's it, the sergeant wants to fire that person. . . . I just don't want to put nobody in that situation, you know?" Evan Worsham, whose appeal had been denied, reflected, "I don't really feel like they were maliciously out to get me . . . I really don't." And Darryl White, who talked about how long the paperwork for a prison job was taking, added, "I'm not saying it's their [officials'] fault because I'm sure they're doing their job as much as possible. Hopefully."

It might be argued that these expressions of empathy and identification are evidence of a kind of Stockholm Syndrome.[7] But, unlike hostages who develop Stockholm Syndrome, most of these prisoners are alternately understanding *and* critical. Further, their selective understanding, identification, and empathy are not isolated phenomena; rather, as we will see, they are part of a larger pattern in which prisoners also express an enduring faith in law and evidence, as well as a respect for key components of carceral logic.

On the surface, too, these rationalizations of officers' conduct appear similar to those of the victims of discrimination in Bumiller's (1987, 431) study, one of whom suggested that her employer might have discriminated against her "without even realizing it." According to Bumiller (1987, 435), her respondents used this downplaying of employer intent to justify not filing discrimination charges against their employers, thereby preserving the "dignity found in their (own) anonymity." In contrast, however, most of these prisoners did mobilize the grievance process, and there was no indication that they sensed any loss of dignity for doing so. Indeed, as we saw in the last chapter, a group of prisoners told one coauthor, when she presented these findings side by ide with Bumiller's work, that they would feel *more* victimized and lose *more* dignity if they did *not* stand up for their rights. It seems likely instead that these prisoners' justifications of and identification with (at least some) officials are part of a larger complex of beliefs about law, justice, and incarceration drawn from the American cultural "tool kit" (Swidler 1986, 273), a possibility that we further explore in the following sections.

THE ENDURING LEGITIMACY OF LAW: "IT'S WRITTEN IN THE TITLE 15"

Just as not all prison officials are discredited despite the dramatically adversarial setting of prison, neither do these prisoners lose all faith in law and the importance of evidence despite their experiences with and cynicism about the 602 process. As we saw in the last chapter, these men sometimes spoke reverently about the rules ("They can't break the rules, cuz that's the rules") and the importance of law in their lives, especially Title 15 ("It's written in the Title 15"). Much like the working-class plaintiffs in Sally Merry's *Getting Justice and Getting Even* (1990, 12; emphasis added), they "are often caught in situations which they cannot alter; yet they do not simply accept these situations as just, nor are they always convinced by the vision of society presented to them by elites. *On the other hand, they rarely doubt the legitimacy of law itself or the value of a legally ordered society.*"

The enduring legitimacy of law and the definitive power of evidence and "the facts" to determine legal outcomes were revealed when we asked these men, "What is the key to writing a successful appeal?" Frank Boutin, the prisoner who told us that staff retaliate against inmates who file appeals by "put[ting] them on a bus and . . . transfer[ing] them up and down the state," nonetheless said unequivocally that to write a successful appeal, one has only to "be articulate about the law, or the Title 15, the rules and regulations, or the DOM." Edward Packer, whose property was confiscated by staff after a bus transfer, had untreated asthma, and had spent time in "the hole," was also sporadically confident of law's justice, telling us, "The key is being truthful and stating the facts."

Adolfo Flores, shackled and in handcuffs, had just finished telling us about an officer kicking another prisoner, when he responded to our question about whether it is possible to win a 602 and how to do it. "Yeah," he said, "you know, quote their Title 15. If you use the DOM and you use what they actually put down on their log books, then you have a way better chance to win. . . . There's certain rules that they go by, the DOM, the Title 15, you know, and so if the Title 15 says that's what we've got coming, then they can't go against it." David Cummings, who had had an untreated ear infection and said derisively that the 602 process was "laughable . . . hilarious," also had not lost faith in law. At the end of a long interview, he told us that officials' responses to 602s were "a bunch of rhetoric" and that filing was "pointless because it just gets you more aggravated." But he still believed in a route to a successful appeal that journeys through the law. He told us, "I believe it's got to be supported by the CCR Title 15, maybe any other legal citations that you could support it with." Over and over again, we heard from men who were profoundly cynical about various aspects of the criminal justice system in general and the prison system and inmate appeals in particular, that the key to writing a successful appeal was simple. As Jorge Bermudez said, the key is "citing the Title 15 [and] citing any other case law."

Some went further to declare that when truth and evidence are on an inmate's side, officials *have* to grant their appeal. Malik Jackson, who had never filed because he does not want to "hurt someone's job" and because he fears retaliation ("You're just causing yourself to make an enemy"), reported in response to our question about how to file a successful appeal, "There's Title 15. . . . Use that code. . . . Be specific about it and they have to grant it." And Evan Worsham, whose interview was replete with references to retaliation, angry comments about officials throwing away 602s, and sarcastic remarks about the 602 "paperwork shuffle," told us that the key to a successful appeal was "back[ing] it up with the Title 15, cuz those ones are almost always passed." Evan's ambivalence is evident at every turn: "But a lot of time, what happens . . . it goes to a clerk, the clerk goes through it, and then god knows what happens after that . . . it takes weeks, months, to resolve a 602. . . . [One time] they lied to my face." But he added, in an apparent non sequitur, "If you can find something where it says, the Title 15 says, we're supposed to get such and such, it's almost always granted."

Sometimes these references to the power of law and evidence to trump otherwise "rigged up" processes came in the context of inmates describing appeals they had won. For example, Darryl White, the man who declared that if we came to prison for a month, "I guarantee you would see things that [you'd say] '*This* can't be right,'" also told us that he had finally won an appeal after much hassle and delay. What he learned from this experience, he said, was "the sense that if I go the extra mile, and go by the steps, that it's a possibility that I can win in the system when it comes to my standing up for my rights." Indicative of the coexistence of enduring belief in law's legitimacy and extreme cynicism, when asked later what he would tell a friend about the appeals process, this same prisoner replied, "That it's unjust, that it's unfair, that it's unreasonable. I'm laughing, but I'm serious."

Edward Packer revealed his commitment to the power of law when he explained how he had won a medical appeal at the final level of review: "They granted it to me because they know that I have a valid reason. . . . They [Sacramento examiners] do a very fine check on every prison. They want to make sure everything is right cuz they . . . that's the constitution of the prison, you feel me? They make sure everything is right. They gonna go by the book." Edward responded to our question "What would you want people on the outside to know about the 602 process?": "That it works for justice for prisoners. It works good. You know, if you know how to write it up, it will work in your favor." José Pena summed up his confidence in the power of law when asked what he would tell a friend: "[I'd say] the law is the law. The law is the law. Use it to your benefit." And Simone Menton, who had never filed a grievance, nonetheless had confidence in the system, telling us, "You know, we can't just write a bunch of BS you know. . . . We get the Title 15, you know, it basically tells us our rights and what we got and what happens. It basically has every scenario in there. If [a violation] happens, then you got a 602, it says what should be on that 602 right there. And you know, people just can't write, 'Cuz I'm locked up, I want my stuff back.'" When asked what he would change about the system, Simone said, "I don't think I'd change anything. I think it's pretty good how it is." Daniel Sanchez, a Mexican American who had spent time in a Mexican prison, said that if a friend asked him about the 602 process, he would tell him, "It works. Even if you are an inmate and you want your voice heard, in the United States it can happen."

It might be argued that such faith in law is to some extent compelled, given that "it's all we've got," to borrow the phrase of the inmate when explaining why he files grievances despite his cynicism. But not all of the prisoners we interviewed expressed even such sporadic and fleeting faith in law and its power to secure rights. Several consistently ridiculed the notion of inmates' rights and the legitimacy of the appeals process. Tom Snider told us:

> You know, inmates think they have rights. . . . The Title 15 . . . it's *guidelines* [not rights], okay? . . . The CDC can take anything in there and they can, they can walk in here and give me a 115 [disciplinary infraction] just because I'm here. . . . Because it doesn't matter. They can do anything they want. These are guidelines and you can interpret it any way you want. They're not rules, they're guidelines. They're not laws. So therefore, like a lawyer, it's crap. And inmates think they've got some powerful tool. They don't.

Comments like this were rare, however. Most of these men expressed some degree of faith in rules and the legal process side by side with a profound cynicism born of their experience.

There is nothing unusual about such variegated attitudes toward law. As scholars who study legal consciousness have shown, our attitudes and beliefs about law are full of inconsistencies and contradictions. Decades ago, Sarat (1990, 355–56) described the legal consciousness of the welfare poor he studied as "an interesting combination of veneration and cynicism. What they venerate, what is 'good' or 'great,' is a law whose power they hope to enlist, while the law about which they express grave doubts is an apparently frustrated legality swimming upstream against bureaucratic resistance and inertia."[8] Ewick and Silbey (1998) found in their study that the same person may think of law as impartial and objective in one instance, boast of manipulating it in another, and then complain of its oppression. Like the people studied by Sarat and by Ewick and Silbey, these prisoners' attitudes toward law and legal processes are multidimensional and fluid, but they are by no means random or capricious. Instead, their dimensions are drawn from "culturally available repertoires" (Harding 2007, 346) that may or may not be consistent. Thus, with no apparent cognitive dissonance, the same respondent can at one moment deride appeals as "a joke" and in another moment explain that being "truthful" is the key to having an appeal granted.

Studies of legal consciousness also reveal the striking capacity of law to roll with the punches, exhibiting a kind of Zen flexibility that strengthens rather than diminishes its power. The survival of law's legitimacy—even in the on-again/off-again form we found in these men's conversations—in the context of prison and in interviews that otherwise focused on problems and grievances, is a testament not only to the chameleon-like quality of legal consciousness but to the enduring power of our "defer[ence] to the law's claim to autonomy" (Ewick and Silbey 1998, 47). As Reginald Thompson put it, "The law is the law."

RESPECT FOR CARCERAL LOGIC: "THIS IS A PRISON AND IT'S NOT DISNEYLAND"

Also present in these inmates' narratives is a measure of respect for the carceral logic that constrains them, even as they chafe against the perceived suppression of their rights. For example, many of these men spoke the same language of security and control that we hear prison management using in later chapters and which scholars have found is the operative language of prison administrators across the United States (Moynihan 2005; Gaes et al. 2004; Lerman 2013). Jesus Avena expressed it simply: "The officers here, they have to run a program too and to have a controlled environment." Later, after discussing problems, he proffered, "We can't blame everything on the department. We're the ones who got ourselves here, and they got to house us somewhere and there's not enough room. .... I would say [it's because of] security issues, because they have to have some kind of controlled movement, now there are so many people and there are less officers, so they have to have some kind of control over movement." Other prisoners went further to suggest security enhancements. Martin Tate recounted stories of violence among prisoners and told us, "It gets scary here," suggesting they "put security cameras up or something."

Also similar to the staff talk we encounter later and underscoring their own commitment to carceral logic, some prisoners insisted that frivolous filers should be disciplined. Harold Steele, the Vietnam veteran who pulled his own teeth because of the long wait for a dentist, told us, "I don't file 602s just in the form of sniveling." Other inmates, he said, see the 602 as "just a place where you can snivel, complain, and be argumentative." When asked what he would do about frivolous appeals, Harold did not hesitate: "I think they should have it in the book [Title 15] that they should be written up, disciplinary action." Trevon Moore, a black prisoner in maximum security for over fifteen years, went further, saying of those who file frivolously, he would "tell 'em if he file another 602, we gonna put you in the hole."

Orlando Martinez, who had said, "As long as we do what we got to do, then they'll leave us alone," complained about prisoners who file grievances against officers who are following prison policy. Reaffirming the legitimacy of carceral policy, Orlando expressed disdain for those who complain about "random searches" of their cells: "They do a random search and they find an extra sheet, an extra pair of pants, extra clothes—in CDC we're only entitled to two pairs of pants, two shirts, and they find extra stuff and they take it. Well, they want to file a 602 because they took extra stuff that they shouldn't have."

These prisoners periodically emphasized the importance of security, much as management did, and they sometimes expressed similar dislike of "sniveling" prisoners who file too many grievances and should be punished. By far, however, the most common refrain that echoed a theme inherent in carceral logic was that prison is *supposed* to be hard. Martin Tate said with some exasperation, "This is a prison and it's not Disneyland. They're not here to make you comfortable. We did a crime and this is what we get." Anthony James, a black man who complained about racial discrimination by prison officials, said the same thing: "You do the crime, you do the time." Daniel Sanchez, who had spent time in a Mexican prison, agreed with this logic that prison is *meant* to punish people for their crimes: "The way I see it, they're doing their job, right? . . . Of course you gonna get punished or you gonna get told, 'Hey don't do this, don't do that.' . . . You gonna get punished for it, for doing wrong." Mark Crenshaw, the white prisoner on a Sensitive Needs Yard, was adamant, telling us of 602s, "I don't believe in them, because we're in here because we're being punished . . . this is our punishment. Our rights are taken away in here for certain things. The minute I came to prison I fully understood that."

We often heard these comments in the context of the kind of self-blame we discussed in the last chapter. Orlando Martinez went on at length:

> We're not really *entitled* to yard. We're really not. That's just a privilege that we have—to go to yard, to go to canteen, everything. . . . I know what's a privilege . . . like TV room, day room, game room, yard, canteen, packages, those are all privileges here. [Sometimes] you get them taken away for a while. . . . I've already done two violations where we really didn't get no yard. . . . We've got our phones taken away. We've gotten everything taken away, so it's like, we get them taken away, we're in *prison*. If you don't like it, don't come back, you know?

Rodrigo Garcia, a Mexican prisoner who had never filed an appeal but had talked about disrespect from guards, told us, "You can't really complain about this [situation] because we committed the crime, we got to do the time. And we gotta deal with whatever's going on in here, you know?"

To summarize these findings, many of these men told us the criminal justice system had been fair to them, and some spoke about understanding the work being done by the officers who guard them. We also heard expressions that revealed the enduring legitimacy of law, the power of facts and evidence, and respect for the carceral principles of punishment, control, and security. In the last chapter, we discussed the complaints of these prisoners and the grievances they had filed. Although we were taken aback by the dramatic nature of some of the stories they told us and the level of medical neglect and psychological abuse they reported, the cynicism and hostility expressed by these men for the system that holds them were not unexpected given that they are inmates in one of the most hierarchical and adversarial institutions of contemporary American society. As Carrabine (2005, 897–98) describes it, there exist "basic antagonisms" of prison life: "The institution [of prison] generates intrinsic and fundamental conflicts, not least since prisoners are confined against their will, with people they would normally not choose to be with, in circumstances they can do little to change and are governed by custodians who police practically every aspect of their daily lives."

What we did *not* expect was that their hostility and anger at prison conditions and the violations of rights they perceive would be regularly interspersed with these altogether different narratives that confer legitimacy on the criminal justice system and imply a commitment to carceral logic. This commitment was evidenced not only through these men's statements about the fairness of the system and their expressed desire for a secure and "legally ordered" environment (Merry 1990, 12); it comes through, too, in their disdain for inmates whom they perceive to be filing frivolous grievances and "sniveling" about minor things when, after all, "this is a prison and it's not Disneyland."

LEGITIMACY AND THE CONTEMPORARY PRISON

Useem and Kimball (1989) introduced the idea that prisoners often see the institution of which they are captive as legitimate. Based on their study of nine prison riots in the United States, they concluded that physical force and coercion are not the critical ingredients in maintaining prison order and averting riots; instead, the key is that the institution be considered legitimate by its inmates. Noting that prisoners *expect* prison to be punishing (just as our respondents did), Useem and Kimball (219) located the source of a prison's legitimacy not in providing "amenities" but in realizing consistent standards and achieving "stability and uniformity":

> Inmates are not propelled to riot merely because they are deprived of the amenities available outside of prison—for punishment is the purpose of prison—but because the prison violates the standards subscribed to concurrently or previously by the state. . . . Well managed prisons, with adequate staffing and physical resources perpetuate a feeling among inmates that the system conforms to reasonable standards of imprisonment. . . . Where administrators and guards are powerful, unified, and competent, the conditions of imprisonment themselves seem more legitimate; the captors are seen as authoritative rather than merely powerful.

Sparks, Bottom, and Hay (1996, 89) expanded on this discussion of prison order and legitimacy, suggesting there are four components of prison legitimacy for inmates: "Amongst these one would certainly have to include the centrality of fair procedures and . . . consistent outcomes. A third component concerns the quality of behavior of officials. . . . Fourthly it is possible that the basic regime of the institution—its accommodation, services, and activities—may itself be regarded as illegitimate in failing to meet commonly expected standards." Sparks and Bottoms (1995, 607) noted in this regard that each act of officer disrespect and misconduct but also "every ignored petition, every unwarranted bureaucratic delay, every inedible meal . . . every petty miscarriage of justice . . . is delegitimising."

This scholarship may advance our understanding of prison riots and is consistent with some of our findings, most notably that prisoners place a high priority on order and security. But there is a conspicuous discrepancy between what these scholars argued are the central bases for legitimacy and our study's findings. The prisoners we spoke with complained repeatedly about the absence of "fair [grievance] procedures," the lack of "consistent outcomes," "ignored petition[s]," "bureaucratic delay[s]," and "petty miscarriage[s] of justice." Yet this does not appear to have delegitimized the institution and the laws that govern it, at least not entirely and not consistently. What we see here is that legitimacy is not all-or-nothing, nor is it fixed; instead, expressions of legitimacy appear, retreat, and reappear throughout these interviews, side by side with eruptions of anger and cynicism. We see also that carceral legitimacy is more robust than this prison literature suggests, and is not altogether eroded by ignored grievances or other perceived miscarriages of justice.

Previous analyses of prison legitimacy tend to treat it in a vacuum, outside of its larger cultural and structural context. But it is wrong to assume that prisoners' belief systems are insulated from those of the broader society. Indeed, the endurance of prison's legitimacy for these men, even if halting and episodic, cannot be understood apart from the ideological strains of this punitive moment, of which the contemporary prison is one major manifestation. As Beetham (1991, 11; emphasis in original) explained, people give power relations legitimacy not because the powerful act legitimately but because they "*can be justified* in terms of [people's] beliefs." Just so, prison, despite all of its "petty miscarriages of justice," may retain some legitimacy in part because it is justifiable within the context of extant cultural belief systems about criminal justice more generally (Jackson et al. 2010).

Consistent with studies of legal consciousness, these men embrace multiple, conflicting views of law and legal practices, with a deep cynicism about law as a rigged game alternating with their enduring faith in law and the power of evidence and truth. In similar fashion, they shift into and out of narrative frames, by turns contesting their perceived rights violations and emphasizing the need for more "controlled movement." And just as they draw from the American cultural tool kit their views of law as both rigged and majestic, so too their conflicting narratives of rights and carceral control are not arbitrary but part and parcel of the defining logics of our post–civil rights era. On the surface, it is a testament to the power of these two cultural narratives that even prisoners—subject to the most repressive version of the culture of control and highly critical of its repercussions in their lives—embrace carceral logic alongside rights discourse. At another level, however, it makes sense that both of these cultural tropes find such prolific expression in prison, where, as we discussed in the last chapter, law is so clearly a master text. For, if rights and repression are the defining logics of our age, it is above all within law that their respective precepts are most vibrantly displayed.

In the next chapters, we turn to the ways these logics also surface in our conversations with CDCR staff as they talk about the grievance process and their practices related to it. As we will see, the contradictions of staff talk are specific to their institutional location; it is a location that is in some ways dramatically removed from that of the prisoners they hold captive but that is embedded in—or more precisely, entangled in—the same cultural web.

CHAPTER 5

"Narcissists," "Liars," Process, and Paper

The Dilemmas and Solutions of Grievance Handlers

The grievances that California prisoners file initiate a process of administrative engagement with the CDCR officials charged with running the prisons that house and control them. This engagement creates considerable work for corrections officials, as line officers, prison appeals coordinators, deputy wardens and wardens, and the chief of inmate appeals and staff in Sacramento must manage and respond to the flood of grievances. We turn our attention now to these institutional actors, their perceptions of prisoners and the grievance system, and their grievance response practices. Serving as both respondent and adjudicator, the CDCR has virtually unilateral power to determine the outcome of these grievances. Yet these officials face a number of dilemmas related to the same contradictory forces that shape prisoners' attitudes and grievance practices, albeit from a diametrically different structural location. In this chapter, we trace these dilemmas and the practical, managerial, and cognitive solutions of these institutional actors, as revealed in our interviews with them.

Since the advent of mass incarceration in the United States and other western countries, increased attention has been paid to the political, economic, and cultural factors that drive it (Alexander 2010; Beckett 1997; Campbell and Schoenfeld 2013; Garland 2001; Lerman 2013; Murakawa 2006; Simon 2007; Wacquant 2010; Weaver 2007). Empirical research on the prisoners themselves is more sparse but growing, with work that explores various dimensions of prisoner culture, strate-

gies of resistance and survival, and attributions of institutional legitimacy (Bosworth 1999; Carrabine 2005; Hunt et al. 1993; Lerman
2013; Rhodes 2004; Sparks and Bottoms 1995). In contrast, there is
relatively little sociological literature on those who oversee these behe-
moth institutions of confinement, and even less that is based on direct
interviews with them.[1]

This relative void, coupled with the usual access issues, made our
interviews with prison employees challenging, for the absence of an
established knowledge base meant that we were starting with a blank
slate. However, this unmarked territory yielded rich veins of quantitative and qualitative information, some of which upends simplistic
notions about the institution of prison and the "thin blue line" of its
officials. In this chapter, we mine our interviews with these officials and
report our sometimes counterintuitive findings regarding their views of
the grievance system, inmates' rights, and prisoners who file appeals, as
well as their tenacious rhetorical commitment to ritualized rules and
procedures. We use direct quotes extensively here, both to give voice to
those who have not been heard from before and because the apparent
inconsistencies and 180-degree turns in their narratives are among the
chief paradoxes this book unpacks.

"THEY HAVE A RIGHT TO FILE": THE LEGITIMACY
AND UTILITY OF APPEALS

The personnel we interviewed included the wardens and deputy wardens of the three prisons, appeals coordinators at these prisons, and
three captains from each prison, as well as the chief and deputy chief of
the Office of Inmate Appeals in Sacramento (also known as the Inmate
Appeals Branch [IAB]) and three IAB examiners. Of these twenty-three
officials, the majority are men (65.2 percent), most have some college
education (86.4 percent), and their ages range from thirty-nine to fifty-
eight years old. They are an ethnically/racially diverse group (40.9 percent Hispanic; 31.8 percent white; 18.2 percent black), and most have a
long history of work in corrections (on average 23.7 years). The vast
majority identify as politically conservative (82.4 percent) and religious
(81.8 percent) (see table 6). Interestingly, over one-third (36.4 percent)
responded yes when asked "Has anyone in your family ever been incarcerated in a prison?"

These officials spoke about prisoners, their grievances, and the grievance system in many ways, but there were a few constants. For one

TABLE 6   CDCR PERSONNEL CHARACTERISTICS*

	Number (%) of Personnel**
Gender	
Male	15 (65.2)
Female	8 (34.8)
Age (mean = 47.5)	
39–45	9 (40.8)
47–50	8 (36.3)
51–58	5 (22.5)
Education	
High school graduate	3 (13.6)
Some college	8 (36.4)
College graduate	9 (40.9)
Any postgraduate	2 (9.1)
Race/ethnicity	
Hispanic	9 (40.9)
White	7 (31.8)
Black	4 (18.2)
Filippino	1 (4.5)
White/Hispanic	1 (4.5)
Political identification	
Conservative	14 (82.4)
Liberal	3 (17.6)
Religiosity	
Yes	18 (81.8)
No	2 (9.1)
Spiritual	2 (9.1)
Years in corrections (mean = 23.7)	
14–19	4 (18.2)
20–29	16 (72.2)
30+	2 (9.1)

* Based on self-reports.
** Valid percent.

thing, almost everyone spoke positively of the legitimacy of the appeals process and prisoners' right to file grievances. This commentary did not appear to be offered merely for the sake of political correctness but was often voiced with, if not passion, then at least conviction. Henry Lopez, an official in the Inmate Appeals Branch (IAB), was among the most adamant: "This is a way of giving voice to people it matters to. . . . We need to ensure they get a voice." Later Henry expanded, "This job plays into my sense of—not equality—but leveling the playing field or something." Inmate appeals coordinator (IAC) John Mansfield explained, "My job is to make sure inmates are afforded an opportunity to be heard." Associate Warden Sandra James told us that appeals are "an individual's opportunity to express, in written form, anything that may be adverse to them." When asked what kinds of problems she thought it was legitimate for an inmate to file about, Lucinda Gray, an examiner at IAB, said, "*Anything*. They have a *right* to file."

Most of these CDCR officers and administrators told us that the appeals they had processed—even those they had denied—were in some sense "legitimate." For example, when asked if she thought an appeal she had just denied was legitimate, Leanna White, an IAC with more than ten years of experience, replied emphatically, "*Absolutely*." Asked why she thought so, Leanna answered without a moment's hesitation, "Because *he* thought so." Later asked about the legitimacy of another appeal, Leanna queried, "To *him* or to *me*? [It was] legitimate for *him*."

These observations about the legitimacy of appeals were sometimes accompanied by general statements about inmate rights, their humanity, and the need to treat them with respect. Examiner Mark Tilden told us unequivocally, "Inmates can, do, and should have rights." Associate Warden Sandra James mused, "We're human, they're human. They make mistakes, we make mistakes." This official, who was one of the few to characterize herself as politically liberal, continued, "Society truly thinks these people [inmates] have horns and long tails. They are not like that." Captain Thomas Jones also acknowledged that prison officials can make mistakes and inmates have a right to file grievances, "because we're not a perfect department. We make mistakes, and there's a lack of training." IAC Stacey Taylor told us she has to keep reminding lower-level correctional officers (COs) that "the inmates are humans, [and] you've got to talk to them like human beings." Captain José Cruz sat back in his chair, reflected for a moment, and considered: "It's a matter of respect for them as a human being. The difference between the inmate and me is I went right at one point and they went left."

These CDCR personnel often recognized the appeals process as not only legitimate but useful. Many saw it as a buffer against legal liability, as we discuss in more detail in the next chapter. All of the IAB staff we interviewed pointed to the role of appeals—and their own administrative role—in protecting the CDCR from lawsuits. Henry Lopez, the IAB official who told us that "this is a way of giving voice to people," later went on at length about his function as a shield against unwanted outside attention, whether from an attorney general or a court. "Wardens want to hear this stuff [our feedback]," he said, "because they don't want to lose a prison, they don't want a murder, or an AG [attorney general] investigating. When things blow up, it's bigger than it had to be." Henry continued, "I like it when we get it right . . . and we can protect the department from vulnerability." Lucinda Gray, an examiner in the same office, echoed the sentiment: "I have great respect for the people who run these institutions [prisons]. It's my job to protect them from liability, and they appreciate that." Chief Deputy Warden Steven Waring also sees the appeals process as protection against liability. He volunteered, "If it goes to court, we have our documentation. The appeals process is a safeguard to the inmate who files the complaint, but also to the institution." IAC Margaret Cummings also foregrounded liability issues: "It helps us see where we're failing. I want to help the warden out of lawsuits where we're representing the institution."

Others, especially prison managers, praised the grievance process as a way to reduce violence. Echoing a theme from the prison-order literature on the importance of achieving legitimacy in the eyes of inmates (Carrabine 2005; Sparks and Bottoms 1995; Sparks, Bottoms, and Hay 1996; Useem and Kimball 1989), these administrators were convinced that a good appeals system is key to avoiding riots.[2] Chief Deputy Warden Steven Waring, who said the 602 process gives him "documentation" in case he ends up in court, also insisted that the appeals system is a critical ingredient of prison order: "I don't know if you've heard of Attica, but that happened because they didn't have an appeals system." Warden Donald Brown reported the same thing. It was, he implied with some exaggeration, the lack of an adequate appeals process that caused the infamous Attica riot in New York State in 1971: "In Attica, when they had that riot, they had a bad appeals system."

In contrast to many prisoners we spoke with, who sometimes declared the system "a joke," the vast majority of these CDCR personnel agreed or strongly agreed that "the 602 process is pretty straightforward and easy to do" (81.8 percent) and "works pretty well" (86.3 percent). Without exception, they lauded the system as fair to prisoners, providing them with a voice and thereby securing order and decreasing violence. Asked what he thought of the California grievance system, Captain Anthony Sanchez told us, "I think it's good. It's an important component that allows inmates to vent." Examiners and others in the Sacramento IAB also credited the system with reducing the chance of riots and other violence. Examiner Sonya Thurman brought up the gruesome

New Mexico prison riot of 1980, telling us, "[The California grievance system] is a good system. I am very aware of what happened in New Mexico—the riot—they didn't have an outlet for their grievances. The inmates [in California] don't always get the response they're after, but they have an outlet." Indicative of this perception that the appeals system is useful as an "outlet" through which prisoners can "vent," these staff told us that prisoners file in part to tell their story (81.8 percent) and also to get something off their chest (90.5 percent).

The advantage of appeals most commonly cited by prison managers was their utility as generators of information. Almost all of them spontaneously offered that grievances were a way to learn what is happening in their prisons as a tool to maintain order and control, not to fix unacceptable conditions (in fact, this was never mentioned). Captain José Cruz said, "I use it as a diagnostic . . . a way to give voice to the inmate population to tell us what is going on." Associate Warden Sandra James used virtually the same words: "This is my way of knowing what's going on. I need to know what's going on to do my job." Warden Sandy Reyes said, "I embrace the appeals process. . . . It tells me the picture of the institution. I have the pulse of the institution." IAC Danielle Garcon went so far as to say, "The appeals office is kind of like the backbone of the institution. This is where you learn about the inmates."

Some CDCR officials spoke of the important role the appeals system plays in allowing inmates to provide critical information surreptitiously. Chief Deputy Warden Steven Waring recounted this story: "Sometimes an inmate uses a 602 to give us information. . . . There was an inmate who wanted to tell a sergeant there were weapons in a certain cell but he couldn't just tell him, so he acted like the 602 form was a grievance and handed it to the sergeant and actually complained loudly to the sergeant as he gave it to him. When the sergeant opened the appeal, he found a note informing about the weapons. This worked well. The weapons were found, and the informant didn't get in trouble with other inmates. No one knew." In the same vein, Captain Anthony Sanchez told us that sometimes gang members write on a 602 form that "'there's gonna be a stabbing fight' or something. . . . And they tell their friends that they're gonna be filing a complaint against some staff member but actually what they write on the 602 is just some information like 'there's gonna be a knife fight' or something."[3]

It would be an exaggeration to say that these officials and administrators exuded enthusiasm for appeals even when speaking about their utility. On occasion, they interspersed their comments about the managerial benefits of the grievance system with bits of sarcasm. For example, when we asked Captain Anthony Sanchez what he enjoyed most about working with appeals, this same man who had told us that gang members sometimes use the 602 to report an imminent knife fight twirled his index finger in the air and, with a sarcastic grin on his face, mock-cheered, "Whoopee! Appeals!" Captain Thomas Jones laughed out loud when we asked him if he enjoyed working with appeals, and if so, what he liked most about it. He responded incredulously, "That I *enjoy?!* Honestly, no. It's just *there.*" John Mansfield, an appeals coordinator who had only been in office six months, said that "inmate appeals is a valuable tool" but "it's not a glamorous thing." This lack of enthusiasm aside, virtually without exception these appeals coordinators, wardens, deputy wardens, captains, and appeals examiners agreed that the grievance process is both an inmate right and a useful tool for maintaining control of their facility.

"SOLID WASTE," "LIARS," AND RIGHTS GONE WRONG

Also prominent in these interviews, however, was a strong theme of hostility toward prisoners, particularly those who actually file appeals. Indeed, much like our interviews with prisoners, which were laced with apparently contradictory narratives, these officials' accounts often took dramatic U-turns. Most conspicuously, while they lauded the utility of appeals and acknowledged in the abstract that filing a grievance is a prisoner's right, they often referred with disdain to those who exercise that right.

Many of these CDCR staff painted with a broad brush the presumed character deficiencies of *all* prisoners. Henry Lopez, the IAB official who earlier told us that "we need to ensure that they [prisoners] get a voice," later theorized, "Inmates aren't good at the regular brokering of life. That's why they're in prison." Dave Manning in the same office went on at length: "You have to think of them as infants and the kind of parents they had. . . . All they know is the *scripts* [of "a good person"], not how to *be* authentic." He continued later about the "dysfunctional" quality of inmates: "You are teetering on the edge of the abyss when you look at prison." Throughout his interview, Dave returned to the theme of prisoner dysfunction: "The inmate culture is to deceive. Inmates are instinctively and reflexively dishonest. . . . Inmates are skillful liars. . . . They're emotionally uncomfortable with telling the truth. . . . Inmates are by definition hyperinsecure. . . . They have an instinctive ability to manipulate information."

Leanna White, the veteran appeals coordinator who told us it is *"absolutely"* legitimate for a prisoner to file an appeal, later launched a soliloquy on what she insisted was prisoners' lack of "logic," beginning, "The inmate population doesn't think like us. There's no logic." In an interview that lasted almost three hours, Leanna volunteered that when she is out in public and someone asks her what she does for a living, she "keeps it vague," saying, "I'm a solid waste man. I'm in solid waste management." When we replied that we thought *solid waste* referred to the waste in sewers, she answered, "No, I mean whole people."

Prison is an adversarial institution of "structured conflict" (Jacobs and Kraft 1978), and it is conventional wisdom that an us-versus-them mentality prevails. However, as we saw in prisoners' unstable and contingent perceptions of the system of which they are captive and of the personnel that guard them, the reality is more nuanced and considerably more complicated than this simplistic "wisdom" implies. And we have seen here that at least some prison officials and administrators acknowledge in the abstract prisoners' humanity and their rights, further challenging a simple us-versus-them paradigm. That said, the vehemence and hostility with which these prison workers denigrated their charges was startling, particularly in the context of other commentary affirming prisoners' basic humanity.

Some of this denigration was aimed at prisoners in general, but the most intense hostility was directed at those who file grievances. Henry Lopez, the IAB official who earlier had proclaimed that the grievance system "is a way of giving voice to people it matters to," expressed contempt for prisoners who use that voice: "Those convicted of the most heinous crimes file the most. . . . Those who file a lot are narcissistic, not accountable. . . . [Pretending to address inmates who file:] 'Why can't you just grow up?'" He picked up the thread again later, weaving it throughout the interview: "They're angry about being in prison. They're narcissistic. They're suffering and want others to suffer too. . . . They tend to be a lot of narcissistic personalities. When they want something, they take it."

After telling us about an appeal he handled from a death row prisoner who was contesting the sometimes faulty injection procedure then in use for executions, Henry could hardly contain his scorn, deriding the claimant: "I thought, 'You're so lucky that we're putting you to sleep. You have been an instrument of torture.' He was a total punk for requesting that he didn't suffer. It was a bunch of hoo-hoo. . . . 'You're a punk for even asking. You did it, don't be a baby. You're gonna get the pinprick of a needle. It's ridiculous to ask not to suffer.'"

The examiner Lucinda Gray was one of the few officials we spoke with whose anger was explicitly racialized: "If there's a three-hundred-pound black inmate who complains he doesn't have enough toilet paper," she said, "I don't want to deal with toilet paper to clean his fat ass." The aversion was echoed later when she mocked black prisoners' claims of racial discrimination. Speaking of a lockdown at one prison after "some blacks tried to murder an officer," Lucinda said that the "whites" and "Hispanics" were released but that the "blacks" stayed locked down while they continued to investigate. A black inmate (Johnson, whose name was on the eventual landmark lawsuit that the entire IAB office was involved in, *Johnson v. California,* 543 U.S. 499 [2005]) filed an appeal claiming racial discrimination. Lucinda was incensed that Johnson "claimed the whole institution hated blacks. . . . This isn't 1854 and we are *not* on a plantation."

Most people were not quite so dramatic or so passionate in their derision, and no one else was this racially explicit, but almost all of the officials we interviewed criticized grievance filers in some way. IAC Leanna White, who said she was in "solid waste management," remarked, "You know, it's [filing grievances is] a scam for them." IAC Danielle Garcon, who had generally been sympathetic toward inmates in her interview, was suspicious about prisoners who file staff complaints, explaining, "They do it [file grievances] to downplay their 115 [disciplinary violation]. Make it look like the person who gave them a 115 is a terrible person." Later Danielle, although she had called the appeals system "the backbone of the institution," said about those who file frequently: "We *do* roll our eyes and think, 'What's he complaining about *now?*' It's gotten out of hand. . . . They appeal about every single little thing. But come on. Life isn't fair. There are a lot of things in *my* life I don't like. . . . A lot of times they feel like *they* are the victims."

An appeals coordinator we conversed with in a prestudy prison visit told us with great confidence that there is a relationship between having committed "manipulative crimes" and filing appeals. He claimed that the "criminal mind" is above all "selfish and manipulative," attempting to illustrate his point with an example of prisoners who use the appeals system "to get ice when it is over 90 degrees in their cells." The theme of manipulative prisoners playing the system was one we heard over and over again and was often expressed in a matter-of-fact manner that implicitly assumed we were in agreement with the interviewee and suggested the unquestioned quality of this institutional truism.

Captain José Cruz, who said he has "respect for them [prisoners] as a human being," touched on another frequent sentiment when he suggested that those who file grievances have not accepted responsibility for being in prison. "It's the ones who believe society did them wrong who file," he claimed. José continued, conflating "abiding by the rules" with not filing grievances, "The ones who accept responsibility—they abide by the rules." This conflation of prison "rules" with not filing grievances is telling, as it exposes the contradiction between the loss of agency inherent in carceral logic (what this official called the prison "rules") on one hand, and the agency exercised in filing grievances on the other. Ironically, despite the fact that the grievance system is part and parcel of the institution and is written into the official rules that govern it, prisoners who use the system are seen as violating "the rules" of prison logic.[4]

The tension in these officials' accounts, which endorsed the appeals process as legitimate but impugned the character of inmate appellants, was sometimes evident in a single statement. Henry Lopez, who earlier called prisoners "a lot of narcissistic personalities," put it this way: "Many inmates are manipulative and exploitative, but they are all deserving of being heard." IAB official Dave Manning struggled with the same tension: "To the best of our ability, we will be fair, irregardless of what we think of them."

Consistent with this disdain for prisoners who file appeals was a general sense that prisoners now have too many rights. Officials who asserted that the grievance process is legitimate and that prisoners have a right to file often also suggested that prisoners' rights have gone too far. Examiner Mark Tilden related what he saw as a major increase in rights during his long career and expressed his ambivalence: "I started back in the department when inmates had no rights at all. I was working as an officer at [prison] in 1973, and we were told they had rights. We were aghast. . . . I don't agree with all the rights they have, but they should have rights." Similarly, Captain Michael Tisdale described what he thought were too many layers of protection for inmates as a result of "mandates from the courts." "It's not as simple as it once was," he said with an air of resignation.[5]

The most vociferous attack on prisoner rights came from Lucinda Gray, who had quipped that "this is *not* a plantation." She began by telling us of a prisoner who had claimed he did not get enough yard time, arguing that this was "cruel and unusual punishment." Lucinda could barely contain her anger, blasting, "*That* has to be pretty extreme to be cruel and unusual punishment." She then gave examples of what she thought qualified as "cruel and unusual": "Not letting you out of your cell in fifteen years, or hog-tying you and throwing you down the stairs." Or "slitting your ankles in the warden's office." Using this as her threshold, Lucinda said, "We very seldom violate their constitutional rights. . . . I tell them, 'You've got your Title 15 rights and *not one second more*. You've got this coming and not one second more." Asked what she would do to improve the appeals process, she did not hesitate: "Shorten scrutiny. Inmates have too many hoops they make us jump through, and they don't have to jump through any hoops. The inmate should have to jump through hoops! . . . I'd say California jumps through a zillion damn hoops to make sure they're happy campers. This isn't Carl's Jr. and 'You have it your way.' . . . We go through a lot to make sure inmates are treated fairly. We're Johnny-on-the-spot, right there making sure they've got everything." Most of our respondents expressed more nuanced views, even as they told us they resented what they saw as an explosion of rights. Chief Deputy Warden Steven Waring, who was relatively measured in his tone, nonetheless complained:

> Inmates have been treated *more* than fairly. . . . We give inmates all ability to sue us. We have to give everyone what everyone else has. It's the only way to show we're impartial if they sue us. *It's gone too far.* They've gotta have whatever's in policy. They complain, "I didn't get my condiment."[6] To me that's extreme. We don't even treat our military people that good. That's putting it to the nth degree.

In their critique of prisoners' rights, several other people also favorably compared the life of prisoners to that of people on the outside. Captain José Cruz, who earlier had ventured that prisoners who take responsibility for their actions do not file appeals, proclaimed, "I don't get three meals a day, not like they do." IAC Margaret Cummings, who had said, "I think the inmates have a lot of rights, too many rights in California," went on to criticize prisoners for feeling entitled: "Me too. I want a full paycheck," she said facetiously, referring to the state furloughs then in effect.

IAC Stacey Taylor joined the chorus. Mimicking inmates, she whined caustically, "'We don't get enough cable in here. And what about our TV?' And I think to myself, 'And you're out robbing and raping people. I mean, *c'mon* man.'" She continued to mock prisoners as self-indulgent and entitled: "'My food wasn't at the right degrees.' *C'mon.* Inmates have way too many things they can file on. They think they're at a hotel. . . . I think the public would be shocked. . . . Inmates have way more rights to things than the public has sometimes. Their medical care is better than some people on the streets."[7]

The master frame here is that, as the appeals coordinator opined after using the example of prisoners asking for ice when the temperature reaches 90 degrees, "the vast majority are frivolous." Lucinda Gray, who had exclaimed that "we are *not* on a plantation," told us unequivocally that almost all grievances are frivolous. She said dismissively: "They're just doing it [filing appeals] because they can do it. Only 10 percent of those cases should even be here. . . . They do it for money or just to be a thorn in your side. Or say I'm a nerd and I write page after page. Or I do it just for attention or to buck the system." To underscore her point, Lucinda said one prisoner had appealed the size of his portion of corn, and she sighed sarcastically, "Oh, well. 'Get a grip.'"

So-called frequent filers, who are thought to file frivolously, are a particular source of scorn for CDCR officials. Well over three-quarters (81.8 percent) of the staff we interviewed agreed or strongly agreed with the statement "Some inmates file too many 602s." Almost one-third (31.8 percent) agreed or strongly agreed that "*most* inmates file 602s for minor or nonexistent issues," and 22.7 percent "neither agreed nor disagreed"; only 45.5 percent *disagreed* that most inmates file for minor or nonexistent issues, and no one strongly disagreed. Further, of the twenty-two CDCR staff asked directly if prisoners file frivolous appeals ("Sometimes people talk about frivolous filing or filing over something relatively minor or nonexistent. Do you think this happens?"), twenty-one said they did.[8]

It should be noted that any depiction of grievance appellants as frequent and frivolous filers is not consistent with the data. According to official data, of the more than 16,000 inmate grievances that made it to the third level of formal review in 2006, 72.1 percent were filed by prisoners with only one such grievance, and more than 92 percent were from inmates who filed fewer than four times. Further, a content analysis of our random sample of written grievances shows that they were predominantly for what our research team coded as "serious" incidents (45.3 percent) or incidents "of concern" (45.3 percent) rather than "minor" incidents (9.4 percent).

Nonetheless, the notion that frivolous filers are a major problem is entrenched in CDCR culture. Chief Deputy Warden Steven Waring, who told us the grievance system "is a safeguard to the inmate . . . [and] to the institution," later went on at length about the problem of prisoners who file over trivial matters: "This one inmate got a sack lunch that was missing a little packet of mayonnaise. So he files a 602 that his lunch was missing the little packet of mayonnaise. . . . Technically the missing mayonnaise is a violation of policy because we post the menus and it says mayonnaise. So he knows what he's supposed to have coming. But that's really silly. Or no cookie." Danielle Garcon, an IAC who self-identified as politically liberal, gave other examples: "'My food's too cold' or 'The officer looked at me the wrong way.'" IAC Leanna White struck the same theme: "So many are frivolous, [just like] 'The teacher called me stupid.'" When asked what her most memorable case was, she recounted a long story about a prisoner who had won a court case giving him the right to a kosher diet. Leanna went on: "He wasn't happy with that. It wasn't enough. It wasn't hot, it wasn't quality food. . . . He was trying to get more. He got kosher. He won. And he thought to himself, 'Let's see what else I can get.' It was never enough." She concluded triumphantly, "But I was able to blow all his arguments out of the water." IAB official Henry Lopez is also convinced that many appeals are frivolous, recollecting a group of "sex offenders who filed a joint appeal." With disgust, Henry described it: "He and all his sex offender buddies wanted sex classes that taught Kama Sutra, videos, and everything."[9]

This theme of frivolous claims, which legal scholars have revealed in other contexts to be sometimes called "garbage cases" by adjudicators (Merry 1990, 16; Yngvesson 1993, 76), was the most common throughout our interviews with officials. In this context, the "broken cookie" story has taken on folkloric status. Speaking both on and off the record, in formal interviews and informal conversations, these CDCR personnel again and again referred to a prisoner who allegedly filed a grievance because he received a broken cookie in the chow line. We were first told this story during a prestudy prison visit to secure endorsement for our research from a prison warden. Upon hearing that we intended to focus on the appeals process, the warden and his team of deputy wardens, appeals coordinators, and various assistants regaled us with details of the "broken cookie" grievance, including their claim that the appellant had won his case at the U.S. Supreme Court. Although we searched and never found concrete evidence of this grievance—much less its court appearance—the truth of the story is less important here than its prominence in prison lore. Much as the McDonald's coffee case and other "fables" of American litigiousness are so entrenched in American cultural knowledge that their names have become a familiar shorthand for legal excess (Haltom and McCann 2009, 3), so the "broken cookie" has become code among these prison staff for all that is wrong with inmate appeals. Universally told with derision, the story has a mantric quality as a tale of rights gone wrong and of the personal and moral deficiencies of prisoners.

CARCERAL LOGIC, "OPERATIONAL REALITIES," AND THE PROBLEM OF RIGHTS

To sum up before going on, most of the staff we interviewed expressed the opinion that the prison grievance system is legitimate—even useful—and prisoners have a right to file. And most paid more than lip service to the concept of prisoners' rights in general. At the same time, many told us that rights have gone too far, and many reserved special disdain for prisoners who file grievances, particularly those they call "frequent filers." One clue to unraveling this apparent inconsistency between the legitimacy of rights and disdain for those who claim them was offered by staff respondents who exclaimed, much like some of our prisoner respondents, that this is *prison* and it is *supposed* to be hard. As Henry Lopez, the IAB official who talked of grievances "leveling the playing field," told us, "There is some truth to each one of these [grievances]. . . . But *it's no fun in prison. You came here, get over it*" (emphasis added).[10]

The inmate appeals process simultaneously embodies the logic of rights and the logic of carceral control—two of the defining principles that form the ideological landscape of the post–civil rights era. The precarious location of inmate appeals at the very intersection of this contradiction may explain both the acceptance of an inmate's right to appeal and the anger and sarcasm with which these narratives are laced ("You came here, get over it"), as these two tectonic ideologies collide.

This tension and its implications become clear if we unpack the concept of carceral logic, which at the level of the prison comprises two related dimensions. At one level, incarceration expropriates much of the captive's autonomy. By definition, freedom of movement is curtailed (at the extreme, as one prisoner in administrative segregation put it, "I'm locked in a cage"), but so are many daily behavioral choices—how to dress and eat, for example—that typically accompany adult personhood in our society and that most of us take for granted. Hence, the quip that "it's no fun in prison" and the commonly expressed notion that if a prisoner takes responsibility for his actions (i.e., accepts imprisonment), he will "abide by the rules" (i.e., not file grievances). For if incarceration is supposed to deny the prisoner autonomy, filing grievances represents an assertion of agency and therefore violates that "rule" of logic.

During a prestudy visit, a warden told us that the inmate appeals process helps reduce violence. He explained, "We tell them when to eat, when to drink, when to sleep—the appeals process relieves tension by letting them vent." As we have seen, other officials also extolled the advantage of allowing prisoners to "vent" through appeals, thereby avoiding riots. It should not be missed, however, that to the extent that it "relieves tension," it does so by allowing inmates a modicum of agency in an environment in which agency is anathema.

If the logic of incarceration entails an assumed loss of autonomy, a second, more practical dimension regards core operating principles of the prison. Gaes et al. (2004) and Moynihan (2005) found that safety and security are the primary goals of contemporary American prisons "regardless of the goals listed in the strategic plan" (Moynihan 2005, 23). Despite increasingly intervening in prison policy toward the end of the last century, the courts still provide a wide swath of discretion to prison administrators "to accommodate the institutional needs and objectives of prison facilities, particularly internal security and safety" (*Hudson v. Palmer*, 468 U.S. 517 [1984]).

A priority on managerial control in the name of security permeated our conversations with CDCR employees and, in their opinions, often explicitly trumped prisoners' rights. Emphasizing the safety issue, examiner Mark Tilden, who began his career "when inmates had no rights at all," went on to say, "They should have rights. I guess we could debate which rights endlessly. . . . We're just trying to ensure the rules, as they are and as I know them, are implemented. *We're also trying to go home alive*" (emphasis added).

When asked how he decides his response to an appeal, IAB official Henry Lopez told us he explores "the larger ramifications—legal, political, and operational. Sometimes it's a correct decision but has bad ramifications, and you have to juggle that." He illustrated with the example of an inmate in solitary confinement who complained that he was not getting the ten hours per week of yard time that regulations require. Henry noted that the prisoner was technically correct, but granting his appeal would be impractical and potentially dangerous because prisoners in solitary confinement are only allowed outside in "stand-alone modules," of which there are a limited supply. Henry asked rhetorically, "If we ordered the prison to give him ten hours of yard, what would the consequence be? Who *doesn't* get yard time if he does?" He continued,

"We use the ubiquitous safety and security card. Sometimes if we did what the regs [regulations] say, someone would be dead." When prompted further, "What do you look for in an appeal?" Henry replied:

> Does it involve life or limb? I look at the protocol, legal and political ramifications, safety and security. [I ask myself] "Is it constitutionally protected? Does it have potential to compromise safety and security?" . . . People *have* to have worked in prison to do the job [of examiner] right. . . . I know how it smells. I know how it seems. I know the operational realities. . . . It's all these subtleties. You have these rules you are supposed to be operating in. . . . But I also look for fundamental fairness. And I think about the operational realities.

Henry also spoke of recurring cases in which black prisoners from Los Angeles do not want to be transferred to facilities in the high desert far from their families (an issue raised by a number of prisoners we interviewed and in some of the written grievances in our sample): "Blacks don't want to go there. But we have to keep a certain racial balance in each prison so one group won't turn on another and take over. This is an operational reality that can trump other considerations."

As a whole, these grievance examiners suggested that the "operational realities" of running a prison are such that prison managers need to be cut substantial slack, even if this means that some rights may be curtailed and official policies circumvented. Consistent with this principle, examiner Sonya Thurman said she looks at "whether or not they [prison officials] did what they did according to policy, and if not, why didn't they? If they didn't do something according to policy, they could have an exemption."[11]

"Operational realities" relating to safety also came up frequently when speaking with prison managers. Chief Deputy Warden Steven Waring talked at length about the conflict between upholding inmates' religious rights and ensuring safety. He began, "Sometimes we have guidelines we can't get around. One guy asked for a sword for his religious rites. Religious rights is a big one." Steven continued, alternating sarcasm with a nod to practicality:

> We have people who practice voodoo here and Wiccans, all kinds, and they want some weird stuff. A Buddhist wanted a special zafu pillow for meditation. But the item can't be searched because it's solid. He had been granted his right to get the pillow, but when it arrived we realized it couldn't be searched and we had to deny it to him. That was frustrating. So we got him a substitute that could be searched, but it wasn't really the right kind. We gotta look at the security behind it. Can I let him have it or is it a breach of

security? . . . It can get crazy because if you satisfy one group, you have to give it to others. Jews got their kosher diet. Muslims want their halal diet. Native Americans want their prayer herbs. One group wanted some powder that explodes. We couldn't give it to them, so we gave them cocoa to sprinkle around.

IAC Danielle Garcon, who was among the most sympathetic to prisoners of the officials we interviewed, summed it up succinctly. She noted that as a Hispanic, she could often see things from the prisoners' perspective, but when responding to appeals, "you have to think about the safety and security of the institution."[12] Overall, almost two-thirds (63.6 percent) of these respondents either "strongly agreed" or "agreed" with the statement "Some of the things inmates complain about on 602s are hard to change because to do so would jeopardize the top priority—safety and security."

These operational realities are part of prison staff's administrative landscape, or what Bittner (1967, 283) calls decision "horizons." In their chapter on the importance of context in administrative decision making, Emerson and Paley (1992, 234) apply Bittner's concept of decision horizons in police/citizen encounters to "organizational horizons" within institutions that "involve distinctively institutional or organizational . . . realities or courses of action." They argue that "retrospective horizons" (knowledge of the origins and sources of referred cases) and "prospective horizons" (knowledge of the predictable "downstream consequences" of various decisions) affect the decisions of institutional actors who come to see their jobs as doing "practical decision tasks" that impact institutional operation. Describing the consideration of downstream consequences, Emerson and Paley say, "Identifying and assessing such consequences build on intimate knowledge of what is likely to happen at future institutional decision points if 'a case of this sort' were to move forward" (1992, 239). It is just such downstream consequences that prison staff refer to when they talk about "operational realities," and it is because of the importance of such intraorganizational knowledge that Henry, who coined the term *operational realities,* told us, "People *have* to have worked in prison to do the job [of examiner] right."

In focusing on the organizational horizons of the institutional actor, Emerson and Paley theorize a critical element of administrative decision making. Their research reveals the institutional restraints on individual decision makers who must apply a vast store of knowledge to anticipate the upstream and downstream consequences of their actions. What is missing from their analysis is the possibility that the "practical decision tasks" of particular institutional contexts may be in tension with, or contradict, extant cultural logics and the downstream consequences associated with those broader logics—a topic we will return to in the next chapter. For now, it is important to note that just as individual administrators make decisions within an institutional context, the institution itself is embedded in a broader cultural and legal context that exerts its own set of pressures—some of which may be in competition with or contradictory to more narrow institutional goals or operational realities. Our interview narratives are replete with evidence of such a tension, with the ambiguity accorded prisoner rights and inmate appeals being its most conspicuous signpost. These institutional actors are caught between managing the practical realities of their carceral organization and attending to its logics on one hand, and acknowledging the powerful cultural logic of rights on the other.

One cognitive solution to this clash between the logics of incarceration and rights is to impugn the character of prisoners who attempt to exercise their rights, and to trivialize their appeals. The disdain of prison staff for prisoners is of course not new (see Jacobs and Kraft 1978; Jurik 1985; Lerman and Page 2012). Prison is in part an echo chamber for tropes that permeate the broader culture, and criminals have long been associated in the public mind with a racialized underclass, whose moral failings are allegedly demonstrated by their disproportionate representation in prison (Gossett 1997; Kennedy 1998; Rafter 1997, 2008; Ward 2012). Today this racist image is coupled with a more subtle but equally powerful trope. In this post–civil rights era, people of color are often depicted as entitlement-assuming beneficiaries of special privileges. The staff's portrayal of prisoners echoes precisely this theme of overentitlement.[13] Characterizing prisoners as dysfunctional liars and narcissists, our respondents above all depicted them as pampered ("We're Johnny-on-the-spot, right there making sure they've got everything") and as enjoying extra rights that ordinary people do not have. It is telling in this regard that 59.1 percent of these personnel agreed or strongly agreed with the statement "I sometimes think inmates feel too entitled," and only 13.6 percent disagreed or strongly disagreed.

The location of the inmate grievance system at the intersection of rights and confinement calls forth this trope in a particularly powerful way, as the institutional response to this collision is to cast the problem as one of excessive rights and a prisoner population composed of entitled whiners. The staff's depiction of prisoners as frequent filers who make frivolous claims is not confirmed either by official data or by our interview data, which reveal that the vast majority of inmate appellants are *not* frequent filers and that their grievances are mostly about rather serious issues. Further, the stark contrast between this portrayal of pampered prisoners and the horrifying prison conditions described in *Brown v. Plata*, 583 U.S. __ (2011), can hardly be overstated and underscores the powerful ideological quality of this racialized image.

RULING OUT UNCERTAINTY AND PROCESSING SCRUPLES

Impugning the character of prisoners and trivializing their grievances constitute one institutional response to the unwieldy logics of incarceration and rights that the prisoner grievance system straddles. But the challenges confronting those charged with processing prisoners' grievances are myriad, as are the strategies for resolving them. At the broadest institutional level, these challenges derive from the need to affirm the carceral logic of control while not negating the prisoners' right to contest the parameters of that control. At the level of the individual actor, there is no escaping the humanity of those one acts upon (as IAC Stacey Taylor put it, "The inmates are human"). Complicating this hapless task, prisoner grievances cover the gamut of everyday life in prison. Applying the neat boundaries of law to the messy contours of life on the ground is never easy. Indeed, subjecting life's disorderliness to the discipline of law is one of the main challenges of any legal practitioner, and the task is all the more daunting in this conflicted total institution. In the sections that follow, we see how cleaving to the rhetoric of strict rules and procedures and a focus fixed on paperwork temper the formidable challenges—both administrative and emotional—faced by these institutional actors.

The Rhetoric of Law, Administrative Certainty, and Emotional Distance

The primary legal tools these CDCR officials have to work with—Title 15 and the DOM—are extensive and stipulate policies, rules, and procedures in sometimes painstaking detail. Like all rules and law, however, they do not cover every conceivable situation and hence require interpretation. Further, rules themselves are of little help in weighing evidence and calculating the credibility of prisoners' claims. Despite these limitations, prison rules and regulations are an abundant source of cognitive certainty for these officials. Faced with appeals that are often a tangle of he said/she said accusations and rebuttals, and which not infrequently involve issues of enormous consequence for prisoners, these CDCR staff repeatedly told us that recourse to rules and established procedures made their task easy. The discursive dominance of law and rules within the prison context is not surprising, as this institution owes its very existence to the formal dictates of law and regiments its charges according to minute rules of behavior.

Less obviously, law and rules have important symbolic and mythological functions and features, as a vast body of literature reveals (Edelman, Uggen, and Erlanger 1999; Meyer and Rowan 1977; Fitzpatrick 1992; Cover 1983; Edwards 2010). Edelman, Uggen, and Erlanger (1999) suggest that organizations which socially construct the "rational myth" that their internal procedures are conducted in strict compliance with the rules they institutionalize to comply with legal mandates, accrue "market benefits" as the organization thereby becomes immune to legal liability. Meyer and Rowan (1977, 340) argue, "Institutional rules function as myths which organizations incorporate, gaining legitimacy, resources, stability, and enhanced survival prospects." They note that employees in institutions whose structures are based on "institutionalized myths" such as the rule of law are more likely to engage in "elaborate displays of confidence, satisfaction, and good faith, internally and externally" (358). These displays, they say, are not false or disingenuous. Rather, "participants not only commit themselves to supporting an organization's ceremonial façade but also commit themselves to making things work out backstage" (358).

The CDCR staff's adherence to the "institutionalized myth" that grievance decisions proceed according to legal strictures and formalized rules not only benefits the institution by keeping things "running smoothly" and holding the courts at bay (Edelman, Uggen, and Erlanger 1999); it also consolidates intellectual and moral confidence among personnel charged with an ambiguous task with powerful human implications. We heard over and over again that making a decision on whether to grant a grievance was, as IAC Leanna White told us, "not that difficult" because "everything we do is in the Title 15. It's right there. . . . We just follow our rules. That's all. We just follow our rules." IAC Margaret Cummings, when asked what she looks for in processing an appeal, or what criteria she uses, said matter-of-factly, "I just look at things. I know the rules. . . . They have the same Title 15 I do." And later in the interview, she explained, "I don't make a conclusion. I find facts." Referring to the simplicity of the process, Margaret said, "[The inmate appeals process] is in-and-out, in-and-out." IAC John Mansfield also made it sound simple when asked how he recognizes legitimate 602s: "You know, when you are in the middle of doing this, you just get the facts and put 'em down. . . . What's right is right. We're obligated to follow the rules." Examiner Mark Tilden showed the same confidence in his decision making and its basis in hard-and-fast rules: "We get to interpret the rules in black and white. Either they [prison officials] followed the rules or they didn't. . . . It's that simple . . . because it all comes down to the rules."

Associate Warden Sandra James also told us that grievance decision making was "cut-and-dried. You just use the rules and regulations." When we asked Warden Sandy Reyes what criteria he uses in making decisions about appeals, he got up from his desk, strode across the room, and grabbed his copy of the Department Operation Manual (DOM). "Have you seen this?" he asked. "Anytime I have a question about an allegation, I go through this to see if the inmate has had an adverse impact or not." Warden Reyes was even more adamant later when he proclaimed, "I look at policies and procedures. . . . Policy is what I live and die for. . . . Policy and procedures. If [the inmate] is wronged and policy says so, then I'm going to grant it." Captain Thomas Jones was succinct: "I'm basing everything on procedure, so it's not hard."

The allegiance to rules and "cut-and-dried" facts is as selective as it is emphatic, but this selectivity does not appear to detract from its utility in shoring up these officials' certainty or their belief that making decisions is "easy." We saw one version of this selectivity earlier, when we discussed the ways operational realities related to safety and security trump even the most established policies and procedures. A second kind of reality that affects decision making, above and beyond what policy requires, is sheer administrative convenience. When we asked officials who had told us some version of "I am basing everything on procedure" whether "how easy it would be for officials to fix a problem" enters into their decision, over half (52.4 percent) said it did.

Another such deviation from a neutral application of policy involves the unwritten rule that when a prisoner makes a claim of fact that is refuted by an official, the official—not the prisoner—is to be believed. While this may call into question the objective quality of fact-finding and the neutrality of the evidence thus uncovered, it has the distinct advantage of reducing the not infrequent "he said/she said" problem to the straightforward question of "*who* said?" For example, IAC Leanna White told us the story of an inmate who said an officer had broken his radio during a cell search. The officer insisted he did not break the radio. When we asked Leanna, "How do you know who to believe?" she replied, "Because the officer said it, that's it. There's no evidence to the contrary. . . . Most of the time it's not that difficult. If there's something damaged and the staff says 'I didn't touch it,' well then, he didn't." Throughout our interviews, staff emphasized that corrections officers must tell the truth because they are sworn to do so; thus their version of events is privileged over versions of prisoners who, by definition, have been convicted of a felony.

Examiner Lucinda Gray gave a revealing illustration. When asked how she recognizes a case that should be denied, she said without hesitation, "When the inmate is wrong, when there is no evidence his case has merit. Like the institution says an inmate had contraband or his TV was already broken. That's cut and dried. I'm gonna take the institution's word for it." Dave Manning, an IAB official, said categorically, "I believe staff over inmates. Always. Always. Always." Captain Peter Dayton revealed how heavy the burden of proof is for inmates: "Sometimes it comes down to the inmate's word against staff's word and then the burden of proof is on the inmate. . . . *Even if there are twelve inmate witnesses, you need something else to go by*" (emphasis added).

The issue of trusting staff over inmates came up most dramatically in discussing staff misconduct grievances. Chief Deputy Warden Steven Waring told us unequivocally, "If the staff says it didn't happen, then it's denied unless there is physical evidence. . . . Let's say an inmate says, '[Officer] Gonzalez socked me up, beat the hell out of me,' and there's no physical injuries, then he didn't." IAC Tanya Harden told us of a case that reveals how profound this trust in staff is. In this case, an inmate claimed he had been sent a money order that he did not receive. The mailroom officer said it never arrived. When Tanya investigated, she found the money order in the mailroom officer's pocket. Ever trusting, she concluded, "The officer forgot he had it in his pocket."

IAC Margaret Cummings, who earlier said, "I don't make a conclusion, I find facts," was convinced that she was "neutral" while stressing that she always believes staff over inmates: "For me it's neutral. You have to be very neutral. . . . The burden of proof is basically on them [inmates]. I tell them, 'I have a sworn peace officer [and here she held out her arms like scales]. On one side I have a sworn peace officer—

what do *you* have by way of evidence?" IAC Stacey Taylor told us, "Nine times out of ten, I believe the officer because they're sworn peace officers." High-ranking prison manager William Landes similarly told us, "I guess denial [of the appeal] is my default," and later, "I give the peace officer the benefit of the doubt." With no apparent irony, he concluded, "I'm the objective reviewer."[14]

Scholars have long noted that judges' use of legal rhetoric obscures the significant discretion they exercise and conceals the indeterminacy of law. Lovell (2006, 298; 2012) explores the use of legal language to "mask discretion" not by judges but by civil servants and other lower-level government officials. Analyzing letters written by ordinary Americans to the Department of Justice between 1939 and 1941 about perceived rights violations and the official responses they received, Lovell found that officials usually reverted to the boilerplate claim that the issue was outside their legal jurisdiction. The use of this legal justification, Lovell (2006) argues, served to dispense with the requests expeditiously rather than to dispense justice. Lovell's argument is particularly persuasive since, as he notes, the fourteenth amendment gives the federal government full authority to become involved in such cases. While Lovell observes that "practical barriers related to a lack of resources" (286) were partly responsible for the Justice Department's refusal to take on these cases, he contends that "the ritualistic claims about jurisdiction" accomplished ideological ends, effectively absolving department personnel of any responsibility for the peremptory dismissal and presumably closing off avenues for redress.[15] Finally, Lovell notes that using formal legal rhetoric to dismiss requests functioned to shore up officials' confidence. In the face of having "to refuse requests from people in very difficult circumstances ... those attorneys had reason to convince *themselves* that they lacked discretion" (2012, 191, emphasis in original). Citing Cover (1986a), Lovell (2006, 287) observes that legal language "is not solely designed to convince or conciliate persons subjected to law. Rather, judges [and other government agents] are trying to convince themselves."

As we have seen, deference of prison staff and examiners to rules, regulations, and policy peppered our interviews with them, as did their insistence that appeals decisions were "simple," "easy," "black-and-white," "cut-and-dried," and "in-and-out."[16] Like the judges discussed by Cover and the Justice Department employees studied by Lovell, their recourse to generic legal justifications is in part strategically aimed at cutting off effective challenges. As Captain Michael Tisdale put it, referring to grievance responses, "If you close all doors and seal it tight, he [the inmate] can't really take it up. . . . What are the regulations and rules? Did my staff violate any policies? Does the inmate have a leg to stand on?" But the repeated reference to rules seems above all designed to invoke cognitive certainty in situations of essential indeterminacy. The selectivity of their allegiance to rules and neutrality is consistent with our reading of their invocation of law as partly ideological. It is ideological in the sense that it justifies and legitimates negative appeals decisions, which serve the institution, but more pertinent here, it instills in decision makers a tidy sense of certainty in a decision-making process that is rife with messy ambiguity.

Relatedly, the emphasis on rules, regulation, and policy does emotional work. In a context where granting or denying an appeal may have dramatic consequences for the prisoner applicant—sometimes meaning life or death, liberty or captivity—shifting responsibility for their decisions onto rigid rules and policies gives decision makers not only cognitive certainty but a moral "alibi" (Berger 1963, 145). Cover (1986a and 1986b) argues that legal decisions always imply a kind of force and violence is the implicit or explicit companion of all legal interpretation: "Legal interpretation takes place in a field of pain and death. . . . Legal interpretive acts signal and occasion the imposition of violence upon others: A judge articulates her understanding of a text, and as a result, somebody loses his freedom, his property, his children, even his life" (1986a,1601).

But if law portends violence, it also provides solace to those who must enact it. Cover (1986b, 819) notes, "There is the internal, psychological, and moral revulsion we feel at the infliction of pain on other people. . . . But there are obvious limitations upon the revulsion against violence. . . . [T]he revulsion in almost all people may be overcome or suppressed," and it is a vital function of law to achieve that suppression among state agents. The organization of law diffuses responsibility among many levels of decision makers and practitioners. And its rituals anesthetize those on the front lines of the violence it decrees, including executioners who must carry out capital punishment (Johnson 1998). Above all, it provides moral cover for decisions and acts that cause others pain and from which we would normally recoil.

Inmate appeals decisions are no less imbued with force and violence than are judicial decisions, having implications for prisoners' medical treatment, release dates, property, confinement conditions, yard time, food quality, and the fulfillment of a variety of daily needs. The decision to deny appeals may result in returning a prisoner to "the hole," with-holding medical treatment, or affirming an infraction that will extend the duration of imprisonment. Even those with apparently less dramatic consequences—from the temperature of mess hall food to the length of hair allowed—inflict a measure of pain on those whose autonomy is severely impaired and whose lives are lived in mind-numbing routine.

Leanna White, the IAC who told us that "most of the time it's not that difficult" because "we just follow our rules," recalled a case that involved a gay prisoner who filed an appeal to be assigned a single cell. She casually relayed to us that she was preparing her negative decision when the prisoner hung himself. When we asked delicately how she felt about this, Leanna replied that she felt no remorse. She explained, "There's a lot of homosexuals in here, and we can't single-cell all of them. . . . We have a rule about single cells. . . . He *chose* that [suicide]. We all make choices." When we asked if she was satisfied with her nega-tive appeals decision in the case, Leanna reported, "*Absolutely.* It was *absolutely* fair because that's the policy."

IAC Danielle Garcon told us of a prisoner's request not to be trans-ferred out of state because it would make family visits impossible. She denied the appeal and explained to us, "To me it [the appeal] wasn't legitimate because visiting is no longer grounds for not being trans-ferred. . . . I don't take the appeals personally. I don't feel anything." She later recounted the story of a prisoner who filed an appeal saying he had been "forced to orally copulate a staff member. He saved the evidence in his mouth and spit it in a plastic baggie." Danielle dis-missed the appeal because the prisoner had been transferred to another prison and had missed the appeal deadline. When we inquired if maybe he had waited to transfer before filing because he feared retaliation, Danielle said, "Yeah, maybe, but he missed the deadline so we couldn't respond." When asked how satisfied she was with the outcome and how it had been managed, and how fair it was, she replied that she was very satisfied, that it was very fair, and that she felt good about it: "I felt good that I did everything I could, in my capability."

Warden Donald Brown, who repeatedly referred to the iconic cookie story as an illustration of frivolous appeals and said "if [prisoners] com-plain a lot, then they lose credibility because there aren't that many things to complain about," also seemed free of stress. Looking back on the hundreds of appeals he had participated in either directly or indi-rectly, he told us with pride, "I never lost an ounce of sleep. . . . I have my management team. I'm very careful to get the right team." Implicitly linking his good health to his clear conscience, he continued, "I never lose sleep. . . . I don't take an ounce of medicine. I got a clean bill of health."

These officials apply law and policy to the appeals before them—for example, is it or is it not consistent with policy to transfer prisoners out of state regardless of its effect on family visits? But many appeals are not about questions of policy but instead are murky debates about who did what and when. Law cannot by itself resolve such issues of fact, but taking rhetorical refuge in law can resolve intellectual and moral dilemmas, sheltering these practitioners from responsibility and protecting them against attacks of conscience. Cover (1986a, 1615) noted that people in Milgram's infamous experiment transcended the human revulsion toward inflicting pain by telling themselves that their actions were the product of commands from authoritative others; so too, he argued, the organization of law shields legal actors from a sense of personal responsibility. Nowhere was this more evident than in the words of IAB official Henry Lopez. Recall that Henry had participated in denying an appeal from a death row prisoner that ultimately paved the way for the prisoner's execution. Henry told us he was satisfied with how things had gone: "I'm satisfied because it was in keeping with law in terms of implementing executions. You're part of the process. I feel fine doing my duty. . . . We all collaborated and we did our duty."

These interview data regarding staff's perceptions of the appeals system and its operation suggest that the rhetoric of law buttresses their intellectual certainty and moral detachment in an environment in which little is certain and much has the potential to cause pain. Their comments about the criminal justice system in general and how fair it is to inmates often invoked the same kind of law-centered discourse, sometimes seeming to come from the truncated Cliff notes of a high school civics lesson. Captain Anthony Sanchez told us the system is fair to inmates: "Yes, it's our Constitution, our laws. Like *Law and Order.* There's police that ensure people who break the law get arrested. And there's courts who process them. And they get sent to prison. It's our Constitution. We have the best system in the world." Answering the same question, IAC Stacey Taylor seemed intent on convincing herself: "Oh, yes. . . you have to believe in your system. It's the law, and the law works. They get their sentence. It's pretty straightforward. It's structured."

Process and Paperwork

These officials' repeated insistence that they simply do their job and follow law and policy often merged with the more bureaucratic issue of following proper *procedures*. The focus on procedure was evident throughout our interviews with staff, as officials explained to us in detail the administrative steps required for each type of appeal. For example, grievances involving missing property require inmates to produce original receipts for the item, confirming that they had owned it. Captain Thomas Jones told us, "You need to get documentation. We're a bureaucracy. We move based on documentation. . . . Technically even if we take their trash, we should give them a receipt for it."

Complaints against staff, medical grievances, Americans with Disabilities Act (ADA) appeals, and so forth are each handled according to strict procedures and require their own document records. These procedures take center stage in any investigation. When we asked Captain Jones whether it was hard to tell a subordinate that he had erred in handling an appeal, he said, "I'm basing everything on procedure, so it's not hard. . . . [I ask,] 'Was the process followed?'" Simultaneously revealing her focus on process and her institutional bias, examiner Lucinda Gray reported matter-of-factly, "I sometimes have to find the details of [a procedure that explains] why they [prison officials] didn't violate due process."

While procedure tends to outweigh the truth-finding mission in officials' handling of most inmate grievances, in the case of grievances related to disciplinary infractions, it is the *sole* focus. Disciplinary infractions (known as "115s" or "128s" for their official form numbers) are of paramount importance to the prisoners charged, as they may carry implications for their release dates. When a prisoner contests a disciplinary action, the grievance is treated much like the judicial appeal of a trial outcome. That is, rather than investigating the circumstances and substance of the infraction charge and whether it was rightfully lodged—which is typically what the prisoner is asking for—the grievance investigation is limited to whether or not correct procedures were followed in assigning the infraction. As IAC Margaret Cummings, who specializes in disciplinary appeals, told us, "I'm not here to retry the complaint but to ensure they were afforded the due process. . . . Process rules. That's the point."

It may not be surprising that these investigations of a disciplinary infraction charge are confined to process and do not revisit the facts, since this is consistent with the emphasis on due process in the American legal system, and appeals in that system typically do not take up substantive trial issues.[17] Surprising or not, the point here is that it shields appeals personnel from having to make difficult decisions in a context of messy uncertainty, indeed making those decisions relatively "easy."

At the practical level of the day-to-day, this emphasis on process often devolves into, and is instantiated by, a focus on the efficient processing of paper. It is this paper-processing aspect of appeals that elicited the most fervor from many of the officials we interviewed, and the inability to keep up the paperwork pace was often mentioned as their primary cause of stress. This frenzy of paperwork and the stress it triggers were graphically portrayed to us one day as we were perusing our sample of written grievances and came across a telling sheet of paper depicting a cartoon, attached to an investigative packet being sent forward with the file from one responder to another. The drawing on the paper, roughly fashioned after a "Cathy" cartoon, depicts a frantic "Cathy" juggling paperwork and screaming, "Everyone quit doing things until I have a chance to catch up." A routine warning at the bottom of the image reads, "DO NOT SEND WITH CORRESPONDENCE" (presumably to the prisoner appellant).

In this setting, where their jobs involve reading prisoners' tales of sometimes unfathomable pain and anguish, the amount of paperwork to be processed was the only source of stress most staff reported. The examiner Lucinda Gray, who told us earlier that she had no sympathy for black prisoners claiming discrimination because "this is *not* a plantation" and they should "get a grip," was clear about what *did* bother her. When we asked her the standard question "Is there anything you don't like about doing appeals?" her answer came quickly: "The pressure of sixty appeals every two weeks. . . . People are on you if you are behind, like you stole something. I'm not going to be behind because it bothers the crap out of me to be behind."

Time after time, examiners in the Inmate Appeals Branch explained their job by detailing the amount of work they face and how they achieve efficiency in their processing of paper. Henry Lopez explained this emphasis on efficiency by telling us that some years ago the office had a backlog of four thousand appeals and the CDCR had "thrown bodies at this office" to try to deal with it. Apparently, the Office of the Inspector General had reported the severe backlog in 2001 and, Henry told us, "we got hammered. If we couldn't reform [eliminate backlog], they were going to abort the appeals process." Later he told us he took great pride in how much they had caught up on his watch, in large part because of increased efficiency in processing cases and forgoing trips to prisons to investigate complicated or ambiguous cases.

Examiner Sonya Thurman began her interview by confirming that they are expected to process sixty appeals every two weeks, and new packets of appeals arrive on their desks every other Friday morning. She approaches this daunting job with impressive discipline and precision, first organizing the piles of paper: "I re-sort everything because I have a certain way of reading it. I scan it by green sheet[18] first, then the second-level response, then the other pages." Her colleague Lucinda Gray told us she has "good days and bad days." She explained, "The repetitiveness is good. I can get a rhythm going. On a good day I can do ten. On a bad day, I can do eight."

Officials at the prison level were just as focused on keeping up the pace. As we saw in chapter 2, the role of inmate appeals coordinators varies somewhat across the three prisons we visited. One constant, however, is their emphasis on quick processing of the numerous appeals they handle. IAC Stacey Taylor told us that she comes in every day to find a stack of about thirty new appeals, and quickly sorts them into piles: to screen out, dismiss altogether, classify as emergency, send to appropriate captains, and so on. Illustrating her sorting procedure, she scanned several and sorted them as we watched, with some taking a few seconds and none taking more than half a minute. Sandra James, one of the high-ranking managers in the prison where Stacey works, told us proudly how efficient these officials were, explaining, "I have zero tolerance—a 'no-late-appeals' tolerance."

When we visited Warden Lawrence Spector to secure his endorsement for our study, he told us that when he was appointed, there was a long backlog of appeals and that the "overdue rate is an indicator of how well we are doing." IAC Danielle Garcon, who had said, "I don't take the appeals personally. I don't feel anything," reported that she was "stressed" about trying to keep up with the paperwork. Captain Michael Tisdale, at the same facility as Danielle, went on at length about the focus on efficiency. He said that every Monday morning there is an announcement over the intercom about which quad "is going good on appeals." "Going good," he said, did not mean that few prisoners in the unit had filed complaints, but rather that staff were up to date in processing them. Admitting to getting "a little competitive," he confided that he "used to get wrapped around the axles" about his quad keeping up the pace.

The fact that the paper chase is mentioned more often than any discomfort at the human suffering at the heart of prisoner appeals is evidence of the centrality of this practical dimension of handling grievances. It is all the more telling that it is mentioned in the relative absence of any discussion of the ability to identify and address problems related to the conditions of confinement. As with its more intellectual cousin—the emphasis on procedures and rules—this obsession with paper processing and the stress it causes hints at its role in emotional distancing.

Cracks in the Wall

If the rhetoric of law, the selective focus on rules, and the emphasis on process and paperwork buttress intellectual confidence and emotional detachment while facilitating decisions that predictably favor the institution, there are leaks in this fortress. As with all things human, there are no airtight quarters here. For one thing, the intellectual certainty that focusing on rules and procedures ostensibly provides occasionally gave way in our interviews to a concession that not everything is clear-cut.

IAC John Mansfield, who insisted that to process an appeal, "you just get the facts and put 'em down" and that he is "obligated to follow the rules," later noted that there are "exceptions." "There are judgment calls," he said. "There's a gray area [in] lots of property appeals." IAC Margaret Cummings, who told us that "process rules" and most decisions are "in-and-out, in-and-out," later added, "A lot of things are open for interpretation." Prison manager Sandra James, who earlier had said that everything was "cut and dried" because "you just use the rules and regulations," subsequently criticized staff who stick too rigidly to rules. "Some people," she confided, "like to be in a box. The rules say they [inmates] don't get this, and that's all they're going to get [sic]. But the black and white becomes gray and the rules need to be changed."

Similarly, Captain Francisco Garcia conceded, "[In] some situations there's no way of knowing. It's he said/she said," before concluding, "But in looking at it, I just want to make sure we covered all our bases." Later he went on at length:

> It's all based on—I don't want to say it's based on interpretation, but it's all based on, you know, what decision you're making with the information you have. . . . I think the appeals system is necessary. I think it serves a purpose. But, uh, it's very, there's so much paperwork, so many reviews, so many hands in the pot, and it's really open to what I alluded to earlier, you know,

what I think, what I interpret, and what somebody else interprets. I may see the appeal one way and feel that granting is appropriate. Where the next level of review may say, based on the same information, you know, "I don't see it that way."

Cracks in the wall of emotional detachment were far more rare. Three interview moments stand out as exceptions. In one interview, when we asked IAC Tanya Harden how she knows when a grievance should be denied, she grimaced and groaned, "It's *hard!*" She gave an example: "In the case of an inmate saying that their legal mail was opened, how am I going to know? He says my legal mail was opened and the mail office says, 'No, it wasn't.' How am I going to know? It's *hard.*" This IAC, who concluded, "I go by what the mailroom says" and had told us earlier of finding a money order in the pocket of a mailroom officer who "forgot" he had it, nonetheless told us several times, each time contorting her face for emphasis, that it was "*hard*" to make decisions.

In our interview with IAB official Henry Lopez, we were surprised by an abrupt and powerful display of emotion. Henry had just finished telling us that denying a grievance which precipitated the execution of a death row prisoner had been "what the law prescribed" and the prisoner "was a punk even for just asking." Suddenly, his face changed, he became somber, his hands began to tremble slightly, and he said in a quiet voice, "On principle, it [the decision] is correct. But you know them, they are people. On a human level, it [facilitating an execution] is bothersome. On a spiritual level, it's very spooky."

Another official in the appeals branch, Dave Manning, surprised us with his comparison of prison to a concentration camp, before regaining his bureaucratic perspective and concluding with a bit of humor. Speaking about a case in which a prisoner was effectively denied family visits when he was transferred to a prison far from his hometown, this official sighed and said, "We understand this is a hardship for you and your family ... but ... if you work in a concentration camp, what do you do—quit? ... You have to ask yourself, does our process support a desirable outcome? The process supports the status quo. As Reagan said, '"Status quo" is Latin for the mess we're in.'"

These were among the few times CDCR staff showed any signs of recognizing the suffering expressed in prisoner grievances. Most were conspicuously detached from the human dramas in which they played a part. Others conveyed some version of what we heard from IAC John Mansfield, who said with an air of resignation, "It's not fun to read grievances all day. You just have to, well, it's your occupation. You do your job. You just deal with it. Do your shift and go home." It may be that prison staff, by virtue of their daily exposure to it, become inured to the pain inflicted by prison. It may also be that they make a concerted effort to protect themselves from the emotional implications of their task. Indeed, many comments reported here suggest not only that they engage in emotional distancing but that they actively do so.

What is clear is that the rhetorical deference to law, rules, procedure, and paperwork not only helps shore up cognitive certainty but facilitates distancing. In the context of ritualized rules and procedures, processing the massive amount of paperwork associated with appeals becomes the primary challenge, and the paper chase stands in as the major stressor. There are inevitably some cracks in this insulating wall, as these people—most of them apparently well intentioned and conscientious—struggle to overcome the "spooky" nature of their task.

We saw earlier that denigrating prisoners and trivializing their grievances is one response to the conflicting logics of captivity and rights. The denigration allows staff ensnared in this contradiction to convince themselves that prisoners are whiners, their suffering is not so great, and their rights in any case have been taken too far. We have seen here a complementary dynamic in which certainty and emotional detachment are further constructed through legal ritual and an obsession with process and paper.

A note of caution is in order here. The terms we have used—*cognitive certainty, emotional distance,* and the *deployment of strategies*—suggest that we are talking about individual psychology and strategic deliberation. However, while they impact individuals, these strategic practices are inscribed in and part of the sociocultural context. As Silbey (2005, 334) has noted, the practices associated with and constituting legal consciousness are "dislodged from the mind of the individual knower" in that they are cultural and social-structural phenomena. This is not to say that the individual is immaterial or insignificant in some existential sense, but that the pattern of these officials' practices is contoured to their location in a nexus of power relations, institutional position, and context (as is that of the prisoner appellants). Indeed, the fact that there *is* such a pronounced pattern—despite the diversity of the staff in terms of gender and race, and to a lesser extent political identification and religiosity—reveals the power of these legal, structural, and institutional forces.

This perspective offers an antidote to the implication that these practices and discourses are utilitarian, deliberately deployed to gain advantage. The strategies we have discussed that produce emotional distance are embedded in institutional practice and power structures and are largely "dislodged" from individual deliberation or artifice. In a way, then, the staff who told us that their job is easy, that they feel little responsibility because they just "follow the rules," may be onto something. While they exercise substantial discretion and even deviate from specific rules on occasion, in doing so they are simply "following the rules" of their institutional position, tracing and retracing a pattern that is cut not by individuals but by the sharp lines of institutional and structural arrangements. The sense of being absolved of responsibility reported by these bureaucratic actors is thus more than a convenient ploy or a moral alibi; at some level, it is an important sociological truth.

Thus far, we have talked rather generically of CDCR staff. In the next chapter, we will look more closely at the CDCR as a bureaucratic organization, at these grievance handlers' locations in the organizational hierarchy, and at their distinctive orientations vis-à-vis the rights/incarceration contradiction by virtue of that location. As we will see, they achieve a remarkable degree of consistency in their grievance responses, yet hints of fissures surface in our conversations with these employees of this most regimented and cohesive of organizations.

CHAPTER 6

Administrative Consistency, Downstream Consequences, and "Knuckleheads"

These corrections officials use a rhetoric of "rules and policy" to justify their decisions, but as we saw in the last chapter, there are vast terrains of exception, and rules are often of little practical use in weighing evidence. In deciding "the relevant 'facts' or 'situation' to which specific rules apply" (Emerson and Paley 1992, 231) and interpreting the kind of he said/she said statements on which many grievances turn, these CDCR staff necessarily exercise substantial discretion. Despite this extensive discretion and the complexity of many grievances, these appeals handlers achieve remarkable consistency across responders and levels of review.

This consistency is most dramatically revealed in the high denial rate at all levels, as detailed in chapter 2. Further, in our interviews, these officials confirmed that their decisions are typically consistent with those of reviewers at other levels. When we asked how often their decisions line up with those before them in the appeals chain, 20 percent of the officials we interviewed told us "always," 75 percent reported "usually," and only 5 percent said "sometimes." The most common answer—"usually"—was often accompanied by some specification of an actual percentage. For example, IAC Leanna White said it was "95 percent of the time."[1] Only one person—a high-ranking prison manager, Sandra James—deviated from this assessment of strict alignment with others, reporting that her decisions "sometimes" are the same as those of her institutional colleagues. Associate Warden William Landes, who has had a long career in the CDCR and had previously been an appeals coordinator, summarized his experience of consistency: "Most of the time, the second level is just a write-up of the first level. Ninety-eight percent of the time, the second level is the same as the first level. It's based on the first level of response. . . . The third level bumps off the second level 99 percent of the time unless they see something that needs tweaking." Somewhat ironically, 90 percent of the CDCR personnel we interviewed reported that it was "easy" to grant an appeal that had been denied at a lower level, and no one said that it was "difficult" to do so (two said it was "neither hard nor easy" and "I don't know," respectively). In other words, they perceived the context as allowing for discretion and independent judgment even as the outcome signals overwhelming conformity.

Legal scholar Keith Hawkins (1992, 28) makes the case "for a view of discretion as part of a sequence of decisions and occurring as part of a network of relationships." This sequential view of decision making and Emerson and Paley's (1992) related concept of the importance of perceived "downstream consequences," as discussed in the last chapter, are critical for understanding this high rate of consistency in appeals outcomes despite the vast discretion involved. Hawkins explains, "Organizations may well shape discretion in ways not necessarily anticipated by law by imposing their own constraints on the way in which their members exercise discretion. . . . The effect of such controls can be to produce decisions which emphasize conformity to regular or expected organizational practices at the expense of an attempt to advance the bureaucracy's broad legal mandate" (38–39).

On occasion, "controls" on appeals personnel come in the form of explicit sanctions for nonconformity. For example, Henry Lopez, the Inmate Appeals Branch official, told us, "When new people come into this office from [working in] the prisons, they think you're weak if you partially grant an appeal. They think you have to deny everything. Another group comes in, and they wish they could have been kinder in prison and take this chance to make it up. They go overboard. They see this as an opportunity [to make up for what they did in prison]. *They grant everything and I have to reel them in* [emphasis added]." When a new examiner was granting 42 percent of her cases, Henry told us he called her in and admonished her, "Now why did you grant all that?"

More often, conformity is achieved through a series of largely invisible social and ideological processes. One mechanism is discrediting prisoner appellants, who have already been stigmatized by their prisoner status. A long tradition of sociolegal research establishes that in legal encounters of all kinds, people of high social status and perceived respectability have an advantage over those whose moral character is impugned by virtue of their class, race, or prior criminal record (Abel 1982; Bell 1987; Baumgartner 1992; Beckett et al. 2005; Chambliss and Seidman 1971; Pager 2007; Provine 2007; Reiman 1979; Western 2006). As Baumgartner (1992, 136) puts it, "People who bring unblemished reputations to their encounters with law generally fare better than those who are already morally stigmatized, whether they appear as complainants or defendants." As we saw in chapter 5, many staff members express considerable disdain for prisoners, especially those who file appeals, who they say are "manipulative," "liars," and "narcissists." In this morally loaded context, it is not surprising that there is substantial consistency in decision making, with prisoner appellants rarely winning at any level of review. Lempert and Sanders (1986, 75) have called this kind of decision making "shallow"; as Lempert (1992, 216) explains, in shallow decision making, administrative actors base their decisions about a case on its stereotypical components rather than any "deep probing of circumstances."

The well-documented "us-versus-them" mentality that pervades much of prison life (and that periodically surfaces and then retreats in prisoners' narratives, as reported in chapters 3 and 4) compounds the shallowness of decision making. Dave Manning, the IAB official who compared prison to a concentration camp, told us, "If you have a culture that's us-versus-them, it's self-evident you don't want to be in a position of not being a team player. . . . [But] it warps your sense of right and wrong. . . . *You know what you should be doing but there is another 'should.'* . . . The environment is one of conflict—us versus them [emphasis added]." He continued, "As long as the public feels the way it does [about inmates and prisons], we will treat inmates as the enemy. When you're at war, do you trust the enemy? The feeling of the staff is you can't be seen as weak." This mentality explains the overwhelming trust that grievance reviewers place in the word of officers when they dispute inmates' charges, discussed in the last chapter. As IAC Stacey Taylor told us, "Nine times out of ten, I believe the officer because they're sworn police officers."

A terminological issue underscores the power of CDCR team loyalty, often captured by the phrase "the green wall."[2] This team spirit was vividly revealed when we inquired about investigations of staff misconduct prompted by prisoner grievances. The first time we asked about such investigations, Captain Anthony Sanchez became uncomfortable, admonishing us gently but firmly not to use the word *investigation:* "I don't use the word *investigation* too loosely. When I say 'investigation,' I use it to refer to gangs or [inmates'] criminal activity. Serious stuff like that. [When referring to alleged staff misconduct,] I use the word *inquiry* or *fact-finding interviews.*" We heard this distinction again and again, always expressed with insistence, as these staff patiently schooled us in the proper terminology. IAC Leanna White was clear: "We don't talk about 'investigations'; we 'inquire.' When we go and we look into [staff misconduct charges] there's not an 'investigation,' there's an 'inquiry.' We use the word *inquiry.*"

To prevent the implication that an officer might have done something wrong (as alleged by an inmate), the term *investigation* is assiduously avoided.[3] In cases where there is overwhelming evidence of extreme misconduct that cannot be ignored, the case is referred out of the appeals system to an Office of Internal Affairs where an "investigation" may be conducted. Thus IAC Danielle Garcon explained, "I wouldn't use that term—*investigate*—because that reminds me of Internal Affairs review." This terminological parsing is a powerful linguistic marker of team playing, and there are consequences for straying from it (as Captain José Cruz told us, "Everyone has a potential career to consider"). The universality of this team sentiment is an example of the kind of organizational control that Hawkins (1992, 39) referred to, and explains much of the conformity in appeals decision making.

This mentality extends beyond privileging an officer's word over that of an inmate to include supporting other staff members' appeals decisions. In *Street-Level Bureaucracy,* Lipsky (1980) developed a "rubber-stamp" model in which those who receive referrals accept without question the recommendations of referring agents. For example, "judges commonly accept the decisions of police officers or probation officers in lower-court criminal cases and . . . ratify these decisions," thereby "adopt[ing] the judgment of others as their own" (Lipsky 1980, 129–30). Emerson (1991, 200) has argued against Lipsky's "rubber-stamping" model and suggests instead that organizational actors who receive referrals apply their "background knowledge of sending agents' referral practices," weighing the trustworthiness and competence of the referring agent and the possible "real" meaning of the referral in making their decisions.

In the context of prisoner appeals, it is at first glance difficult to avoid the conclusion that officials and examiners rubber-stamp each other's decisions, and the us-versus-them language that is sometimes used suggests this is at least in part due to an institutional ethos of loyalty. IAC Stacey Taylor proudly told us that in many years on the job, she had never had a third-level reviewer grant an appeal she had denied. She said the third level always supports her decision and declared with confidence, "They're going to back me," her choice of words revealing that she considers this a matter of loyalty and team playing. IAC Leanna White reported that if she finds a staff person made a mistake in responding to an inmate's grievance, she may tell the inmate, "It's unfortunate you were told such and such." But she does not tell them the staff was mistaken: "We never say that the other staff person lied or it was a mistake. I don't want to make trouble for staff. I would never do that. I would never do that to a staff person."

This does not mean, however, that prior decisions are simply rubber-stamped. For one thing, there is substantial communication between levels of review that is not always evident from the official paper trail. We heard repeatedly that when there are potential differences of opinion between staff about a particular appeal, an effort is made to resolve the differences informally. Associate Warden William Landes told us that if he is thinking of denying an appeal but is concerned that the third level in Sacramento might grant it—or, more likely, partially grant it—he telephones them and discusses it, and as a result a reversal "doesn't happen very often." He went on to say that he is teaching his staff to do the same: "I'm trying to teach our ACs [Inmate Appeals Coordinators, IACs] to call third level and get a sense of whether they would grant or deny. I don't think it's good to get it wrong here and have them overturn it there." Associate Warden Sandra James said she "imagines" how the third level might respond and recommends accordingly. Warden Donald Brown told us that he reads the third-level decisions that come back from Sacramento to "focus on trends and patterns," presumably in an effort to avoid inconsistencies in the future. He proudly relayed to us that Sacramento almost always affirms his prison's appeals responses, and this is an indication that "obviously, we're doing good." Similarly, IAC Stacey Taylor, who said the third level always "backs" her, went on to explain that she telephones them about once every ten days to get a sense of how they would respond to an appeal: "If I have a question, I'll call them." This avoids the awkwardness and conflict of a Modification Order ("Mod Order")—the formal document issued by the Inmate Appeals Branch to the prison facility reversing their appeals decision and ordering them to implement, at least in part, the remedies requested by the inmate.

This is not to say that if prison officials anticipate the third-level review resulting in a grant or partial grant, they passively fall into line. Given the low rate of even partial grants, it is safe to assume that the prison staff's proclivity to deny carries at least as much weight as Sacramento's pushback in the relatively rare cases where there is initial disagreement. Indeed, the lines of communication go both ways. Examiner Sonya Thurman responded to a question about whether the prison she receives appeals from (each examiner deals with grievances from a specific set of prisons) sees her as "friend or foe." She told us, "We're normally seen as helping these institutions, but we're also seen as watchdogs. We try to avoid being seen as Monday-morning quarterbacks by calling an institution [before issuing a written correction]." This gives them an opportunity to either correct themselves without receiving a written order or to explain why they denied the appeal. Indicative of her team loyalty, Sonya revealed that on the rare occasion when she has to reverse a decision made by the prison, she keeps it general: "I like that it can be vague. I want to be real careful not to violate some staff member's rights." Sonya expressed a more practical reason for consistency in outcomes too. Presumably related to the need to explain a contrary decision diplomatically, with advance communication to avoid "being seen as a Monday-morning quarterback," Sonya reflected, "It takes twice as long to grant." This examiner, who told us she had only fully granted one grievance in ten years, continued, "It's more work, but I will do it."

Examiner Lucinda Gray explained that she always calls the prison before reversing a second-level denial to see if they can meet partway, thereby avoiding a Mod Order. She said this is "cuz I have to work with these people every day. We have to get along." In explaining her need for caution in this attempt to "get along," she emphasized the issue of her inferior rank relative to prison wardens: "Because *no* warden wants to be told what to do. I do *not* tell them what to do. I give them some information [on the telephone in a pre-Mod Order call] and then I wait quietly for his response. He wants to know that you respect him and respect his rank, and that he knows how to run his own prison. It goes a long way, especially if I want to promote back out there [to the prison]. You don't want to *tell* them what to do." On occasion, Lucinda said, "they [prison officials] are dead wrong." Revealing how rare full grants are, even when the officials "are dead wrong," Lucinda concluded by telling us that in such a case, "It's gonna get partially granted." This examiner was adamant that she would never intervene when there is a lockdown of prisoners: "I don't supersede the warden on a lockdown. Who am I to say, 'Take this guy off lockdown'?"

Besides team loyalty, professional collegiality, the importance of rank in this paramilitary organization, and deference to those who run the prison on the ground level, Lucinda expressed concern about the message a reversal at the third level would send inmates. As quoted in chapter 2, she explained with some agitation that "the inmate gets a copy of the Mod Order. You can imagine what happens then. He runs down to his cellies and says, '*See! I told you I was right!*'" Such a "downstream consequence" (Emerson and Paley 1992, 239) of a potential third-level grant was clearly unacceptable to this examiner, who told us, "I *never* grant in full. I only grant in part." To underscore the point, she described a group of women prisoners who filed a grievance because they were not paid for work they had done. She conceded to us that after speaking to officials at the prison, she concluded the women were right, but she only issued a partial grant. She explained that this was "because they [the inmates] implied it was done on purpose. It was granted *in part* because it was *not* done on purpose. It was an oversight." Later Lucinda confided that it was sometimes a challenge to figure out an angle that would allow her to reach a decision favoring the institution, or at least not giving prisoners the satisfaction of a full grant.

It should be noted that these repeated expressions of the challenges of achieving some consistency across levels of appeal—and the multiple strategies employed to arrive at it—appear to be at odds with these same staff's statements, reported earlier, that it is "easy" to grant an appeal that has been denied at a lower level. Our data are replete with such apparent ambivalences, and they probably reflect the complex reality these administrative actors confront, with layers of professional commitments, institutional protocols, formal policies, hierarchical obligations, and practical downstream consequences vying for attention. It is also worth thinking briefly about the methodological implications of such fluctuations across data and the advantages of the kind of mixed data we have here. For when these staff were allowed to expand on their answers to brief survey-type questions ("Is it difficult or easy to grant an appeal that has been denied at a lower level?"), their free-wheeling discussions often exposed complexities and ambivalences that would otherwise have been overlooked.

To sum up, the mechanisms that produce consistency across levels of appeal include reprimands for deviations, "shallow decision making" (Lempert and Sanders 1986, 75) based on stereotypes of prisoner appellants, an us-versus-them mentality, and intraorganizational communication. It is a sequential process in which each level of appeal ratifies prior (mostly) denials, but this is no rubber-stamping. It is a ratification grounded in shared organizational knowledge and meaning, along with a concerted effort to reach conformity. That said, this behavioral conformity masks underlying tensions and subterranean conflicts that are at work even in this paramilitary organization that prioritizes loyalty and team spirit. A close look at the nature of these tensions and their distribution gives us a more complex picture of administrative decision making than a simple ratification model implies.

DISCORD IN THE RANKS

One set of tensions derives from the peculiar organizational structure of appeals, in the context of the strict hierarchy of the corrections department. The hierarchy of the CDCR, like that of most correctional agencies across the United States, parallels that of the military in both nomenclature and rigidity. The importance of rank was stressed to us throughout our conversations with these personnel. The examiner Lucinda Gray, for example, in discussing the diplomacy and care with which she approaches wardens when she needs to question them about an appeals decision, proudly informed us that she is "authorized to speak to the warden." She explained that only those with the rank of captain or above have authorization to initiate an administrative conversation with a warden, and that is why examiners such as herself are almost always appointed at the level of captain.

In this strict hierarchical system, conflict is inevitable because inmate appeals coordinators—who are usually appointed at the midlevel rank of correctional officer II (CCO II)—are often responsible for making second-level decisions; they thus have the authority to reverse the decisions of officials who might be more highly ranked than they are. IAC Danielle Green remembered how difficult her early days as an appeals coordinator were, emphasizing this awkward ranking issue. She explained, "I'm a CCO II, and I'm sometimes making decisions that override the AW [associate warden]." To survive on the job, she said, you have to "get thick skin."

IAC Tanya Harden added gender politics to the mix. When we asked her if it was difficult or easy to grant an appeal that had been denied at a lower level, she said, "I don't have a problem." Then she rocked back in her office chair with what appeared to be nervous energy and added, "But then, you know, we are three females here [in the appeals office] and all the captains and sergeants and lieutenants are male, and I kind of see it as their male ego. Maybe if I was a male, they wouldn't argue with me. But they argue with me and sometimes I e-mail the third level to try to figure it out. Make sure I'm right." Tanya went on to describe a case in which inmates had appealed disciplinary infraction charges related to urinalysis drug tests that they alleged had been misclassified. She concluded that the inmates were right about the misclassification and told us ruefully, "That took a lot of energy and time. They [the captains] are resisting, and sometimes it's hard. I feel pressure. . . . You get pressure from the third level. You get pressure from the inmates. And you get pressure from the staff. And that's why I'm trying to get out of appeals." Later Tanya told us, "A person in this position has to develop assertiveness and not back down. It's hard. You've got captains telling you—and actually captains outrank us. You see them as a higher authority than you are, and it's hard. It takes a while to get thick skin and to, uh, not back down."

IAC Stacey Taylor also complained about the push-back she gets if she has to correct male prison staff, especially those who outrank her. She recalled the time she had to go to the yard to tell a group of officers they had done an appeal wrong:

> We went to the yard and we told them. We had a hard time getting it through their thick skulls. As you ladies [the interviewers] know, men are a lot of time intimidated by women who have smarts. Sometimes the male ego—it just kills me! "C'mon guys! I didn't just fall off the bus." They can be stubborn. It's the male ego. . . . I'm not intimidated. I've always been a level 4 [maximum security]. . . . I simply say, "No, you're wrong." But it takes up a lot of time during the day. That's what's exhausting. . . . Sometimes they just take a shortcut. It's laziness. . . . But you have to correct them. You know they got it wrong. And they don't like that. You don't have many women in the higher ranks. . . . They kept on beating the same dead horse, and I said, "How long are you gonna let this horse die?" Yeah, and he outranks you. Lately the male egos have been going rampant.

Several male captains confirmed that they had on occasion wrangled with appeals coordinators. Captain Peter Dayton, with a half grin, answered a question about his relationship with appeals coordinators: "I've gotten in some good arguments with them a few times. But sometimes they get the AW [associate warden] on their side first and then contact us, and they have the AW in their pocket, so that helps." While officials highlighted the rank-related risks faced by appeals coordinators, our interviews made it clear that such tensions also confront other officials who handle appeals. Captain José Cruz, while speaking of something else altogether, spontaneously interjected, "In Sacramento [at the Inmate Appeals Branch], you know, they are all captains. Isn't it odd that a captain is overruling the warden?"

Another captain, Thomas Jones, said he tries to remember that appeals coordinators have "positional authority." That is, even though lower-ranked than he is, they are what he called "the subject matter expert" when it comes to appeals. Although he is acutely aware of rank, Captain Jones said he defers to appeals coordinators when they disagree about a grievance: "I don't want to use the word *bow down*, but I will acknowledge their authority." After a pause, he added, "I will have a discussion with them, though, and tell them my perception."[4]

Another captain, Francisco Garcia, took a protective stance vis-à-vis the lieutenants he supervises, going on at length about his resentment of appeals coordinators who tell his lieutenants how to write their first-level grievance responses:

> My lieutenant will do 'em and he'll write it as he sees it. . . . Then they [appeals coordinators] will get 'em and they'll write all over it in red ink, saying, "Well, this needs to be first person or third person. You need to add a little more information. . . . It needs to be changed," or, you know, "This is the way that IAB wants it." . . . It just seems like it's up to the appeals office. . . . I even have an example of an appeal that went back to my lieutenant five times. . . . You have a lieutenant or a captain or an AW [associate warden], while the person in appeals is a [lower-level] staff. So that creates a little more tension.

This ranking issue, sometimes amplified by gender politics, is compounded by the perception that appeals coordinators are akin to ombudsmen. Dave Manning, an official in the Inmate Appeals Branch in Sacramento, made the spontaneous comment that "appeals coordinators are at risk because they have to interface between inmates and staff" and "nobody wants to be in that interface." Most people, he said, approach it with the idea, "Get out of the job as fast as you can before your career is over." Dave went on, "There are ways of managing the risk. . . . One is overlooking things and minimizing staff misconduct."[5] Some examiners, too, are concerned with the perception that they do not always side with the institution. Examiner Sonya Thurman complained, "Sometimes the [prison] staff think we're all 'inmate lovers' because sometimes we side with the inmates."

We were occasionally told secondhand of such tensions. For example, Sonya revealed that when she calls appeals coordinators to tell them an official at their prison has made a mistake on an appeal, the appeals coordinator sometimes tells the examiner, "'I know. I figured *you* could tell them. I figured *you* could do that. *You* tell them.' The AC [IAC] doesn't want to get crosswise with the staff." Henry Lopez at the IAB also mentioned this practice: "Sometimes at first and second level the prison staff denies [a grievance] so as not to confront their peers, and they let the third level play the heavy. Sometimes the appeals coordinator calls us to let us know that's the case."

It is not only appeals coordinators who are caught in these status inversions. As the examiner Lucinda Gray made clear in earlier comments, examiners must be delicate in their disagreements with wardens. Henry Lopez spoke of the same tension, although he seemed less concerned with diplomacy. When asked what he did not enjoy about the appeals process, Henry said, "When conflicts are intense and hostile with wardens. Sometimes they [wardens] say, 'You don't have a right to tell me what to do!' The winner is the person who gets the last word and is least bloodied."

Beyond the tensions provoked by status inversions and the reluctance "to get crosswise" with other staff, we sometimes encountered surprisingly blunt criticisms of lower-level staff. Captain Peter Dayton, who told us he had some "good arguments" with appeals coordinators, was more overtly hostile toward guards. Suggesting that some prisoner grievances may be valid, he minced no words: "Some of these guys [guards] are knuckleheads or lazy and they do some stuff inmates complain about. . . . A lot of staff are lazy or don't do their job, and the inmate doesn't get what he's got coming to him. And he's got every right to appeal." IAC Tanya Harden echoed the sentiment when describing the mailroom practice of sometimes ruining photographs that arrive in the mail for prisoners by stamping them with the CDCR "receipt" seal in the middle of the picture. With a disdainful roll of her eyes, she said, "See what I'm dealing with?"

Henry Lopez similarly told us that "some COs are an impediment," going on at length about the "stupid" guard who mishandled a situation involving fermented fruit juice. Apparently, the guard found the contraband pruno in a large, black trash bag in a cell and punched a hole in the bag. The pruno poured out all over the floor, leaving the place smelling rancid for days and infuriating everyone. IAC John Mansfield also described instances of officer misconduct and noted, "None of us likes working with those people. They make us all look bad."

IAC Stacey Taylor cringed when telling us about an appeal she had dealt with in which a prisoner had been put in solitary confinement after having been erroneously found guilty of dealing drugs in prison. She explained to us that this prisoner was the *informant* rather than the guilty party. Stacey was incensed: "I don't know how that happened without a hearing because there were no hearing documents. This blows my mind. I still don't understand how they did that. . . . And worse, he [the prisoner] got a SHU [solitary confinement] term for this. . . . Some people [staff] aren't very bright." Later in the interview, she told us there are "blanket violations of due process and policy and procedure. We've got rules and we're supposed to follow them. I'm appalled sometimes at what I see. People [officers] going out and doing stupid things. They're talking crazy. I tell them the inmates are humans, and you got to talk to them like they're human beings."

In a different kind of example, in which she thought a CO had been too candid, Stacey recalled a lower-level officer who wrote on his response to a missing property grievance, "I know you had your property [before going to Ad Seg]. Your cellmate packed it for you." Stacey fumed because writing that on the response form validated the inmate's complaint: "That's a crazy response. [That confirmed] it's a CDCR violation of property, of policy. And he put it in writing, making it worse."

Captain José Cruz was at first more nuanced in his criticism of low-level CDCR staff, complaining, "There's a culture among COs—'Don't ever admit you did anything wrong.' The inmates have a code of conduct, and the officers have a code of conduct." Later, when asked if there was anything he did not enjoy about doing appeals, he said without hesitation, "The lack of communication, the culture at large where people don't take responsibility." Growing increasingly agitated, he insisted that this is not an abstract concern: "The potential for violence is imminent, and I don't want an appeal to be the powder keg that sets off violence. There's a fuse burning out there, and I don't want an appeal that's been denied to be the powder keg."

Operating at the highest level of prison administration, Warden Donald Brown joined the critical chorus, telling us that sometimes the CO on the ground doing the first-level review "is a bad cop with prejudice" and that "the second level is needed in case there's some prejudice." In a rare instance in which we heard of disagreements between a captain and his superior, Chief Deputy Warden Steven Waring told us, "I had this argument with a captain. I had to tell him it wasn't his job to back up his staff [on an appeal]." He added, "The purpose of the appeals process isn't to back up the staff. . . . In a case where black-and-white evidence is there, then it has to be granted."

Examiner Sonya Thurman's tone was biting when talking about prison staff who do appeals wrong. They are "knuckleheads," she said, using the same vernacular that Captain Dayton applied to COs. As an example, Sonya talked about a grievance involving missing property. The inmate had provided evidence that his property was missing and had explained in detail what had happened, but his grievance was denied at the first and second levels. Sonya said she told the prison staff who handled the grievance, "C'mon guys. You're just double-talking."

These are not simply interpersonal squabbles, territorial and status rivalries, or intelligence gaps. And while there may be gender politics at work, none of this is the whole story. Instead, these CDCR officials are sharply aware of the potential downstream consequences of their decisions, and their criticisms are generally targeted at lower-level personnel whose orientation is more custodial and who do not share the "big picture."

A central feature of this big picture is court liability, a potential downstream consequence that is of paramount concern to these grievance handlers. Attention from the courts is an organizational future (Emerson and Paley 1992, 239) that these administrators and officials anticipate and strive to avoid, within the constraints of the institutional features outlined earlier, which consistently bend the grievance process toward denials. This was most obvious in our conversations with examiners and officials at the third level of review in the Inmate Appeals Branch, who see themselves above all as protecting the CDCR from lawsuits. Sometimes this involves informal communication between the IAB and prison officials, when red flags suggest persistent problems. As we saw in the last chapter, IAB official Henry Lopez believes that wardens want to be told of problems because "they don't want to lose a prison, they don't want a murder, don't want an AG [attorney general] investigating. . . . They *want* to hear from me" (even if, as Henry later relayed, wardens on occasion attack him when he tries to tell them what to do).

Highlighting the concern with legal liability, Henry revealed that a Legal Awareness Notice (LAN) is placed on appeals considered at risk for ending up in court. A LAN, which Henry estimated applies to approximately one of every seventy-five appeals, "suggests we messed up, and it red-flags [the grievance]" for special treatment. The LAN flags are primarily used for alleged violations of the Americans with Disabilities Act, staff complaints, and medical grievances. With his characteristic ability to turn a phrase, Henry explained, "These have greater potential to be a vulnerability. . . . You pick and choose what's going to eat you for dinner and what just snaps at your ankle."

Later Henry surprised us when he said that frequent filers elicit more attention from him than those who rarely file (even though other officials told us that frequent filers lose credibility).[6] This does not necessarily mean they are successful in their appeals, but their denials are handled with special care. Henry explained, "If he files a lot of appeals, he automatically gets my attention. It says, 'My appeal is up for litigation.' . . . We have to defend what we do if it goes to court. I have a greater vigilance for frequent filers. When I get an appeal from a litigious inmate, it's gonna have my full attention . . . so we don't hand ourselves on a platter when we try to defend it in court." Examiner Mark Tilden told us the same thing. At first he responded to an interview question by saying that all appeals get equal treatment from him, but then he had second thoughts. When an appeal comes across his desk under the name S. Roland Smith (a pseudonym), he said he snaps to attention. Calling Smith an "inmate appeals litigator" and "a formidable foe," Mark explained, "He's beat us a few times, so when I get one of his, I take a close look because he's shown us to be wrong."

Lucinda Gray, the examiner who earlier told us that she does not "tell [wardens] what to do," a few minutes later outlined her predicament, emphasizing her function as protection against liability: "I just don't want to go to court. [Referring to her caution with wardens,] I can be very tactfully up in your face about it." "It's a style," she said later. "It depends on who I'm talking to. I'll pull rank if they're a subordinate."

On rare occasions, this focus on the downstream possibility of having to go to court can mean that a grievance is granted, or partially granted, that otherwise might be denied. As Henry Lopez told us, "I like it when . . . we can protect the department from vulnerability, and the inmates are going to feel like they get heard and get treated fairly. [I like it] when we can do things on behalf of the whole organization that helps minimize risk and vulnerability—for inmates and for the CDCR." In considering whether a case might go to court, he asks himself, "Is it constitutionally protected? Is it a sensitized subject near and dear to someone's heart? I look at the larger context. Who's bringing the issue? Is the prison wholesale cutting people off? I also look at the individuals involved, both inmate and staff."

Our random sample of written grievances provides one striking example of the perceived potential of legal liability to affect the outcome of a case. The appellant in this case had argued that the CDCR inappropriately added 120 days to his prison time based on an infraction of which he had been found guilty. The infraction was contemporaneous with a change in policy regarding such misbehavior and subsequent losses of time credit. The appellant cited a Ninth Circuit Court of Appeals case to buttress his claim that the 120 days credit should be restored because of the new policy. He was denied at the lower levels of inmate appeals, but the director's level granted his grievance in part. The decision was based largely on the director's perception that the inmate could win in court. It read, "Considering the high potential for the appellant's position to prevail in court, the DLR [director's level decision] finds that the interests of all concerned are best served by a partial grant and restoration of 50% of the 120 days credit that were assessed as a penalty for the RVR [Rules Violation Report] cited herein."

Such cases of (partial) appellant success are rare, and more often these grievance responders focus on crossing the t's and dotting the i's on the appeals they *deny* as they orient to their work as potentially being reviewed by the courts. As we see in chapter 7, this often means adhering to prescribed formats and precise wording. Formats and verbiage that have been carefully constructed with an eye to court liability are particularly formulaic at the final level of review but also prevail at lower levels. IAC John Mansfield told us he even borrows templates and verbatim wording from third-level responses for his second-level appeals, to make sure they are properly done. Lucinda Gray, who had said unequivocally that she "*never* grant[s] in full," said her job is to "answer an appeal correctly so that it can stand up to court scrutiny." Mincing no words, at another point she declared, "I'm just trying to save face for the institution, because this could go to court." When asked how cognizant she is of the possibility of court when she reviews an appeal, Lucinda replied without hesitation: "*Very* cognizant! Every appeal, every single day. I've been under the duress of being at court's door, dealing with the DAG [deputy attorney general]. In the end, those cases were settled, and I didn't have to go to court. But I have had to redo, rehone my work. But I don't let it stop me from denying it. Now, if I go to court I am very prepared."

Examiner Mark Tilden told us that prisoners are understandably cynical about the process: "I don't think they think it's viable. I don't know the numbers, but the denials are much greater than the grants, so they believe we are rubber-stamping the lower level." He countered, "But we're not. They don't see what's going on up here—how much time, energy, and work goes into assessing where errors and wrongs need to be fixed." Despite his apparent empathy for prisoners, his decisions reflect the same skewed credulity as that of other examiners, and for him too, preparation for court is an ever-present concern. Echoing his colleagues and combining his concern with the courts and his loyalty to CDCR personnel, Mark told us, "A sworn officer's word is going to be taken over an inmate's. It's what I'll testify to in court. I'll write it down."

Examiner Sonya Thurman reported always being aware of liability issues when she writes her responses. She told us, "I want to be able to justify my response. Every time I answer one, I think of it [court]. I keep in mind if a judge and jury read my appeal response. If the second level completely messes up and gets silly with it, I want my response to be able to explain it. This is why I do lengthy responses." She added that the concern about going to court is not to be underestimated, once again suggesting that "silly" official responses are problematic for the institution: "Courts are more sympathetic now because we've been stupid in the past," she told us. Even in cases where she believes the inmate does not have a legitimate complaint, she said, "I still put 100 percent into it. You never know where it's going to go."

Sonya considers some staff "knuckleheads" (as she referred to them on several occasions during our interview) precisely because they create problems of liability for the CDCR. She complained that low-level officers on occasion handwrite something next to the informal level complaint on the 602 form that is "uninformed, and the inmate points to it later on in court and says, 'See, see right here what it says right here?'" Along these lines, she told us about how a sergeant had bungled the case of a prisoner in administrative segregation who filed a 602 alleging that the officer had broken his television. The sergeant in question had apparently written at the first level, "Well, it was time for you to get a new one anyway." "That was stupid," Sonya declared. "It could go to court. And that comment sticks in people's minds. The sergeant was stupid." Henry Lopez in the IAB echoed the concern after he likened dealing with appeals coordinators and other prison staff to "herding cats." He added that there is "more and more liability and vulnerability. There are more and more inmate advocates [attorneys] too."

While IAB staff provide the last level of review before a potential lawsuit, prison officials are also perpetually concerned with a possible court appearance downstream. IAC Margaret Cummings told us, "I want to help the warden out of lawsuits where we're representing the institution. We need to think about the legal ramifications." Later Margaret explained that Americans with Disabilities Act (ADA) grievances raise a special red flag in this regard: "If it's an ADA issue, that's big business. That's big. That's legal." IAC Leanna White, who was dispassionate about the homosexual who hung himself, in contrast was incensed by inexperienced staff and the legal liability they open up. She told us what bothers her is "when I see new appeals coordinators screen out something without knowing the rules. It will come back to haunt you later, especially in court. Not all inmates are stupid." Chief Deputy Warden Steven Waring explained, "If it goes to court, we have to have our documentation. The appeals process is a safeguard to the inmate who files the complaint, but also to the institution."

We have argued that the contemporary prison incorporates two conflicting cultural logics and that the inmate appeals system embodies this conflict in sharp relief, with the rhetoric of rights jostling for position within a context of captivity. It makes sense that this tension between rights and confinement is felt particularly acutely by those whose job it is to handle inmate grievances, especially appeals coordinators and examiners and officials in the IAB. While the logic of incarceration is clearly the master text for these state officials, the basic rights inscribed in and represented by the appeals system cannot be ignored, because the presence of the courts looms large on the horizon. It makes sense too that high-ranking prison administrators are caught within the same tension, while those who are lower ranked have the luxury of privileging more exclusively their narrow custody functions. IAC Danielle Garcon reminisced, "I used to be concerned about my little area. But as you promote you get the bigger picture." IAC Leanna White had a slightly different take, but she made the same point when she explained that "management" is concerned about legal liability and the "money" associated with it, but that "the ground-level officers are worried about keeping people and prison safe."

In other words, institutional position impacts one's relative orientation to the rhetoric of rights, with the downstream consequence of embarrassing and inconvenient court reversals and subsequent mandates primarily of concern to those whose job it is to cope with the "bigger picture." This institutional divide—which follows the contours of the rights/confinement tension—is so powerful that it occasionally trumps the collective solidarity and team spirit of this militaristic institution and is expressed as hostility toward custodial "knuckleheads" who engage in behavior that provokes appeals or incorrectly construct grievance responses, opening the institution up to legal liability and adverse court scrutiny.

BETTER TRAINING AND COMMUNICATION FOR THE "KNUCKLEHEADS"

These expressions of hostility surprised us at first, given the reputation for circling the wagons that correctional officials have earned. We took them not only as an indication of the underlying tension described above but as a sign of our respondents' candor and their level of comfort in the interview. But their conflict narratives should not be overstated. For one thing, the solution these staff proposed to the problem of "knucklehead" officers was always some version of more training or better communication, with no one imputing malicious intent or deliberate malfeasance.

Captain Thomas Jones said repeatedly, "It all goes back to how you train your staff" and "Some of my staff are better communicators than others." Even in extreme cases of apparent officer misconduct, he was confident that the misbehavior indicated only insufficient training or a lack of good communication. He gave the example of an officer whom a number of inmates said had "trashed their cells," and he concluded, "It comes back to a training issue." He had the same perspective on lower-level officers who do not respond to appeals in a timely manner. "Sometimes," he told us, "even when I can get them to respond . . . it's like [and here he winced and handed over a piece of paper, suggesting the response was begrudging]." He continued, "We're not at a level where all staff appropriately communicate with inmates."

Captain José Cruz, who had told us earlier that "there's a fuse burning out there," also emphasized that when the process does not work right, it is because of "lack of training by staff. The employees are so naïve about how it works. They really don't know how to communicate." He noted further that when "the treatment of the appeals process is violated, it's because they [lower-level staff] don't know what they need to know." This captain, who was among the most highly educated of the staff we interviewed, was convinced that much of the problem was that "some of these guys only have GEDs." Associate Warden William Landes was also convinced that any problems with staff misbehavior could be fixed by training. Focusing not on education per se but on on-the-job training, he complained that many staff arrive straight "from the academy": "There's a lack of experience in the custody staff. There's a lot of new staff. They have to be trained."[7]

In the most extreme example of this, Examiner Mark Tilden told us of a good friend who asked him to deny a prisoner's grievance of proven staff misconduct (he said he lost the friendship when he refused). Despite this egregious incident, Mark later claimed the problem was that "we still don't do enough training about appeals and how to handle them informally. The line staff don't understand that it could be a legal document. Rarely does that person 'get it' when it comes to the consequences up here and beyond."[8]

The implication of this emphasis on better training and communication skills is that staff deficiencies are a matter of innocent mistakes. Staff who deal with grievances may periodically criticize other personnel for making their jobs harder, but we never heard a report or any insinuation of deliberate wrongdoing. Indeed, the term *knucklehead* used for lower-level officers may suggest a lack of respect and carries a hint of class condescension, but it also has connotations of protective affection (the two possible exceptions being IACs Stacey Taylor and Tanya Harden, who noted gender politics at work in their relations with male staff who sometimes outranked them). Unlike the "whiners," "liars," and "narcissists" among the inmate population, "knuckleheads" are mostly innocent mess-ups, nothing that could not be fixed with a little more education and training.

It is interesting to note that the vast majority (78.3 percent) of the personnel we spoke with said they had not "received any kind of specific training to do work related to inmate appeals," with many adding that the training occurs on the job through experience. The paramount role of on-the-job experience in attuning these staff members to downstream consequences, in contrast to their perception that those in more purely custodial positions must be trained into that awareness, once again underscores the importance of institutional location and its associated "organizational horizons" (Emerson and Paley 1992, 234) in shaping administrative behavior.

That said, this tension roiling beneath the surface does not translate into any significant discontinuities in grievance outcomes. While upper-level managers, appeals coordinators, and examiners may need to attend to rights discourse, and their position gives them the authority to reprimand those who are oblivious to downstream consequences, we end this chapter where we began: noting the remarkable consistency of grievance denials. These officials may grapple with the tension between rights and carceral logic, but it is the latter—pivoting on the operational realities of prison—that prevails when it comes to the substance of grievance responses, with concerns about court liability primarily affecting the careful formatting and phrasing of denials.

In the next chapter, we return to the written record, in the form of hundreds of formal grievances, as we continue to explore prisoners' and officials' attitudes and practices relating to the grievance process and the turbulent ideological, legal, and institutional terrain into which it is inserted and which it reflects. In sharp contrast to the interview narratives at the center of recent chapters, in which we heard prisoners and officials sometimes express surprisingly converging views, in these written grievances we find strikingly adversarial postures, an entrenched duality, and disputing "dialogues" that are anything but.

CHAPTER 7

Grievance Narratives as Frames of Meaning, Profiles of Power

Previous chapters have focused primarily on our interviews with prisoners and CDCR officials as windows into prison life and lenses through which to understand the sometimes complex institutional processes and power dynamics involved in disputing on this highly uneven terrain. In this chapter, we return to our sample of specific grievances filed by California prisoners, which include the official responses they received. Combined with our interview data, these written grievances reveal a great deal about how people in different institutional locations perceive law and engage in legal practices, and how these perceptions and practices shift with changes in venue and occasion. As we will see, changes across data sites, from interviews to the grievance documents themselves, speak powerfully to the fluidity and contingency of these participants' construction of meaning and to the critical roles of culture, institutional location, and context in shaping that construction.

Our grievance analysis focuses on our random sample of 292 appeals that reached the third formal level of review in fiscal year 2005–2006. This random sample includes grievances from twenty-nine of the thirty prisons for men in California.[1] As discussed in chapter 2, the complaints raised in these written grievances range widely. An inmate on death row alleges surgical errors and negligence in treating painful lumps; another appellant says the cans of tobacco he purchased at the canteen were confiscated as contraband; another requests a transfer to be closer to his elderly father; another one contests the termination of his visiting privileges; and yet another prisoner writes that his fund account was errone-ously debited. These grievance narratives give us a glimpse of prison's ordinary routines and practices, often through their disruptions; they also evoke a sense of the "totality" of this total institution and its awe-some power, in things both large and small, over those whose lives are lived within its walls.

Our analytical focus is on the ways these grievances and their official responses are composed and what this can tell us about the disputing perceptions and strategies of their authors, as well as the socially struc-tured and contingent quality of legal discourse and disputing more gen-erally. A number of sociolegal scholars have documented how language in a legal context is a weapon in the fight to construct meaning (Frohm-ann 1998; Lovell 2012; Merry 1990; Yngvesson 1993). Frohmann (1998, 394), in her study of the strategies of prosecutors interacting with victims of sexual assault, reveals "how people use language to accomplish their practical interests and activities in particular settings." And Lovell (2012, x) shows "how ordinary people appropriate the lan-guage of law . . . to frame expansive demands for new entitlements." Language, in other words, is a way of framing meaning and is part and parcel of that frame.

FRAMES AS REPERTOIRES OF MEANING

Goffman (1974, 10) coined the term *frame* to apply to "definitions of the situation" that "are built up in accordance with principles of orga-nization which govern events . . . and our subjective involvement in them." Gitlin (1980, 6) explains, "Frames are principles of selection, emphasis and presentation composed of little tacit theories about what exists, what happens, and what matters." More recently, Harding (2007, 346), quoting Young (2004), argues that frames are ways of under-standing "how the world works. A frame is a lens through which one interprets events. . . . Frames identify problems and assign blame, pro-vide solutions or strategies, and provide a rationale for engaging in action."

Goffman (1974) showed that social interaction often involves a struggle for the dominance of one's frame. This is arguably all the more the case in disputing, where conflicting frames may be employed for strategic purposes by parties in opposing locations. Lovell's (2006, 285) study reveals that both officials and ordinary people are "savvy" in their choices of frames. Following Cover's (1983) argument that legal rhetoric is used to deflate oppositional frames, Lovell shows that officials' use of a technical-legal frame provided the justification for them to reject the vast majority of citizens' complaints. In contrast, the lower courts in Merry's (1990, 10–11) study often "reframe[d] the discourse of rights and evidence" of the citizen plaintiffs into a "discourse of morality and treatment" as a way to dispense with these cases, revealing once again the strategic nature of frame deployment.

Consistent with this scholarship, the frames used by prisoners and staff in the grievance dialogue—or the "lens[es] through which [they] interpret events" (Harding 2007, 346)—can be seen as critical elements in their struggle to construct the meaning of the events they describe. With this in mind, we systematically coded the grievances for the types of frames advanced by prisoners and CDCR officials. For a description of our coding procedures, including a list of frames, see appendix C. Our findings in this chapter derive in large part from a close reading of each of these grievances and our coding of the frames deployed across four levels (a first "informal" level[2] and three formal levels). As with the interviews in previous chapters, we quote extensively here from appellants' narratives and from those of official responders.[3]

Prisoners use a range of frames to narrate their complaints and demand redress. However, two primary frames are most common: a legalistic frame focused on rights (e.g., "Exposure to deadly extreme heat [is] in violation of the Eighth Amendment Cruel and Unusual Punishment Clause") and a frame that asserts basic human needs ("In order for me to get the help that I so badly need"). Myriad other lenses are used to interpret the situation about which they file and to justify their requested remedy, including frames focusing on accountability ("You owe me something beside a bunch of lame excuses"), which emerge more frequently as grievances reach higher levels of review; procedural justice ("The hearing officer seemed to have a predetermined belief of my guilt"); fairness ("CDC took advantage of my limited knowledge of the English language"); and discrimination ("Post 9/11 discrimination against Muslim inmates is illuminated for all to see").

The range of frames deployed by CDCR respondents was narrower. Like the prisoners, CDCR staff frequently framed their responses through a legal lens, which in their case often involved quoting from Title 15 and policies and procedures stipulated by the Department Operation Manual. A bureaucratic frame was also used frequently, with CDCR responders prioritizing the findings of internal administrative committees ("On [date], you appeared before C Squad UCC for your

Annual/CSR/Transfer review based on the CDC memorandum dated September 1, 2005, titled Institutional Bed Management"). Together, legalistic and bureaucratic frames characterize the vast majority of CDCR responses.

In the sections that follow, we examine in detail the nature and dynamic character of these frames, including shifts over time as the dialogue progresses through a series of reviews. Further, more than one frame may be deployed at the same time. In her study of how women talk about sexual harassment, Marshall (2003) observes that they may use several frames to describe the same event, weaving them seamlessly in and out of their narrative. Just as the stories we tell in everyday life—or in narrating sometimes dramatic events such as sexual harassment—may incorporate different frames simultaneously, so too inmates and the CDCR sometimes adopt more than one frame at any given level of review. In recognition of this possibility of multiple-frame deployment as well as shifts in framing across the course of a dispute dialogue, we discuss primary and possible secondary frames at each level.

Among the major themes of this chapter, we note that previous analyses of disputes as sites of discursive struggle imply a kind of competitive contest. However, the reality here is of grossly unequal contestants, with one side retaining all the power to call the shots and—at least at the level of tangible results—ultimately to decide meaning.[4] This, then, is hardly a "competition" in the usual sense, and only one side is really "struggling." The patterns we find in how these grievances are constructed and the frames that are deployed cannot be explained outside of this context of the dramatically unequal nature of these disputes.

THE CENTRALITY OF LAW

As might be expected in this quasi-legal venue, one of the most common frames prisoners use to construct their grievances is that of law and legal rights (see tables 7 and 8). Whether the issue is medical care or a disciplinary infraction or any of the many other topics of complaint, prisoners often use legal frames and cite case law and the U.S. Constitution, particularly the Eighth Amendment's prohibition of cruel and unusual punishment. Some appellants are more literate and articulate than others, and there is a range of legal sophistication, but across types of grievances and sophistication levels, prisoners often cast their grievances as legal issues and use legal justifications for the remedies they request.

TABLE 7   PRIMARY FRAMES USED BY PRISONERS TO ARTICULATE GRIEVANCES*

Type of Frame	Informal Level	1st Level**	2nd Level	3rd Level
Legalistic/legal rights	86 (30.8)	27 (25.0)	36 (19.7)	74 (26.2)
Needs	71 (25.4)	34 (31.5)	49 (26.8)	57 (20.2)
Accountability	31 (11.1)	16 (14.8)	42 (23.0)	55 (19.5)
Procedural justice	28 (10.0)	2 (1.9)	6 (3.3)	32 (11.3)
Fairness	21 (7.5)	12 (11.1)	15 (8.2)	19 (6.7)
Discrimination	13 (4.7)	2 (1.9)	9 (4.9)	18 (6.4)
Deservedness	8 (2.9)	3 (2.8)	3 (1.6)	3 (1.1)
Mistake made	7 (2.5)	5 (4.6)	5 (2.7)	8 (2.8)
Safety	4 (1.4)	0 (0.0)	2 (1.1)	4 (1.4)
Compassion	4 (1.4)	2 (1.9)	3 (1.6)	5 (1.8)
Human rights	2 (0.7)	0 (0.0)	1 (0.5)	1 (0.4)
Importance of principle	2 (0.7)	3 (2.8)	10 (5.5)	4 (1.4)
Other	2 (0.7)	2 (1.9)	2 (1.1)	2 (0.7)
Total	279	108	183	282

* The data presented in this table include raw counts and valid percentages (in parentheses) based on the 292 grievances in the random sample. Cases with missing data (usually because of review bypasses) are excluded.

** When a grievance bypassed the informal level response from the CDCR, the appellant did not write a first-level narrative because there was nothing at that level for him to respond to. Hence the number of first-level prisoner narratives entered here is fewer than at other levels.

Their narratives are most detailed at the informal level, for it is here that they provide the initial description of their complaints and their requested remedies. The appellant not infrequently writes only a few sentences at subsequent levels, as the 602 form already contains a full description of the complaint and requested redress. In some ways, then, it is at the first, informal level that we get the most complete picture of how an appellant views the problem and justifies the remedy.[5] As we see in table 7, almost 31 percent of prisoners deployed a legal lens as their primary frame at the informal level of review, making it the most common way of narrating a grievance at that level. If we also consider secondary frames (i.e., if we look at prisoners who use a legal lens as either their primary *or* secondary frame at the informal level), the proportion rises to 48 percent (see table 8).

Ronaldo Rivera reported in his grievance that he has chronic pain from a degenerative disc and argued that CDCR medical personnel denied him the pain medication he said a staff doctor had prescribed. In his description of the problem, Rivera wrote, "I will never be pain free. [Medical staff's name] again has denied me the proper medical attention

TABLE 8 PRIMARY AND SECONDARY FRAMES USED BY PRISONERS TO ARTICULATE
GRIEVANCES*

Type of Frame	Informal Level	1st Level	2nd Level	3rd Level
Legalistic/legal rights	134 (48.0)	39 (36.1)	48 (26.2)	110 (39.0)
Needs	82 (29.4)	40 (37.0)	60 (32.8)	72 (25.5)
Accountability	73 (26.2)	36 (33.3)	85 (46.4)	110 (39.0)
Procedural justice	49 (17.6)	8 (7.4)	11 (6.0)	48 (17.0)
Fairness	38 (13.6)	22 (20.4)	25 (13.7)	45 (16.0)
Discrimination	25 (9.0)	3 (2.8)	15 (8.2)	25 (8.9)
Mistake made	22 (7.9)	8 (7.4)	13 (7.1)	26 (9.2)
Deservedness	20 (7.2)	9 (8.3)	12 (6.6)	15 (5.3)
Importance of principle	12 (4.3)	9 (8.3)	20 (10.9)	19 (6.7)
Compassion	11(3.9)	5 (4.6)	6 (3.3)	17 (6.0)
Human rights	9 (3.2)	1 (0.9)	4 (2.2)	9 (3.2)
Safety	6 (2.2)	0 (0.0)	5 (2.7)	10 (3.5)
Other	6 (2.2)	3 (2.8)	5 (2.7)	9 (3.2)

* The data presented in this table include raw counts and valid percentages (in parentheses) based on
the 292 grievances in the random sample. Cases with missing data (usually because of review bypasses)
are excluded. The total numbers exceed 100% because when a grievance includes a secondary frame
as well as a primary frame, it appears twice. The denominators used to compute percentages are as
follows: 279 for the informal level, 108 for the first level, 183 for the second level, and 282 for the third
level (as reported in table 7).

required under 42 U.S.C. §1981, §1983, §1985, §1986, §1988." He
concluded his "Requested Remedy" section: "[Medical staff's name]
will be held responsible for her non actions in this matter."

In another medical grievance, Jason Darrell cited Supreme Court
findings as well as the human rights code of the United Nations.
Darrell, a prisoner with a documented disability, began by describing
his problem: "I sustained a broken ankle while attempting to get on
the top bunk in a 'makeshift' wheelchair cell. Upon being sent to
the M.T.A [medical personnel, neither an RN nor an MD], I was told
to fill out a medical request as opposed to being sent for X-rays and
a cast. On [next day's date] I told/showed M.T.A that my ankle was
swelling further and that the pain is excruciating and unbearable. I was
again told to fill out a medical request form and maybe I'd be seen
next week." Darrell continued, citing *Plata v. Davis* (329 F. 3d 1101 [9th
Cir. 2003]):

Re Plata, I was supposed to have my foot tended to as follows: A RN or a
physician must decide "every case" of urgent or emergency care. . . . Upon

arriving at the M.T.A's office on [date] M.T.A. [name] told me nothing was wrong; note she's not an RN, LVN, OT, NP, or a physician. She only visually assessed my injury; blocked all access to the RN and physician, and to add insult to injury, made me walk back to the unit on my broken ankle. M.T.A. [name] is in direct violation of my civil, human rights as well as, willingly and knowingly violating "Plata." ... Further violations of my rights under the code of the United Nations, General Assembly: A/Res/43/173, are as follows: Principle 1: All persons under any form of detention or in prison shall be treated in a 'humane manner' and with respect for the inherent dignity of the human person. ... Principle 6: No person under any form of detention shall be subjected to torture or to cruel, inhuman or degrading treatment or punishment. The term 'cruel, inhuman or degrading treatment or punishment' shall be interpreted so as to extend the widest possible protection against abuses, whether physical or mental.

In a similarly legalistic grievance, David Hansen contested a disciplinary infraction he had incurred for refusing a cellmate in administrative segregation. Framing his concerns as a legal issue, he argued that the floor space was inadequate for two men in the small cell and noted that double-celling in such a confined space violated judicial rulings: "Inmate was improperly found guilty [for] 'Refusing to House,' double cell within Administrative Segregation Unit. Said unit with the X-BED in the down position leaves well less than 24 sq. ft. per person of floor space. ... These findings are in opposition to the findings in TOUSSAINT v. MCCARTHY, 597 F. Supp. 13, 88 (N.D. Cal 1984) (801 F. 2d. 1080 (9th Cir. 1986); 481 U.S. 1069 (1987); DOHNER v. MCCARTHY, 635 F. Supp. 408 (C.D. Cal (1985))."

Many appellants attached additional pages to the 602 form, where they enumerated constitutional rights, laws, and judicial findings they believed were relevant to the disputed issue. In his grievance, José Rubio reported that he had become a vegetarian; as a Catholic, he always had eschewed meat during Lent and on Fridays, but he had been studying other religions and had decided to adopt a wholly vegetarian diet (although he remained a Catholic). When his request was denied, partly on the grounds of the prison priest's recommendation, he filed a grievance, emphasizing his First Amendment rights. He wrote:

> With all due respect, Father [priest name's] argument is both flawed and unconstitutional. On the following page you will note specific case citations, and their wording as related to this specific case. First of all, we have the "Free Exercise Clause" of the First Amendment. The U.S. Supreme Court detailed in *O'Lone v. Estate of Shabazz*, 482 U.S. 342 (1987), that if a belief is (1) religious in nature; (2) sincerely held; and (3) does not interrupt a legitimate penological interest, it must be allowed. It also held in *Thomas v.*

Review Board of Indiana Employment Sec. Div., 450 U.S. 707, 714 (1981), that "religious beliefs need not be acceptable, logical, consistent, or comprehensible to others in order to merit First Amendment protection."

Rubio continued in this vein for a single-spaced page, citing eleven other U.S. Supreme Court and lower court decisions. He concluded his description of the problem: "Remember, the key word here is 'rehabilitation,' not deprivation of civil rights. Please do the right thing . . . Respectfully, [appellant's name]" (ellipsis in original).

It is not only the citation of laws and judicial findings that constitute the legal frame; many of these prisoners adopt a legalistic style, referring to themselves in the third person or as "appellant" and carefully parsing out and numbering the relevant legal principles. Ronaldo Flemming, an African American prisoner with a life sentence, had recently been indefinitely placed in a Security Housing Unit (SHU) for his alleged gang affiliation. He had been released from a SHU several years earlier but was returned there when a search of his cell found a magazine considered to be gang-related. At thirty-six pages, Flemming's grievance file is one of the most extensive in our sample—much of it composed of his handwritten details of events and meticulously numbered and lettered allegations and responses. He began:

> This inmate/parolee appeal form arises from the California State Prison [name] Institutional Gang Investigation (IGI) Unit's and Institutional Classification Committee's as well as Law Enforcement Investigation Unit's in Sacramento practices and policies which has caused me (appellant) to be wrongly placed and retained in Administrative Segregation Unit (ASU) and referred for an indeterminate placement in the Security Housing Unit (SHU) on the basis of alleged active prison gang membership. I (appellant) have wrongly been placed and retained in ASU and referred for an indeterminate placement in the ASU:
> a) without due process;
> b) when I (appellant) has not been active in prison gang activity;
> c) in retaliation for . . . legitimate freedom of speech and expression, activities that do not violate any prison rules;
> d) when appellant has not been found guilty of violating Title 15;
> e) on the basis of coerced, erroneous, false, and/or unreliable information.

Flemming continued with a long section he titled "Statement of Facts," ending with more detailed allegations of his perceived due process violations, "(a)" through "(g)."

Another prisoner, Matthew Jenkins, had been charged with possessing inmate-manufactured alcohol, had incurred a disciplinary infraction, and had lost time credits. He described the problem this way:

> On [date], Appellant submitted Five (5) Application for Restoration of Credits to his assigned Correctional Counselor [name]. Correctional Counselor denied all Five (5) Applications and justified her denial as being consistent with CCR Title 15, Pursuant to Sec. 3327 (a)(10 AND 3327(2)(4). The aforementioned Applications for Restoration of Credits are incorporated hereto as Exhibits "A," "B," "C," "D," & "E." Appellant Incorporate with each aforementioned Exhibit the Rules Violation Report with the Final Disposition. The Exhibits are submitted as supporting documents pursuant to CCR Title 15 Sec. 3084.2(a)(2). The Department Regulation set forth pursuant to CCR Title 15, Sec. 3084.1(2) Guarantee any Inmate under its jurisdiction the right to Appeal any Department Decision, Action Condition or Policy when it have an adverse effect upon his welfare. The denial of Restoration of credit loss is an adverse effect and raise a Liberty interest by illegally and unconstitutionally extending Appellant Release date for a total of 541 days and refusing to restore the credits in full.

Jenkins appended a sheet on which he meticulously organized the long body of his appeal into two sections: "Introduction" and "Legal Argument." At the heart of his argument, he noted:

> It appears that counselor is not familiar with the Ruling in *In re Dikes* 121 Cal. App. 4th 825; 18 Cal. Rptr. 3d 9 (2004). The court of Appeals held in *In re Dikes* . . . : "Not more than 30 days of credit may be denied or loss for a single act of misconduct defined by the Regulations as a serious disciplinary offense by the CDCR." Only if the act of misconduct can be prosecuted as a felony or a misdemeanor can the disciplinary action involve a loss of more than 30 days credit. Here the appellant could not be prosecuted for a felony or misdemeanor, therefore the 541 forfeited was in error and shall have been restored upon request.

CDCR responses were also frequently cast in a legal frame, with their first response at the informal level written primarily through a legal lens in 40.6 percent of the 101 grievances that were reviewed at that level (see table 9). In 54.5 percent of all informal responses, CDCR officials adopted a legal lens as either their primary *or* secondary frame (see table 10). The informal-level response is often bypassed by the CDCR, and when it is not bypassed, it usually consists of a short statement by a lower-level official. Therefore, the first substantive response to a prisoner's appeal frequently comes at the first formal level. Here, the legal frame is the most common, characterizing 47.4 percent of the 175 responses (see table 9). In fully 62.3 percent of these first-level responses, the legal frame was used as either a primary *or* a secondary lens (see table 10).

The responses to the prisoner grievances cited above are illustrative of the CDCR's reliance on a legal frame. The grievance filed by Ronaldo

TABLE 9 PRIMARY FRAMES USED BY CDCR OFFICIALS TO RESPOND TO
PRISONERS' GRIEVANCES*

Type of Frame	Informal Level	1st Level**	2nd Level	3rd Level
Bureaucratic	48 (47.5)	60 (34.3)	103 (35.9)	108 (38.4)
Legalistic/policy	41 (40.6)	83 (47.4)	126 (43.9)	131 (46.6)
Medical expertise	4 (4.0)	9 (5.1)	8 (2.8)	11 (3.9)
Other	3 (3.0)	13 (7.4)	30 (10.5)	16 (5.7)
Needs	2 (2.0)	1 (0.6)	0 (0.0)	0 (0.0)
Safety/security	2 (2.0)	5 (2.9)	10 (3.5)	9 (3.2)
Budget	1 (1.0)	1 (0.6)	1 (0.3)	2 (0.7)
Human mistake	0 (0.0)	2 (1.1)	0 (0.0)	0 (0.0)
Logic/reason	0 (0.0)	1 (0.6)	4 (1.4)	3 (1.1)
Overcrowding	0 (0.0)	0 (0.0)	5 (1.7)	1 (0.4)
Total	101	175	287	281

* The data presented in this table include raw counts and valid percentages (in parentheses) based on the 292 grievances in the random sample. Cases with missing data (usually because of review bypasses) are excluded.
** The number of informal responses entered here is smaller than at other levels because this level was often bypassed.

TABLE 10 PRIMARY AND SECONDARY FRAMES USED BY CDCR OFFICIALS TO
RESPOND TO PRISONERS' GRIEVANCES*

Type of Frame	Informal Level	1st Level	2nd Level	3rd Level
Bureaucratic	63 (62.4)	95 (54.3)	161 (56.1)	167 (59.4)
Legalistic/policy	55 (54.5)	109 (62.3)	207 (72.1)	203 (72.2)
Medical expertise	5 (5.0)	12 (6.9)	15 (5.2)	21 (7.5)
Safety/security	5 (5.0)	13 (7.4)	26 (9.1)	24 (8.5)
Other	4 (4.0)	18 (10.3)	43 (15.0)	32 (11.4)
Needs	4 (4.0)	2 (1.1)	0 (0.0)	1 (0.4)
Budget	2 (2.0)	1 (0.6)	4 (1.4)	3 (1.1)
Human mistake	0 (0.0)	5 (2.9)	1 (0.3)	1 (0.4)
Logic/reason	0 (0.0)	4 (2.3)	6 (2.1)	5 (1.8)
Overcrowding	0 (0.0)	4 (2.3)	7 (2.4)	5 (1.8)

* The data presented in this table include raw counts and valid percentages (in parentheses) based on the 292 grievances in the random sample. Cases with missing data (usually because of review bypasses) are excluded. The total numbers exceed 100% because when a response includes a secondary frame as well as a primary frame, it appears twice. The denominator used to compute percentages are as follows: 101 for the informal level, 175 for the first level, 287 for the second level, and 281 for the third level (as reported in table 9).

Flemming, in which he contested his indeterminate placement in a SHU, bypassed informal responders. At the first formal level, after noting that he had been interviewed and given an opportunity to provide additional information at his gang validation hearing, a lieutenant and the captain responsible for his cell block dismissed his allegations, emphasizing Title 15 of the California Code of Regulations (CCR): "A review of all gang validation documents in your Central file indicates no due process violations. All confidential information was disclosed pursuant to CCR §3321. Additionally, the review indicates you were afforded appropriate due process related to defending yourself, which included your handwritten validation rebuttal. This rebuttal was submitted and considered by LEIU [Law Enforcement Investigation Unit] regarding your validation status. . . . The decision by LEIU regarding your validation status has been rendered. . . . Therefore, this portion of your appeal is DENIED."

Flemming was subsequently transferred to a SHU to begin his indeterminate placement in solitary confinement. When he continued to appeal, second-level responders reaffirmed the first-level justification. The final review in Sacramento focused on information allegedly provided by a confidential CDCR informant—information that Flemming had contested—and once again argued that Flemming's due process rights had *not* been violated: "A further review of the CDC 1030s [confidential information disclosure form] indicate that sufficient information was disclosed to provide the appellant with an understanding of the information that is contained in the confidential documents. The CDC 1030s meet the criteria established in the California Code of Regulations, Title 15, Section (CCR) 3321."

The informal response was similarly bypassed in José Rubio's grievance requesting a vegetarian diet. At the first level, a short memorandum denied his appeal based on "The California Code of Regulations, Title 15, Section 3054 (a) (1) (A) (B) (c)." A longer response memorandum was signed by the warden at the second level, spelling out the provisions of Title 15, Sections 3084 and 3054, and concluded, "Review of CCR 3052 reveals that you do not meet the criteria for a Religious Diet Card at this institution."

Jenkins's legalistic appeal of his forfeiture of 541 days' credit for possession of alcohol elicited a comparably legalistic response from the CDCR. After asserting that Jenkins's interpretation of *In re Dikes* was inaccurate, first-level responders stated that in any case it is not only federal law that applies here: "Every person confined or residing in facilities of the department is subject to the rules and regulations of the director, and to the procedures established by the warden, superintendent, or parole region administrator responsible for the operation of the facility." Citing two pages of regulations from Title 15, they concluded, "Your claim that this [alcohol possession] cannot be referred for felony prosecution is incorrect. The California Code of Regulations, Title 15, Section 3316, allows each institution discretion in referring individuals for felony prosecution." Because, they said, the institution had discretion and thus *could* have referred his alcohol possession for prosecution (but chose not to), it was permissible to penalize him with more than thirty days' credit loss. While no restoration of credit was forthcoming, the appeal was "granted in part": the reviewers noted that the appellant was correct that "the Department of Corrections and Rehabilitation is required to abide by all laws, regulations, and policies set forth by the Penal Code."

A CLOSE-UP OF THE LEGAL FRAME

While a legal frame, broadly defined, dominates many of these prisoners' grievances as well as CDCR responses, a closer look reveals that this frame is multidimensional and varies considerably across locations. Indeed, prisoners and the CDCR rarely spoke the same legal language, with the former far more likely to refer to constitutional rights, federal lawsuits, and even international law, while the latter almost uniformly drew on local policies and procedures such as those stipulated in Title 15, the DOM, and administrative bulletins. Prisoners who deployed a legal frame occasionally referenced Title 15 and the DOM, as well as broader national and international legal principles; in contrast, the CDCR used a more circumscribed legal frame, dominated by local policies and procedures. At the first formal level, where 47.4 percent of CDCR responses were framed primarily through a legal lens, 40.6 percent focused specifically on policy and procedure, while only 6.8 percent emphasized statutes and judicial decisions. The pattern continued to prevail at subsequent levels, with 36.6 percent (policy and procedure) compared to 7.3 percent (statutes and legal cases) at the second level, and 40.2 percent to 6.4 percent at the third level.

Further, previous scholarship has shown that legal language is eminently versatile, doing the disparate work of judges, prosecutors, plaintiffs, ordinary citizens, and civil servants alike (Cover 1983; Frohmann 1998; Lovell 2012; Merry 1990). Much as the ordinary citizens and

Justice Department employees chronicled by Lovell (2012) used legal justifications to extend rights arguments and dismiss rights claims, respectively, so these prisoner appellants and CDCR responders adopted legal frames for diametrically opposite ends and to establish altogether different meanings.

As we saw in the grievances of Rivera, Darrell, Hansen, Rubio, and Flemming, the appellants deployed the language of legal rights in their efforts to secure better physical conditions and living arrangements while in prison. Whether citing the U.S. Constitution, federal law, or Title 15 of the California Code of Regulations, their legal frames were used to establish that a right had been violated or an entitlement denied. The institution instead used Title 15, the DOM, and administrative bulletins to *limit* the extension of rights and reaffirm prison authority. One illustration of this principle is the frequent reiteration at the director's level in the case of medical appeals: "The appellant . . . will not dictate the type of treatment he will receive or that which is afforded him. The appellant's medical condition has been considered and pursuant to the California Code of Regulations, Title 15, Section (CCR) 3350, the Department shall only provide medical services for inmates which are based on medical necessity." Part and parcel of the priority CDCR placed on resisting the extension of rights and maintaining prison authority was the reaffirmation of its established order and the minimization of any disruption or necessary modification to it. In this context, it is significant that grievance denial orders issued by the director's level routinely conclude with one sentence: "No changes or modifications are required by the institution."

The institution's task in minimizing disruptions or modifications should not be underestimated or summarily critiqued as plain authoritarianism. This total institution encompasses all the messy minutiae of everyday life compounded by security concerns and the hyperlegal nature of prison. It is always one of the most stubborn challenges of legal practitioners to impose the rigid boundaries of law on the infinite variety and complexity of human social life. The challenge is magnified many times over when that life transpires in a total institution among people who do not chose to be there and where law is meant to govern every detail of their existence.

In *Getting Justice and Getting Even*, Merry (1990, 16) documents the struggles of working-class Americans to get justice in lower courts, as well as the courts' efforts to dispense with those cases expeditiously. She writes, "The court endeavors to manage chaos, to contain emotion, to blunt the impression of injustice . . . , while the plaintiff fights for recognition of his problem as he or she experiences it and for the legal relief to which he or she feels entitled." The "endeavor to manage chaos" through law and policy is striking in these CDCR responses to prisoner grievances, no less so for their failures or for the apparent callousness of some of their decisions.

Among the grievances in our sample, one stands out as emblematic of many of the dynamics discussed thus far and serves as a particularly graphic illustration of the tangled complexities of daily life and CDCR attempts to manage the always impending chaos with law—and the bizarre turns such efforts may take. David Monrose was a maximum-security prisoner with a disability. In his grievance, he wrote that he required a wheelchair to shower, but that when he showered with other inmates, "their privite parts are . . . in my face." To avoid this, he waited to shower until after the other prisoners had finished. But, he wrote, "Officer [name] locks me in the shower area." Further, Monrose contended that the officer locked him in "because I've written him up for breaking my T.V." during a cell search. His requested action was "that I be treated like other inmates and not locked away like a dog. Also shower with the same respect as other inmates."

A facility lieutenant responded to Monrose's grievance at the first level, noting that he had interviewed Monrose about his complaint. He wrote, "I informed you that it is not [prison name] policy to place additional restriction and/or security precautions on inmates who are mobility impaired. In speaking to Officer [name], he stated that he does not secure you in the shower area. . . . At times staff may institute additional security precautions due to a myriad of custodial variables such as, lockdown, code alarms, medical emergencies etc. . . . I invite you to review California Code of Regulations, Title 15, Article 2, Security, Section 3270."

The second-level response by the prison warden cited two pages of regulations from Title 15 regarding ADA accommodations, personal hygiene, employee conduct, and security. It concluded by referring to an interview with the officer in question: "He reported that he does not lock you in the shower area; however, he indicated that he does provide you with the necessary devices, including a chair to accommodate you during your shower and that he allows you to participate in the shower program at the proscribed times and intervals. . . . He indicated that at times, you may have been locked in the shower, as he or other correctional staff had other assigned duties to perform." Monrose would no longer be locked in the shower area, the warden announced, because "Officer [name] stated that the practice of showering you at separate times has been discontinued as it is not practical or feasible in consideration of providing necessary coverage by the correctional staff." Nowhere in any of the responses was there mention of the more delicate "coverage" issue that Monrose had originally raised, which was the principal reason for his late showers and the problems that ensued. The final review noted only that the complaint classification should be changed from "living conditions" to "staff complaint."

People showering en masse, the particularities of ADA circumstances, cell searches, damaged property, lockdowns, security alarms, perceived retaliation, and controversies over complaint classification converge in this archetypical grievance. It highlights much about the reality of daily life in prison, made up in quick succession of the mundane and the extraordinary. Above all, it speaks to the chaotic minutiae of life in this total institution and the challenges and ultimate failures of CDCR's efforts to harness law to impose order on it, much less "to blunt the impression of injustice" (Merry 1990, 16).

As we have seen here, these prisoner appellants and the CDCR both use a legal lens in pursuit of their goals; however, the dimensions of law they deploy and the purposes to which they apply them diverge, often radically. We follow this divergence into the next section, where we examine these participants' languages of human needs on one side and bureaucratic mandates on the other, and the disconnect this cross-talk generates.

NEEDS, BUREAUCRACY, AND THE DISPUTE
"DIALOGUE"

The divergent framing and corresponding grievance goals of prisoners and the CDCR are most starkly revealed when we examine the other common frames used. We have seen that prisoners often construct their grievances as legal issues, but they almost as frequently frame them as simple human needs. At the informal level, over a quarter (25.4 percent) of inmate grievances are framed primarily as needs; at the first formal level, the percentage rises to almost a third of the grievances (31.5 percent), making needs the frame most commonly used by prisoners at that level (table 7). The percentage of prisoners who frame their grievances either primarily or secondarily through a needs lens reaches almost 30 percent at the informal level and 37 percent at the first formal level (table 8). This percentage declines somewhat at the second and, especially, the third formal levels, where "accountability" becomes a powerful secondary frame. It is perhaps not surprising that appellants—after having been denied at lower levels—subsequently put a strong secondary emphasis on accountability. However, even at the final review and considering both primary and secondary frames, the needs frame is apparent in over one–quarter of grievances (table 8). In some cases, grievances based on a needs frame also include a legal frame. In other cases, prisoner appellants refrain altogether from using legal language or rationales and, by virtue of emphasizing needs, push back against the carceral logic of regimentation and control.

Many prisoners who base their grievances on needs are concerned about transfers. Joseph Sonora was worried that he was scheduled to be transferred to a prison far from his mother—a concern that was unmitigated by the fact that the transfer was to a prison with a lower custody level, and therefore usually more desirable. Sonora described the problem in plain, heartfelt language:

> This is an emergency 602 filed in order to hopefully halt/prevent my transfer to a level II facility which would cause an extreme hardship on my only family member who visits me on a very regular basis . . . my mother. My mother is 73 years old, in poor health . . . and I am her only child and the reason she is able to stay alive & strong. My father passed away in [date] and my mom has been alone ever since. She is very dedicated towards me and me towards her. The only thing in life that keeps us both going is the ability to spend those precious Sundays together. Moving me away up north would severely limit her ability to visit me and would devastate her emotionally. I plead with you to consider my family ties and that transferring me elsewhere would cause an unusual hardship upon my mother, who I love & care for so very much.

Other prisoners wrote to *request* transfers for reasons related to maintaining family ties. Ricardo Jimenez, in a SHU unit in a maximum-security prison for active gang members, neatly printed a long, hand-written grievance describing his need to be closer to his ailing father:

> My father . . . is a [war] veteran and he has shrapnel . . . which is hindering his [mobility]. Over ten years ago my father had an operation for [gall bladder]. . . . My father is not in the best of health and it is not healthy for him to be traveling long distances and having to stay away from home for more than a day or two which visitors have to do if they wish to visit an inmate here at [prison name]. . . . My brother [has medical problems] and he needs constant care and supervision . . . and my parents cannot be away from him for more than a day.

At his final level review, Jimenez wrote that his father had recently visited and that it took a full day of travel each way and two days away from home. He appealed to the director's compassion: "This form of travel caused my father much discomfort and strain."

Stephen Sterling also framed his transfer request in the language of needs. Sterling wrote that the parole board (Board of Prison Terms [BPT]) had recommended that he receive help for his mental problems, and he asked to be transferred to a prison where he believed such help was available. He wrote, "In order for me to get the help that I so badly need . . . I request that I be transferred to [prison name]. . . . The staff here is hindering me from getting the rehabilitation that I would need in order for me to receive a date [for parole] by the BPT." When he was denied, he persisted, writing at the first formal level, "It is clear that I'm in need of mental help. This is not something that I'm making up. It is a well-known fact. The BPT sees that I'm in need how come you refuse to see it? You are denying me a chance to receive the help that I need."

Many of the grievances framed as needs deal with medical and mental health issues. Leonard Lipsky, a death row inmate who reported having lumps on his [arm and back], requested that they be removed. In a harrowing account, Lipsky said he had surgery in prison, and "a large lump formed on my [arm] after [doctor's name] torn the screw loose that [other doctor's name] had installed to repair the joint he fractured when his digital saw slipped during the surgery." He said the doctor told him he would remove the lump on his [back]. "Since then," Lipsky wrote, "I have made repeated requests to have these lumps removed. . . . It is now over 5 years since I began requesting to have these lumps in my [back] removed. . . . It is very painful. The large lump on my [arm] . . . has gotten larger and causes me severe pain."

David Thomas similarly foregrounded his pain and medical need. In a relatively brief, handwritten description of his problem, Thomas wrote that he is a hearing-impaired inmate with ADA status, that he had an ear infection and had been twice ducated for prison medical appointments, but the doctor had not shown up. He requested "to see an EENT [eyes, ears, nose, throat specialist] either here or outside of prison ASAP so this emergency medical problem can be addressed." At the first formal level, he continued to request an appointment with a specialist: "Still have not been seen by EENT & have developed severe pain to right ear & leakage of infection out of ear on a continual basis. Need to be seen immediately." At the final review, he wrote, "7 months with an ear infection is way too long."

Confronted by these appellants who spoke the language of needs, the CDCR often responded using the altogether different vocabulary of bureaucratic mandates. In response to Lipsky's request to have lumps surgically removed, the informal reviewer wrote, "You have been referred to a surgeon & will be seen @ the next available appointment" (to which Lipsky replied skeptically that he had "been given promises of treatment for the past five years. . . . Promises are not an accepted form of medical treatment"). The first formal reviewer also cited scheduling problems: "We have not been able to find a surgeon to do this procedure. . . . When we can get you scheduled we will notify you." Months later, Lipsky received surgery for one problem but was denied treatment for the other. His persistent request for surgery was "granted in part" at the director's level—not because he had prevailed but because the director, who pointedly noted that he had not received the necessary information and paperwork from prison officials, ordered them to provide it.

The response to Thomas's request to see an EENT specialist followed a similar pattern and was similarly framed, with CDCR reviewers initially justifying their inaction on grounds of scheduling problems. At the informal level, Thomas was told, "We will schedule you in accordance with numerical order of consults." Three months later, he was sent to an outside hospital for a CAT scan. By the time of his second review, Thomas had been referred to a specialist (but did not receive any treatment), and his appeal was thus technically "granted." In response to Thomas's subsequent plea that he was still "in a lot of pain," the chief medical officer wrote, "Your appeal was already granted because you were evaluated by an EENT specialist . . . and [received] a CAT scan." Thomas later received surgery on his ear, but his appeal was officially denied at the director's level, where they pushed back against his assertiveness in demanding treatment. The director concluded his review, "Only qualified medical personnel shall be permitted to diagnose illness for inmates."

While Lipsky and Thomas eventually received some medical treatment despite bureaucratic hurdles and delays, the transfer grievances were met with unilateral rejection. In response to Sonora's plea that "transferring me . . . would cause an unusual hardship upon my mother, who I love & care for so very much," the informal-level denial was accompanied by two brief sentences, concluding, "Due to population pressures the CSR [Classification Staff Representative] endorsed you to [transfer prison] consistent with your classification score." Sonora retorted, "I was hoping that CSR would show some compassion as family ties are supposed to be important in rehabilitation." The first formal level was bypassed, and the second level was more legalistic, consisting of seven pages of citations from Title 15. At the final review, the director returned to an emphasis on bureaucratic processes:

> The appellant's initial requested institutions were not available. His placement was based upon the availability of institutional programs and housing. . . . The institution has shown that UCC [Unit Classification Committee] members were appropriately concerned about the appellant's requirements for Correctional Clinical Case Management System level of Mental Health Services Delivery System care. . . . Population pressures and case factors dictated the action of the CSR who appropriately endorsed the appellant to a facility commensurate with his case factors, placement needs and available bed-space at that time. . . . No changes or modifications are required by the institution.

At no point in the CDCR review of Sonora's file was there any reference to his mother's health or the impact of a transfer on family visits.

Jimenez's request to be transferred to a prison closer to his ill father was similarly denied mostly on bureaucratic grounds. In response to Jimenez's lengthy description of his aging father's health woes and his medically dependent brother, the informal response was one sentence: "Per ICC [Institutional Classification Committee] action of [date] your request has been denied." First-level reviewers elaborated: "Your hardship transfer request and the ICC decision to deny your request was documented in the aforementioned CDC Form 1280G. You were informed during the ICC hearing that based on your current validation as a prison gang associate and the fact that [prison name] is currently the institution of choice for validated gang members and associates, you were appropriately housed. . . . There is no evidence to support your claim that the ICC decision to retain you in [prison name] on Indeterminate [indefinite status] is inappropriate." The warden reiterated these first-level findings, concluding his response with a not-so-veiled suggestion that if Jimenez wished to be transferred, he could deactivate as a gang member: "The inmate has been housed at [prison name] since [date] and the inmate has options available to him for release from SHU. The inmate is encouraged to review these options so that he can be housed closer to family." This is the only point in this grievance "dialogue" where the CDCR made any mention of the family basis for Jimenez's request.

The CDCR denial of Sterling's request to be transferred "in order to get the help that I so badly need" was also justified on the grounds of bureaucratic principles. At the informal level, the lieutenant who responded wrote one hand-penned sentence on the 602 form: "Denied. You are appropriately endorsed to [prison name]." At the next level, another officer submitted a paragraph, beginning by noting the number of "points" the inmate had and his security level. Next he stated, "You are a participant in the mental health system at the level of CCCMS [Correctional Clinical Case Management System] and are receiving the treatment that corresponds with that level. . . . There are no in-level transfers at this time." The warden's review and the director-level review followed suit, reiterating that "you are appropriately housed" and no "in-level transfers" were available.

Affirming the authority of the Institutional Classification Committee, the Unit Classification Committee, the Correctional Clinical Case Management System, and other such administrative bodies, citing scheduling problems and the "numerical order of consults," referencing inmates' "points," and deferring to internal memoranda regarding "in-level transfers" and other matters—these bureaucratic rationales recurred repeatedly in CDCR responses. Often accompanied by and woven through with legalistic references to Title 15, this bureaucratic lens characterized 47.5 percent of CDCR responses at the informal level and never fell below 34 percent at any level (table 9). Looking at both primary and secondary frames, the bureaucratic lens was used in 62.4 percent of grievances at the informal level, 54.3 percent at the first formal level, 56.1 percent at the second level, and 59.4 percent at the final review (table 10).

The disconnect between the needs frame these prisoner appellants deployed and the bureaucratic response constructed by the CDCR is notable. Even more conspicuous, however, is the absence of anything resembling a dialogue (as opposed to iterative turn-taking between parties). These participants speak past each other, as their two languages of needs and bureaucratic mandates entail not only distinct vocabulary but altogether different syntaxes of meaning. Sonora pleads with the CDCR not to transfer him because that would "cause an unusual hardship upon my mother, who I love & care for so very much." The CDCR responds with reference to the Unit Classification Committee and available bed space. Jimenez's efforts to be transferred to enable his ailing veteran father to visit him were answered by the CDCR reiterating his gang classification. Not only was his father's health status not mentioned, but it was erased altogether, as the institution declared that "there is no evidence to support" the need for such a hardship transfer. And Lipsky's request for surgery was "granted in part" not because he was to receive his requested remedy, but because the director issued a Modification Order telling the prison to complete the paperwork.

It is not only these particular needs/bureaucracy frames that stymy meaningful conversation. As we saw earlier, prisoners who speak the language of law talk of the Eighth Amendment, and the CDCR replies with verbiage from Title 15 and the Department Operation Manual. Recall the inmates housed in a converted gym with triple-deck bunks, discussed in chapter 2. They filed a group appeal contesting overcrowding and its effect on ventilation, violence, sanitation, and noise. They argued that conditions such as "toilets placed 15 inches apart . . . without any kind of separation and/or protection from urine splashes" and noise levels making sleep impossible, among other harsh conditions, violated the Eighth Amendment's prohibition against cruel and unusual punishment. Their appeal was screened out at the first level of review because it "covers too many complexed issues." After the appellants explained in their follow-up that the single overarching issue was overcrowding, the institution reverted to a recitation of policy, interspersed with references to administrative-bureaucratic concerns: "It appears that no violation of Department rules, regulations, or policies has occurred. Housing capacity is the CDCR's system-wide bed count utilizing occupancy standards, classification levels, special housing designations, and the institution's program needs." The final reviewer concluded that the appellants had not presented any evidence or documentation that they had "suffered adversely"[6] from the overcrowding.

The CDCR's strict adherence to formulaic legal and bureaucratic frames may be administratively useful, closing off dialogue and creating an illusion of certainty, but it can have grave human consequences. David Pastor wrote in his grievance that he had fallen and suffered severe injuries. He had originally filed a grievance alleging that two scheduled surgeries had been canceled without explanation. His appeal was granted at the first level, and he eventually received surgery. Pastor subsequently requested follow-up attention in a second-level appeal that was framed as an urgent need, saying that he was in pain and pleading, "I respectfully ask for help." The official response at the second level was to decline any further help, referring to the official policy on keeping grievances narrow and self-contained: "The additional requested action is not addressed [by CDCR] herein, as it is not appropriate [for the inmate] to expand the appeal beyond the initial problem and the initially requested action." We turned the page expecting to find the third-level decision and were startled to read: "The appellant has deceased rendering the issues under appeal moot."

It is not only on high-stakes issues that the parties frame their concerns in dramatically different languages and speak past each other. Whether the grievance involves a disputed $1.00 in a trust account, framed by the appellant as a matter of principle, or an urgent medical issue that may be fatal, these disputes are remarkable for their dialogic disconnects. And these non sequiturs go both ways. If the institution conspicuously refuses to engage the issues of ailing family members and chronic pain, prisoners do not engage the CDCR's preferred subjects of bed space and scheduling headaches.

In *Getting Justice and Getting Even* (1990, 93), Sally Merry says of disputing, "The conflict is a form of communication, a kind of extended conversation. . . . The parties exchange messages which express their interests, feelings, and their interpretation of the situation." What we see here, however, is two parties differing not only in their interests but in the very languages they speak. Under these circumstances, communication is limited and conversation aborted. Indeed, these disputes resemble not so much conversations as efforts to establish the language of currency and, hence, meaning.

Even this, however, is misleading, for to refer to these sequences of opposing soliloquies as struggles for meaning is to imply a competitive contest. But while prisoners may struggle to assert the primacy of their language and the validity of their meaning, the CDCR—as both defendant and judge—speaks the language of authority and determines the outcome of the exchange. While the prisoner appellants are not likely to be convinced of the CDCR interpretation of events—and thus in a sense, neither side succeeds in establishing its meaning—the CDCR controls the parameters of the exchange, its pace, and perhaps most importantly, its consequences. They quite literally have the last word, with the director's review routinely concluding with one final sentence: "This decision exhausts the administrative remedy available to the appellant within the CDCR." Technically, the prisoner may attempt to bring a lawsuit, but in reality the vast majority of prisoner grievances end here. The following section examines in more detail evidence of the one-sided quality of this "struggle" through the patterns of the parties' respective frames and telling deviations from script as prisoners express their frustration.

POWER, THE SEARCH FOR MEANING, AND "RESISTANCE"

One of the most compelling indicators of the CDCR's power to define this exchange is found in the consistency of their frames. Together, two frames—legal and bureaucratic—dominate CDCR responses, accounting for all but a small fraction of the primary and secondary frames the CDCR used. Further, the use of these frames remains relatively constant across all four levels of review when inventorying primary and secondary frames (table 10).

As we saw in the last chapter, consistency of response outcomes across levels is achieved through a variety of institutional, ideological, and interpersonal processes, including a focus on downstream consequences, implicit and explicit sanctions for nonconformity, a shared discrediting of prisoner appellants, and intraorganizational communication. Consistency in the framing of responses is no doubt in part the product of these same processes. In addition, however, there is a more prosaic reason for the CDCR's frame consistency. At the first and second formal levels, respectively, the same format is used for every grievance (for example, at the second level, sections are titled "Appeal Issue," "Regulations Governing the Issue," and "Decision"); when substantial deviations occur, prison officials are instructed by the Inmate Appeals Branch to adopt the conventional format.

This rote approach is even more pronounced at the director's level. In our interviews with CDCR examiners, they revealed that computerized "libraries" provide them with generic verbiage for specific types of grievance responses. Thus director-level responses to staff complaints, for example, are formatted exactly the same way, contain the same reasoning, cite the same sections from Title 15, and end with the same concluding paragraph—all drawn from these "libraries" of responses, which include not only routine formats but also precise wording.

Given the volume of work these reviewers and examiners face, it is not surprising that they have devised such efficiencies. However understandable the reasons, this boilerplate formatting and rote verbiage further reduce the potential for a substantive dialogue. More relevant here, the consistency achieved reveals the inaccuracy of any reading of the CDCR as *struggling* to achieve their preferred meaning. Confident in their ability to define the situation, these CDCR responders stick to their script. This confidence is all the more apparent when contrasted with prisoner appellants' search for a winning strategy.

In contrast to the institution's frame consistency, prisoners as a group tried out a plethora of different strategies. While a legal lens and the urgency of needs were the two most common primary frames through which prisoners narrated their claims, these two characterized only approximately half (51.4 percent) of their grievances if we average all levels of review (table 7) Not only did accountability emerge as important, especially as a secondary frame (table 8), but procedural justice, fairness, discrimination, and a host of other framing strategies were also engaged.

While these aggregate numbers provide a view of the landscape of frames and their consistency of usage across prisoners and staff, it is even more revealing to examine whether *individuals* shifted the primary frame they deployed. Looking only at the first, informal level, where appellants originally tell their story in full, and the final level, where they make their last plea to Sacramento, well over a third (42.2 percent) of these prisoner appellants shifted their primary frames (table 11). It is powerful to consider that the *same* prisoner switched primary frames almost as often as *different* CDCR responders did. When we examine the first formal level, where CDCR officials most frequently enter their first response, and the final level of review in Sacramento, these different institutional responders changed primary frames 43 percent of the time (table 11). More telling still, when we examine the number of individual prisoners who deployed the dominant legalistic and needs frames at the informal level but reached beyond these dominant frames to engage more peripheral ones by the final review, we find that almost one-third (30.3 percent) did so (table 11). In contrast, fewer than half as many (13.6 percent) CDCR responders deviated from their dominant legalistic and bureaucratic staples at the first level to try out more peripheral framings at the third and final review. Unlike individual prisoners, these CDCR responders apparently felt little need to deviate from well-worn scripts.

This picture of prisoner-appellants trying out a wide variety of frames to narrate their grievances is consistent with much of what previous scholars have found. Frohmann (1998, 401, citing Merry 1990; Sarat and Felstiner 1995; Yngvesson 1993; White 1990) summarizes an argument made in the literature: "Participants . . . shift between legal, moral, and therapeutic discourses to frame problems in an advantageous way." Just so, these prisoners often changed frames as the dispute progressed in search of a winning strategy. But as with the prosecutors and sexual assault victims that Frohmann studied, there is a clear "asymmetry of

TABLE 11   PRISONER AND STAFF PRIMARY FRAME CONSISTENCY*

	Individual Prisoners		CDCR Staff	
	No	Yes	No	Yes
The same primary frame is used at the initial and final levels of review.**	116 (42.2)	159 (57.8)	74 (43.0)	98 (57.0)
A dominant frame at the initial level is replaced by a peripheral frame at the final review.***	108 (69.7)	47 (30.3)	121 (86.4)	19 (13.6)

* The data presented in this table include raw counts and valid percentages (in parentheses) based on the 292 grievances in the random sample. Cases with missing data (usually because of review bypasses) are excluded.

** For prisoners, we treat the informal level as the initial level, and for staff the initial level is the first formal level of review (because the informal review is so often bypassed by the CDCR).

*** The dominant frames for prisoners are legalistic and needs, while the dominant frames for staff are legalistic and bureaucratic.

troubles management" (401) here. One indication of this asymmetry is the degree to which prisoners, compared to CDCR staff, reached beyond the dominant narrative frames over the course of the dispute in their struggle to secure a victory. Considering that our random sample included no full grants at the final level, we must conclude that whatever they did, prisoners were not able "to frame problems in an advantageous way."

This asymmetry was further evidenced in the relative frequency with which prisoners adopted angry or contemptuous tones in their appeals, while CDCR responses were for the most part affectless.[7] While most prisoners initiated their grievances matter-of-factly, anger sometimes became evident as the dispute progressed. Edward Tamigran had not been allowed to have the prayer oil that he said "is an essential part of the Muslim faith." After being denied at the informal and first formal levels, Tamigran attached a long, handwritten page in which his anger was palpable: "This is nothing but Muslim discrimination, post 9-11 hate by prison officials towards Muslims. . . . You people have nothing better to do but harass the Muslim inmates and play these stupid games as if it will make you appear more patriotic by doing so. Stopping me from getting prayer oil doesn't seem a significant contribution, but 'whatever.'"

In another case, Samuel Sparks requested a transfer to a lower-security prison, maintaining a matter-of-fact tone through three levels of review where he was repeatedly denied. In appealing to the director's level, his frustration erupted. Sparks complained that the CDCR imposed their rules selectively and deviated from them when convenient, a complaint other prisoners made in their grievances and one we often heard in our interviews. He fired off his final appeal: "Since coming to [prison name], I come to find out that certain rules *do not* apply and that certain rules does when it's to there benefit."

Richard Hallaway wrote that while working his prison job, he was loading food carts onto a truck and a limb got caught in the mechanism. He complained of severe pain, but, he stated, no X-rays were taken nor cast applied before permanent damage had been done. As his requested remedy, he demanded compensation and punitive damages. When informed at the first level that "monetary compensation is not within the scope of the appeals process," Hallaway filed his second-level review: "Oh, no I don't think so. You all messed up and you should pay through the nose." At the director's level, he blasted, "Because of the fact I incurred permanent injury to my [ankle] from the lack of medical attention don't you people think you owe me something beside a bunch of lame excuses."

José Pereira had been sent to administrative segregation, and he wrote in his grievance, "I was not given a 1083 receipt for my property. After repeated attempts to get a copy of my 1083, I was told that I have no property." He supplied an inventory of the missing items and asked that his property be replaced. When he was answered at the informal level that only those items for which he had receipts would be replaced, he replied, "Completely unacceptable. Nowhere close to compensating me for missing items." When the next CDCR reviewer reiterated the original review response, Pereira wrote, "I bought a hot pot. I want it replaced. Also my cable for my TV. I will consider the rest a learning experience at [this prison]. Also, for the record, I was not interviewed by [officer's name]. I was threatened to take what he's offering or else he would make my life 'a living hell.' Quote!" At the director's level, he continued, "Of course I'm dissatisfied. I have not been compensated for all my family photos, legal transcripts and hot pot, along with my TV splitter, 6 ft. cable. CDCR staff are thieves. [Prison name] staff threatens inmates and intimidates inmates into doing there will. Sacramento is aware of these out of control employees ([officer's name]). You are just as guilty as they are for turning your head."

Madison King expressed similar outrage in his grievance. King had been given a 115 for distribution of heroin and other drugs in prison, and the officer who brought the charge argued that King's wife dealt drugs on the street and was implicated in smuggling them into prison. King hand-printed two dense, single-spaced pages underscoring the lack of evidence for his drug charge and blasting the institution for implicating his wife. Regarding the officer's statement that he had seen his wife dealing drugs on the street, King declared, "This statement is a lie. Plan and simple. . . . The [officer] was clearly very prejudicial. . . . My hearing was a sham hearing."

David Stanton was a prisoner with a life sentence coming up for parole, and his mother had written a letter supporting him, which was to go in his parole board file. Because the letter was unsigned, an official telephoned the mother to confirm that she had written it. Following the phone call, the official wrote on the bottom of the mother's letter with an apparent typo, "Called to confirm if she sent it since she *did not* [blank space] it. Confirmed."[8] A note presumably misinterpreting this communication was placed in the prisoner's file indicating the mother had not *written* the letter (though the mother confirmed that she had). The prisoner requested that officials write his mother an apology and send a letter to the parole board clarifying the mistake. When he was denied, he wrote, "This is a letter from my mother we are talking about. To even insinuate that my mother is lying by 'changing her story' is outrageous. . . . What's next, are you going to write that my mom really hates me but doesn't want me to know and see if you can get someone to buy that?"

Sometimes the anger is laced through with desperation. Donald Flemming had complained repeatedly of a variety of physical problems. In the first section of his 602, he estimated that he had "put in over 60 sick call slips and have always been denied the requested & necessary medical help." Increasingly desperate and combative, Flemming threatened, "Your medical department will be held liabel when I start cutting on myself or decide to hang myself. . . . Just a matter of days." Another inmate who said he had been denied medical treatment later charged the CDCR with a "magnitude of unprofessionalism, immoral, and unethical conduct," before concluding that they were perpetrating a "form of attempted murder."

It is easy to understand these appellants' anger and frustration, but side by side with these eruptions of anger, it is jarring to find routine articulations of conventional etiquette. Indeed, most of these same appellants concluded their appeals with "Thank you" and signed them "Respectfully." Tamigran ended his appeal to the director, "This is clear discrimination. Please review these claims. Thank you." After demanding compensation beyond "a bunch of lame excuses," Hallaway signed off, "God Bless." King, who called his hearing a sham and said the officer who accused him of drug dealing was "a liar," signed all four levels of his long appeal, "Respectfully, [name]." And after threatening suicide because of the CDCR's withholding of medical treatment, Flemming carefully drew two lines for his signature: "Respectfully Submitted [name]."

There were no comparable shows of emotion in CDCR responses, which maintained a consistently flat tone and bureaucratic tenor. Even in the face of these prisoners' angry allegations and threats, the institutional responders were unflappable. Flemming's demand for medical treatment was bypassed at the first two levels and denied at the last two levels, despite his threats to hang himself. At the director's level, the library of responses for medical appeals was employed: "The evidence presented provides that the appellant has access to medical services deemed appropriate by medical personnel. California Code of Regulations, Title 15, Section (CCR) 3354 establishes that only qualified medical personnel shall be permitted to diagnose illness for inmates. It is not appropriate for the appellant to self-diagnose."

Faced with Stanton's anger in response to the CDCR insinuation that his mother was a liar, the institution again stuck to its script, with the director adopting routine language: "The request for administrative action regarding staff [presumably Stanton's request for an apology] . . . is beyond the scope of the appeals process." In response to Pereira's charges that "CDCR staff are thieves" and "you are as guilty as they are," the director's level replied coolly, "It has been determined that no liability on the part of the Department has been established for the hot-pot and other miscellaneous items."

It might be argued that this difference in prisoner and CDCR tones is related to the fact that prisoners are a diverse group with varying temperaments and levels of sophistication, while CDCR staff are a more or less coherent group of trained professionals. During our interview with prisoner David Miller, he volunteered his theory of why prisoner appellants are rarely successful: "The appeals coordinator is pretty much like an attorney, cuz they do this [appeals] all day long. They're smart, they're well educated most of the time. That's why they got that job. And you know, that's up against, you know, Tyrone the crack dealer." David's focus on education and training overlooks not only the high level of sophistication of some appellants—even some who become angry and contemptuous in their appeals—but also the institutional basis for grievance asymmetries. David's stereotypical "Tyrone the crack dealer" may in fact be a capable jailhouse lawyer. Nonetheless, this may not determine either the outcome of his appeal or whether he maintains a matter-of-fact tone.

It might also be argued that these outbursts by appellants are not evidence of desperation but are in fact illustrations of agentive resistance. Much as "Mrs. G.," the welfare mother chronicled by Lucie White (1990), went off script to declare forthrightly that she had bought Sunday shoes for her children with a disputed insurance payment, so these prisoners may be exerting agency in an otherwise hopelessly asymmetrical context. In other words, these expressions of anger and even contempt can be seen as empowering acts of resistance.

Whatever they are called, such displays of emotion by prisoner appellants—particularly contrasted to the CDCR's seemingly emotionless tone—speak to prisoners' relative powerlessness. After all, as James Scott (1985) noted, resistance is a weapon of the "weak." It is a weapon that may restore self-dignity to those armed with it, but it does not alter the terrain of the conflict, the structural locations of combatants, or even who might accurately be referred to as "combatants" in such predetermined contests. As we watch prisoners deploying a variety of frames and tones and occasionally lashing out against those who calmly deny them, it is clear that this is neither a two-sided "conversation" nor a combative "struggle." Rather, it is an exchange between those armed with structural and institutional power and those who fight on despite the odds.

As we have seen throughout this book, the prisoner grievance process in California is heavily asymmetrical in design and outcome, and those who use it to make claims are usually denied. As revealed in this chapter, the grievance process cannot even be considered a dialogue, because the institution is tone-deaf to the language of the appellant and the parties speak past each other, often going four rounds that can last for months. But the failure to score a victory does not seem to defeat these prisoners. Instead, as we have argued in previous chapters, the very presence of the 602 system is a daily reminder to prisoners of their rights and their identities as rights-bearing subjects. Alfonso Lopez, the appellant quoted in chapter 2 who had been diagnosed alternately with pneumonia and valley fever, put it best when he wrote in his grievance: "I want what anyone else would want and expect. . . . I want to be sure and for them to be sure I am getting the definitive test to diagnose what ails me. . . . *All I know is that my rights are protected by law.* And if I'm not being given the best care, there are . . . mechanisms that I can invoke [emphasis added]." Despite the limitations of these mechanisms, they keep alive the promise of rights and the sense among prisoners that they are entitled to them like "anyone else."

IMPLICATIONS

Together, the findings presented here point to a number of conclusions regarding the nature of disputing, the fluidity of legal consciousness, and the importance of methodological approach in their discovery. First, much previous scholarship has revealed that legal rhetoric is a weapon in the struggle to control meaning. But as this analysis of grievances in prison makes clear, it is a weapon that is loaded unequally. Not only are the professionals who respond to prisoner grievances trained to do so, as David Miller told us, but they are armed with the authority to impose meaning and decide outcomes. It is impossible to understand prisoners' deployment of frames and their struggle to construct a winning strategy, or at least a strategy that restores dignity, without recognizing this dramatically unequal structure of power within which the dispute takes place. Indeed, this inequality must be considered a principal actor—perhaps the lead actor—in shaping these disputes.

Swidler (1986, 277) conceptualizes culture as a "tool kit" from which people build "strategies of action." She argues, "People do not, indeed cannot, build up a sequence of actions piece by piece, striving with each act to maximize a given outcome. Action is necessarily integrated into larger assemblages, called here 'strategies of action.' Culture has an important causal role because it shapes the capacities from which such strategies of action are constructed. The term 'strategy' is not used here in the conventional sense of a plan consciously devised to attain a goal. It is, rather, a general way of organizing action." While culture broadly construed is often formative, at least as important in understanding the pattern of frames we uncover here is the way the structure of power differentially "shapes the capacities" of prisoners and CDCR staff.

Second, our findings confirm the argument of much scholarship that legal consciousness is fluid, multifaceted, and contingent (Ewick and Silbey 1998; Marshall 2003; Silbey 2005). As Silbey (2005, 334) notes, consciousness is "a type of social practice," and it is dependent on the social-structural and institutional context in which it is practiced and one's location within that context. The disputing frames and tones of prisoners and staff constitute just such "social practices" and are integrally linked to the institutional locations of the participants and the structural context of the dispute. Further, these frames and tones may shift as the conflict evolves, shifts that are exposed only by following the entire arc of the dispute. The patterns we trace reveal that participants' frames may be fluid and zigzag or may be more constant and persistent depending in part on actors' institutional location and purpose. Specifically, the greater fluidity of prisoners' frames and tones compared to those of the CDCR is a reflection of their relative institutional powerlessness. In other words, while legal consciousness as a social practice is indeed fluid and contingent, the degree of that fluidity and contingency is not uniformly distributed but varies with structural context and actor location.

Third, prisoner and CDCR narratives—empirical markers of their legal consciousness, if we want to call it that—shift markedly across research venues. In our interviews with prisoners and CDCR personnel, discussed in earlier chapters, we often found surprising convergences. Woven through prisoners' interview narratives were periodic references to the humanity of guards and the difficult job they have, as well as nods to the exigencies of running a prison and affirmations of carceral logic. CDCR staff in turn almost uniformly endorsed the idea of prisoners' rights—at least in the abstract—and occasionally lambasted colleagues for being "knuckleheads" when they were not adequately cognizant of those rights. These convergences should not be overstated, as the interviews mostly revealed the parties' predictably adversarial positions, but neither should they be missed.

Our analysis of the written grievances presents a radical contrast to these discursive moments of convergence. Adopting different frames for different purposes, these prisoner appellants and institutional responders rarely had a dialogue, much less any convergence or overlapping meanings. Even when each adopted a legalistic frame, they focused on different dimensions of law. Prisoners, who in their conversations with us often spoke of Title 15 and barely mentioned constitutional rights, in their grievances adopted a legal frame that focused almost entirely on the Constitution and federal law. In contrast, the CDCR did not engage issues of constitutional rights in their grievance responses, focusing instead on Title 15 and its implications for carceral management. The discrepancy of frames is even more pronounced in the case of prisoners who emphasized their needs and were responded to in the language of bureaucracy.

Furthermore, these diverse frames were deployed for altogether different purposes. In these grievances, we find prisoners pushing for an extension of rights and the fulfillment of needs—and thus pushing against carceral logic. In its turn, the CDCR consistently pushes back against rights claims, affirms carceral authority, and prioritizes the "operational realities" of prison. Gone is any hint of convergence or any indication that these two sides inhabit the same cultural world. Instead, prisoners' and officials' grievance narratives are crystallized versions of the two sides of the rights/carceral control tension.

It may be that the more formal legal context, the stakes involved, and the written form taken by grievances evoke this oppositional posture. The absence of the kind of convergences we discovered in our interviews is certainly understandable given the adversarial context of an official dispute. However understandable they are, these shifts in narratives across venues underscore not only the fluidity of legal consciousness but the importance of methodology in tracking it. Most scholars of legal consciousness, legal mobilization, or disputing employ interviews, with a few—such as Lovell (2012)—revealing the advantages of the written record. What we see here, however, are the benefits of an inclusive methodology that shifts data sites to capture the contingencies of participants' narratives and their implications for how disputes and legal meaning in general are constructed.

CHAPTER 8

Conclusion

This is a book about prisons in California at a particular historical moment and about the implications of that institutional context and sociohistorical moment for disputing and more generally for the attitudes and practices of those inside, both captives and captors. The power of institutional context beyond the particulars of any individual is a persistent theme throughout. We began by noting the paradox that these prisoners—among the most stigmatized and vulnerable of populations—name problems and claim redress far beyond what one might expect from the literature on disputing and legal mobilization. While not contesting the general pattern reported in these literatures, we show that particular institutional features can trump the forces that otherwise tend to tamp down legal mobilization. We thus draw attention to the contingency of the effects of self-blame, stigmatization, vulnerability, and the American "ethic of survival" (Bumiller 1988) on legal mobilization, and to the awesome power of institutional context.

We have seen that prisoners' extensive use of the grievance system is the result of not only the considerable array of problems they confront, but also the hyperlegal nature of the total institution that holds them. As Justice Stewart said, for these prisoners, the state prison system is their "landlord," "employer," "tailor," "neighbor," and "banker" (*Preiser v. Rodriguez*, 411 U.S. 475 [1973]). But the state is also their legal captor and, as such, law personified. In this institutional context, law is an unavoidable master text. Borrowing a concept from Goffman (1961) and from DeLand's

(2013, 657) recent study of pick-up basketball players' emphasis on rules and the related prevalence of disputes on the (basketball) court, we found that in prison virtually all behavior is "played in 'the key of law.'" As with DeLand's basketball games, the prevalence of disputes in prison is both a reflection and a constitutive chord of the dominant legal key.

In the total legal institution of the prison, there is extensive naming and claiming despite a heavy dose of cynicism about the process. Because of this cynicism regarding the grievance system and the starkly adversarial nature of the prison context,[1] we were taken by surprise when these prisoners expressed empathy for guards, faith in the power of law and evidence, and respect for the logic of the carceral institution of which they are captive. These men who called the appeals system "a joke," who complained of guards "on some kind of power trip," and who spoke bitterly of being "a bird in a cage" also said—often in the next breath—that officers "are just people like the rest of us," that any unfairness in the system "evens out," that to win an appeal, "the key is being truthful and stating the facts," and that prison is *supposed* to be hard ("This is prison and it's not Disneyland").

Prisoners' conflicting narratives ran parallel to, and sometimes converged with, the U-turns found in our interviews with CDCR staff. Examiners and prison officials lauded the grievance system as "a way of giving voice to people it matters to," "an informational tool," and a hedge against legal liability; and they emphasized that prisoners "have a *right* to file," that "we make mistakes," and that "we're human, they're human." But these affirmations of prisoners' rights and their humanity were laced with potent counterthemes of hostility toward prisoners who exercise their rights, the perception that rights have "gone too far," and the view that the "operational realities" of running a prison "can trump" prisoner rights.

The logics of rights and control are two of the defining ideologies of our age, with their dominance eloquently expressed in Bumiller's *The Civil Rights Society* (1988) and Garland's *The Culture of Control* (2001), respectively. It makes sense that both prisoners and staff articulate the dominant themes of this cultural-ideological context. It makes sense, too, that these themes collide in sometimes starkly contradictory narratives, reflecting the oppositional logics undergirding them, because rights and control are not only dominant cultural strains; they pull in opposite directions at once.

The complex relationship between rights and "penality" was the focus of David Garland's (2013) Sutherland Address to the American

Society of Criminology. In his address, Garland notes that the United States is a "liberal democracy" and that "'liberalism' and 'democracy' are different traditions, involving different political principles and practices." He points out that while "liberalism" promotes freedom and autonomy and restraints on state power, "democracies" give governing power to the people, a power that at the state and local levels often translates into what he calls "penality," and sometimes "full-on punishment" (507). Thus he concludes, "Liberal institutions tend to constrain state punishment in the name of limited government and the rights of individuals. Democratic institutions punish in accordance with majority preferences, whatever these may be. What we call 'liberal democracy' is a merger of (specific kinds of) liberal institutions and (specific kinds of) democratic institutions" (507). Garland implies but does not state outright that the "merger" of these two traditions is a rocky union of potential opposites. As we have seen here, the full force of this tumultuous marriage and its associated tensions came to fruition in the last four decades of the twentieth century, as adherence to their respective tenets intensified simultaneously. Garland argues that the dominance of penality in some states is due to "the declining power of liberalism and liberal elites from the 1970s onward" (507). But while "liberal elites" may no longer hold sway, the rights discourse associated with liberalism is evident in the wide array of movements that continue to deploy it. Indeed, this union of two conflicting logics forms the big picture here; it is reflected in, and helps make sense of, the narratives and counternarratives of our prisoner and staff respondents as they engage the grievance process.

The prisoner grievance system, born of the incarceration explosion and the litigation of a surging population of rights-conscious prisoners, embodies this broad sociocultural tension. The tension reverberates in the conflicting narratives of prisoners and their keepers, as they simultaneously affirm both the validity of prisoner rights and the legitimacy of punishing control. And it percolates beneath the surface of the CDCR hierarchy as grievance responders are alert to the potential downstream legal consequences of flagrant, "stupid" rights violations and mishandled appeals by "knucklehead" personnel whose sole focus is on custody.

If prisoners' and staff's interview narratives incorporate both sides of this tension, in the written grievances the duality is split apart as appellants and responders line up on opposite sides to stake their positions and defend their territory. Using different frames, speaking different languages, and pursuing different purposes, the disputants in this "dialogue" mostly talk past each other, as prisoners push for an extension of rights and fulfillment of needs while the CDCR pushes back, asserting carceral authority and privileging the operational realities of prison. In this crystallized version of the dialectic, the convergences so evident in our interview conversations have vanished as the two embattled sides clash head-on.

The tension between the logics of rights and carceral control is thus revealed in both our interviews and the written documents, albeit in starkly different forms. But as with all things dialectical, these oppositional forces not only conflict but meet in moments of coproduction and synthesis. For example, prison managers told us that the need to prioritize the most fundamental operating principle of prison—ensuring safety and security—sometimes meant that rights must be curtailed and appeals denied. At the same time, however, they were adamant that allowing prisoners to "vent" reduces the possibility of riots and that the information gleaned from 602s can be "a diagnostic" and a tool of order. From this perspective, the two logics intersect, as prisoners' right to appeal the conditions of their confinement becomes an important element of carceral control.

In perhaps the best example of such dialectical synthesis, the grievance system mandated by Congress to limit prisoners' legal mobilization has now become an institutionalized feature of prison life. While the system usually leaves appellants dissatisfied with its outcomes and, more broadly, represents a depoliticalization and narrowing of reform efforts, at the same time its institutionalization, its local instantiation in every prison and jail, and its very physicality in the form of mandated 602 boxes in their cell blocks, stoke prisoners' rights consciousness. Ironically, it may be in prison—this iconic institution of control—that members of our civil rights society are most likely to mobilize for their rights. Indeed, as we have seen, it is in this total institution of law that otherwise disempowered people overcome many of the usual barriers to naming and claiming, and "go get that book and . . . write it up" when a perceived violation occurs.

One of our aims in this study of the inmate grievance process was to explore disputing in this most asymmetrical setting and advance our theoretical understanding of the implications of such asymmetries. In addition to the specific findings outlined above, our research suggests both a narrowing of how we describe such disputes and a broadening out of what they mean for the participants and for rights consciousness. Scholars have often described the dispute as a "site of struggle" (Merry 1990, 16) and a contest over meaning (Frohmann 1998; Lovell 2012; Merry 1990; Yngvesson 1993), characterizations that offer important insights. But it is clear from our findings that the prisoner grievance process is hardly a contest in the usual sense, as the parameters, rules, and outcomes are dictated by the CDCR, and substantive prisoner victories are predictably rare. As Yngvesson (1993, 10) observed over two decades ago, "The analysis of disputes is always an analysis of power relations." In the prison context, where extreme power inequality and appellant vulnerability are defining features, the very term *dispute* seems quaintly euphemistic.

While individual prisoners almost never succeed in incorporating their meaning of events or situations into the outcomes of their claims, the larger meaning of the process may lie elsewhere. For, the very existence of the grievance system affirms to prisoners their identities as rights-bearing subjects. As Alfonso Lopez, alternately diagnosed with pneumonia and valley fever, wrote, "All I know is that my rights are protected by law. And if I'm not being given the best care, there are . . . mechanisms that I can invoke." Some will say these mechanisms are symbolic at best, and officials may tout their utility for managerial control, but at the same time this grievance system keeps alive the promise—if not the fulfillment—of rights.

Clearly, if we are to advance our understanding of the conditions under which people recognize injurious conditions and launch claims, we need to move beyond establishing broad patterns to explore the precise institutional and structural settings that facilitate or inhibit disputing and legal mobilization, as we have begun to do here. Future research might add further detail, for example by specifying the different relationships between racial identification and legal mobilization in varying institutional and social environments.

More broadly, while it is difficult to imagine an institution as overtly regimented by law as the prison, if we think of a continuum along which institutions can be sorted according to the overt or subterranean quality of their legal regimens, we might trace the relationship between this aspect of the institutional environment and legal claims making. Such a continuum would include institutional environments that are physically circumscribed, such as prisons, but also those that are socially, culturally, and legally bounded, such as the world of the welfare poor described by Sarat (1990) and others (Cowan 2004; White 1990).

The present study also has implications for the fluidity and contingency of legal consciousness, affirming much of what previous scholars have reported while adding several theoretical and methodological complexities and caveats. Much as Ewick and Silbey (1998) found that people shift seamlessly from views of law as majestic and neutral to see-ing it as a con game or an oppressive apparatus to be resisted, so too these prisoners and CDCR staff in interviews adopted shifting stances vis-à-vis the grievance system, rights, and criminal justice. However, their apparently inchoate views were not arbitrary nor were their narra-tive U-turns capricious. Instead, our interview respondents—prisoners and officials alike—were drawing from the American cultural tool kit, articulating its tropes and logics, its fissures, cracks, and contradictions.

We found a different kind of fluidity and a different pattern when we looked across sources of data. For while both prisoners and staff in interviews articulated their versions of the extant cultural contradiction between the logics of rights and control, written grievance documents revealed a sharp schism. In contrast to the narratives and counternarra-tives permeating the interviews, in the formal disputes neither side wavered far from a position dictated by their strategic goal. What we learn, once again, is that context matters. The larger cultural context matters in terms of how we interpret the shifts and apparent contradic-tions of the interview narratives, and so too the data context matters if we are to accurately assess the legal consciousness of social actors. Much current research on legal consciousness and on disputing relies on interviews, but we see here that an altogether different picture emerges and interesting fluidities and shifts are uncovered by looking *across* data sources, from interviews to written documents and back. Lovell (2012, 19) says of the letters written by ordinary citizens to the U.S. Justice Department, "Analyzing a large number of these encounters . . . pro-vides an illuminating picture of people's complicated ideas about poli-tics, power, and the legitimacy of law." Analyzing such written docu-ments in conjunction with personal interviews exposes not only the complications and nuances of ideas, but also their fundamental contex-tual contingency.

This methodological approach thus reveals previously understudied contingencies of legal consciousness across data venues. It also invites us to rethink its conceptualization. Most contemporary scholars implic-itly or explicitly define legal consciousness as entailing both attitudes and practice—how people talk but also what they do (Ewick and Silbey 1998; Kirkland 2008; Lovell 2012; Marshall 2003; Nielsen 2004; Silbey 2005). Quite apart from the methodological concern this raises—suggesting that it is not sufficient to base our studies solely on interviews, by definition relying on what people say—the question arises as to the cohesiveness of saying and doing. We have seen here that the way people talk about law in interviews and the way they deploy law in grievances are not necessarily coterminous. To be fair, many scholars acknowledge disconnects in the way people talk about law and how they engage it.[2] However, the prevailing definition of legal consciousness, encompassing in one concept both talk and engagement, implies a coherence that may rarely exist and in any case does little to facilitate empirical examination of their potential dualities. Alternating the data collection context from interviews to archived written grievances exposes the need for precision in our analytical concepts and provides empirical grist for the task.

The context of data collection also matters in another way. In the introduction, we said that it is critical to get inside prison walls to do research in this era of mass incarceration. But a legitimate methodological question arises as to what the benefits of *in*-prison research are, especially in an environment in which researchers find it so hard to gain access (Simon 2000; Wacquant 2002). The answer largely depends, as such answers always do, on what the goal is. A vast sociological and criminological literature on prisons and incarceration reveals that excellent research can be conducted through archives, official statistics, and interviews with formerly incarcerated people. However, for the purposes of some research questions, our experience convinces us that interviewing people in the environments of interest—in this case, prison and the offices of the grievance examiners—delivers an immediacy and a richness that may be flattened out in more physically and temporally distant settings. The icy dismissal of one coauthor by examiner Lucinda Gray; the gender bonding that IAC Stacey Taylor engaged us in ("As you ladies know, . . ."); the abrupt chastening of one of us by prisoner Raymond Sterling over a playful reference to "trouble"—not only do these serendipities of the research context add narrative depth, but they prompt analytical insights and help confirm hunches; in fact, many of the insights presented in our analyses originated in the field as we engaged with the prisoners and institutional staff who occupy center stage in this book.

Further, although there is no way to measure this empirically, the physicality of the setting in which our respondents were interviewed seemed palpably relevant. Interviewing a prisoner in 90-degree heat while ants crawled around us in an infamously infested prison, or another one who was eager to talk to us even though his cuffs chafed his raw wrists and his ankles were shackled to his chair, and yet another who wore only boxer shorts in his cage—these conditions were immediate, raw, and all too "accessible." Above all, they were visceral reminders of the harshness of the conditions to which these prisoners are routinely subjected.

Although not as intense an experience, interviewing CDCR officials at their workplaces was also revealing. The overwhelming nature of officials' task as we interrupted their work flow to interview them was constantly apparent to us. The stacks upon stacks of paperwork in the Sacramento filing room, where shelves of appeals six feet high lined walls fifty feet long and snaked up and down the central aisles, were constant physical reminders to both interviewers and staff respondents of the challenging and hapless task at hand. Beyond the workload issue, the appeals coordinator who flipped her neck scarf and playfully spun around in her swivel chair as she assured us that she was not disturbed by the incident of the gay inmate who hung himself because, after all, "we all make choices," and the official whose hand began to tremble as he conceded that it is "spooky" to facilitate an execution—such field experiences yield insights rarely accessible through more remote means.

In addition to enriching the interview data and allowing for direct observation of prisoners' conditions and staff's work routines, conducting research inside prison produced a number of revealing images. For example, we encountered in cell blocks prisoner grievance boxes complete with padlocks, which served as a compelling symbol of the challenges of the grievance system as well as the locked-in status of those who use it. Another powerful image appeared serendipitously one day during an interview session. As one of us battled the army of ants at her feet in an empty closet-sized lunchroom for custody officials that had been provided us for interviewing prisoners, she noticed a hand-drawn picture taped to the wall, yellowed from age. Its four dog-eared corners satirized a logo of the Legal Defense Fund featuring the scales of justice. Inside the paper square anchored by these logos was written, "If you came here TO BITCH, you can leave now." It was not entirely evident who originally put it there or who the intended audience was—presumably correctional officers in both cases because this was their space—but its message of visceral hostility to rights mobilization came across loud and clear.

Leaving behind these methodological issues, a more substantive point bears addressing before we conclude. Specifically, given the predominance of people of color behind bars and the well-documented racialized nature of criminal justice processes, the relative absence of race in our story may seem surprising. Ideologies of race make an appearance as part of our explanation of staff's perception of prisoners as overentitled whiners, and we have made reference periodically to inmates' race/ethnic self-identifications, including in one case a Mexican prisoner's belief that "we're a hush-hush type of people" as compared to "the blacks." But race and explicitly racialized processes are not a dominant theme in this narrative, which is based closely on our interviews and our sample of written grievances. Indeed, one of the many surprises we encountered as we conducted this research was that, with a few notable exceptions, neither prisoners nor staff spoke much about race in our conversations with them or in the 602 documents. We might expect that prisoners of color (or white prisoners, for that matter, given their minority status in prison [see Smith 2012; and Kruttschnitt and Hussemann 2008]) would sometimes mention race when complaining about treatment by officers or CDCR practices, or that we would find claims of racial discrimination in the grievance files. While a few prisoners talked about race-based gangs and the related challenges of daily interaction, complaints about racist staff were conspicuous in their absence. Similarly, almost none of the official grievances in our sample directly involved questions of race.

It is possible that the relative absence of discussions of race in our interviews with prisoners reflects their reticence to engage the issue in this post–civil rights era, a reticence that arguably could be compounded by perceived racial difference with the interviewer. We cannot discount this possibility, although we are not altogether convinced, given that these men broached a wide range of other controversial topics and their written grievances *also* rarely involved issues related to race (the two exceptions being the Muslim prisoner who wrote that staff discriminated against him post-9/11 and the black prisoner who contested barring his Swahili dictionary as "cultural/racial discrimination"). Whatever the reason for the scant mention of race in these prisoners' verbal complaints and the sample of written grievances, it is indicative of our fidelity to the data that race remains mostly unspoken here.

That said, it should not be missed that approximately three-quarters of the prisoners we interviewed were men of color (and almost two-thirds of staff were people of color), as is the overall California prison population from which our sample of grievances comes—a percentage that has risen in tandem with the incarceration boom of the last four decades. Further, these men are largely segregated by race in prison. In this context, race makes its appearance as an embedded feature of the institution, if not an individual topic of conversation or issue of formal dispute. Race may not have had many speaking parts here, but it set the stage, provided the players, and worked behind the scenes to keep the production running.

It is a production that disproportionately affects marginalized and racialized people, as we know from the vast store of scholarship on racial inequality and the criminal justice system, as well as from much sociological work on the collateral effects of prison and the aftermath of incarceration (Comfort 2008; Goffman 2014; Pager 2007; Pettit and Western 2004). But we should not lose sight of the fact that this ongoing production affects us all in one way or another. Borrowing from the public health domain, where it is well understood that human communities share microbial space, it is clear that we too share the fallout of social practices that marginalize and justice systems that perpetrate injustice.

This notion that, for better or for worse, our social space is shared (much as we share our biological habitat) was brought home to us in a powerful way as we were writing this conclusion. An article in *The New York Times*, "In Texas, Inmates and Officers Swelter" (Lowry 2013, A29), brought us back to the issue of dangerously hot prison cells with which we began our book. Noting that it is sometimes 130 degrees inside Texas prisons and that fourteen prisoners have died from the heat in the last six years, the article's author observes that the new $750,000 swine-production facilities at these prisons are to be climate controlled. The dangerous conditions the author describes—with the added indignity that air conditioning is provided for animals housed at the prisons—are much like those reported by California prisoner James Williams. Strikingly, however, in this case the author is a correctional officer. Underscoring their shared predicament, he writes, "The correctional officers, whose working conditions are the same as the inmates' living conditions, have taken note," and their union is supporting the wrongful-death lawsuits launched by the families of the deceased inmates. He concludes, "Texas needs to ensure humane conditions for the inmates who live in prisons and the officers who work there. After all, people shouldn't be treated worse than the livestock" (A29). The point is not that prisoners and officers suffer equally—of course they do not, most obviously because the latter return home every day after their shift. But this Texas case serves as both a metaphor for the shared physical and social space that we ultimately all inhabit—albeit with dramatically different degrees of privilege—and as a fitting end to our story about the tangled logics of incarceration and rights and the sometimes surprising convergences that surface from deep within.

We conclude by offering a word of caution and drawing out its implications for future research and policy. As we explained in the introduction, our focus on the tension between the rights revolution of the late twentieth century and the simultaneously advancing culture of control by no means implies that these conflicting logics are always mutually exclusive, even in the prison context. Examples of relatively open prisons that incorporate unusual levels of freedom exist around the world and throughout history, including the United States. The fact that the United States is now in an era of unusual "penal excess" (Pratt 2008, 119) in terms of the numbers incarcerated and the conditions of confinement itself attests to this variability. To expose the tension, in other words, does not imply that it is hopeless to advocate for rights in the context of prison. Quite the opposite. It underscores the importance of vigilance, of getting into these mammoth institutions to analyze the dynamics of life inside, to make visible the usually invisible contest transpiring there between the promise of rights and the awesome power of carceral logic, and to propose reforms that may temper the excesses of the latter.

Systemic improvements in the way prisoners' grievances are processed must be one priority. The conditions the U.S. Supreme Court found unconstitutional in *Brown v. Plata* (2011) have been appealed for years to no avail by prisoners through their grievances. Nor has the Supreme Court decision radically altered these conditions. In February 2014, inspectors in California's newest correctional institution, the California Health Care Facility in Stockton, found grossly unsanitary facilities, an outbreak of scabies, and the death of a prisoner whose calls for help went unanswered (St. John 2014, AA1). According to one reporter, inmates "had been left overnight in their own feces, confined to broken wheelchairs or forced to go without shoes . . . and incontinent men . . . received catheters that did not fit" (St. John 2014, AA1, AA6). The facility remains open but has been prohibited by a court overseer from accepting new admissions.

If these conditions are to be remedied, it will be in part through pushback from those who inhabit these places of confinement using an appeals process that works. An effective appeals process would necessarily involve an entity with institutional independence from the CDCR, for the objective adjudication of any case is well-nigh impossible when the outcome is determined entirely by one of the parties to the case. An independent agency modeled on the parliamentary ombudsman in England might respond to prisoner grievances as well as exercising broad oversight of the prison system (Deitch 2012, 239–40). In the absence of such full institutional independence, the participation of a panel that includes both prisoner and third-party representatives at each level of review could help partially offset the built-in bias. Of course, such reforms would multiply the work involved in processing the thousands of appeals filed each year and, given the already daunting workload of grievance responders—not to mention the lack of political will—are probably unfeasible.

In the long run, a prerequisite to any real improvement in the grievance system and in the conditions contested by its prisoner appellants is a significant reversal of the trend toward mass incarceration that triggered the PLRA's institutionalization of internal remedies in the first place. A dramatic reduction in the number of people in prison is not a guarantee of improved conditions, but it is a necessary step for any meaningful improvements in either the conditions or the grievance system through which those conditions are contested. In the meantime, as Nathaniel Forest told us, "They decide. You just complain."

Procedures for Interviews with Prisoners

Before any interviewing began, we engaged in extensive training with our research team to address procedures for obtaining informed consent, maintaining confidentiality, and responding to the kind of special circumstances that researchers encounter when conducting research in prison settings, as well as standard interviewing techniques and probing strategies. Above all, we aimed to reduce interviewer bias and ensure that all subjects were approached in a similar fashion to participate in the study, were asked standard questions in similar ways, and—as much as possible in this most coercive of settings—did not feel required to participate.

Prisoner interviewing began in July 2009 and ended in late September 2009. During this time, members of the interview team traveled to each of the three prisons and completed 120 face-to-face interviews with prisoners, including some who were confined to administrative segregation ("Ad Seg," or what prisoners call "the hole"). The two coauthors did the majority (60 percent) of these prisoner interviews. Once these interviews were complete, the coauthors returned to these same prisons and interviewed CDCR staff who participate in processing inmate grievances—including all wardens, deputy wardens, and appeals coordinators, as well as two randomly chosen captains in each prison. Finally, we traveled to Sacramento to interview key administrative officials and randomly selected examiners in the Inmate Appeals Branch, which conducts the final review of grievances.

For the prisoner interviews, we made every effort to secure a random sample and ensure that officials did not interfere with sample selection either on purpose or inadvertently. About ten days prior to the first day of interviewing at a particular prison, we requested from the CDCR Office of Research the official roster that identified every person housed in the prison by name and CDCR number. From this roster, we used Statistical Package for the Social Sciences

(SPSS) to randomly select fifty inmates to serve as potential study participants, with the goal of interviewing the first forty (the other ten would serve as backup candidates for interviews in case of denials or when a prisoner in our original sample had been transferred or released by the time we arrived to conduct interviews). We then sent the list to our liaison at the prison, typically the public information officer or another lieutenant, so that the first forty prisoners could be notified by a ducat that they were invited to meet with an interviewer. This process resulted in a 93 percent participation rate, an unusually high rate of participation in any research setting, and one that may have been enhanced by our "outsider" status, as discussed in the introduction.

Two practices were key to protecting the integrity of random selection, guaranteeing prisoner privacy and confidentiality, and ensuring that participation was as voluntary as possible in a prison setting. First, ducats stated the appointment was for "research on prison life" or "interview," and officers were asked not to discuss the research with inmates. Although we briefed upper-level prison administrators on why the research team was at the facility and why they were there for multiple days, we made an effort to keep rank-and-file officers, especially those who escorted prisoners to and from interviews, unaware of the purpose of the study. We did so to minimize the degree to which they could intentionally or unintentionally contaminate the field or otherwise undermine the research. Despite our best efforts, on occasion it was clear that rank-and-file officers had a (in some cases erroneous) sense of why we were there; we did not confirm or deny their assumptions. Second, if an inmate could not be scheduled for the interview—for example, because he had been paroled, transferred, or was in the hospital—the CDCR staff was instructed to note the reason and then proceed to the next randomly selected person on the list until all interview appointments were filled. A few people who were scheduled for interviews did not show up for the meeting, in which case they were given the opportunity to be interviewed on a subsequent day. They occasionally had another appointment at the same time (e.g., a medical appointment or a work assignment), and sometimes we were told that an inmate chose not to leave his cell.

These one-on-one interviews were conducted in strictly confidential settings where only the interviewer and interviewee were present and they could not be overheard. The location varied depending on available space. For example, we interviewed in correctional counselors' offices, staff lunch rooms, chapels, and visiting rooms, as well as conference rooms and what appeared to be custodial closets. Once inmate respondents had given their informed consent to be interviewed,[1] we asked their permission to record the interview—with the understanding that the recorder could be turned off at any time—and 91 percent of them agreed to be recorded.

The interviewer asked prisoners both closed and open-ended questions about housing arrangements, daily prison life, problematic or bothersome conditions, perceptions of the inmate appeals process, involvement with the appeals process, assessments of the legitimacy of the appeals process, perceived fairness of the criminal justice system, and recommendations for improving the grievance system. After a few initial rapport-building questions, we asked about any problems in prison and how they dealt with those problems. Later in the interview, we asked if they had filed any grievances and, if they had, what they were about. At this point, we inquired specifically about and completed an "incident form" that we developed to capture data on specific instances of grievance filing. The incident form we created for the purpose of this study focused on (1) a grievance the respondent had filed that was resolved informally, (2) the most recent grievance he had filed, (3) the most important grievance he had filed, and (4) a grievance he had filed, if any, that had been granted. In addition, at the end of the interview, we read a series of statements (e.g., , "The inmate grievance process works pretty well," "Staff retaliate against inmates who file," etc.), to which we asked respondents to "strongly agree, agree, disagree, strongly disagree, or neither agree nor disagree." The interview instrument was semistructured in format and included follow-up questions that led to free-flowing exchanges. This allowed the prisoners, who are often restricted from speaking with outsiders, to share their personal stories and have their voices heard. The average interview length was slightly over one hour, with the shortest interview lasting just under half an hour, and some interviews extending well over two hours.

As a final step, we concatenated official data from the CDCR's database on inmates (OBIS) to the interview data. Because privacy concerns required that the identities of participants be kept confidential, we requested and received central file information on eighty prisoners from each of the prisons (our sample of forty per prison, plus forty "decoys").

The coding process began with the authors taking notes during the data collection period to track emergent ideas and themes. Once prisoner interviewing was complete, we read through a subset of transcribed interviews to develop preliminary coding categories designed to capture, among other things, (1) what prisoners identified as problems; (2) how they made sense of those problems, including attributions of blame for problems associated with prison life; (3) what grievances they had filed; and (4) whether they felt fairly treated by the criminal justice system. A team of four advanced graduate students then did "focused coding" (Charmaz 2006) of all the transcribed interviews—coding that was subjected to multiple checks by members of the research team. These coded data, coupled with the quantitative data from our interviews, concatenated official data, and research notes, form the basis for our analyses and arguments relating to the extent and nature of prisoner grievance filing, its meaning to the prisoner appellants, how and why it differs from disputing patterns in other stigmatized and vulnerable populations, and how to make sense of these differences.

Procedures for Interviews with CDCR Personnel

After the research team had interviewed all 120 prisoners in our sample, the two coauthors returned to interview key CDCR personnel in these three prisons and went to the Inmate Appeals Branch in Sacramento to interview appeals officials and examiners. Table 6 provides a summary profile of the CDCR staff we interviewed. We followed the same protocol for these interviews as for those with prisoners, with regard to obtaining informed consent, maintaining confidentiality, and minimizing interviewer bias.

There were, however, several notable differences between our prisoner and staff interviews. First, not all of our CDCR interview subjects were randomly chosen. While we interviewed a random sample of two captains at each prison and three examiners at the Inmate Appeals Branch, we interviewed all three wardens, all deputy wardens, and all appeals coordinators at each prison, as well as the director and deputy director of the Inmate Appeals Branch. Second, we were not authorized by the CDCR to audio-record the staff interviews. For this reason, the coauthors personally conducted all of these interviews and did so jointly. In this way, one of us was able to take extensive notes—including direct quotes—and filled in the interview instrument, while the other also took notes but more actively engaged with the respondent. At the end of each day, we spent hours discussing and audio-recording our field notes. Finally, these interviews tended to take longer than the prisoner interviews, not infrequently lasting several hours or more. If not everyone was at first eager to participate, once they began talking, many respondents were clearly happy to continue the conversation as long as we would listen.

Our staff interview questions followed many of the same substantive themes, often using the same wording, as those for our prisoner interviews. We began with rapport-building questions, then moved to a discussion of the details of the grievance processing system—including how it works both in theory and in fact. This was followed by questions about specific grievances they had participated in and their opinions about the legitimacy and fairness of the system. The interview ended with the same set of "agree/disagree" statements we used with prisoners.

Coding the Sample of Grievances

The coauthors initially read a subset of twenty-five prisoner narratives from the grievance sample and provided the research team with a short list of narrative "frames" with which to begin coding the prisoner grievances. This initial list included "legalistic/legal rights," "needs," and "accountability." As the team coded the complete sample, "procedural justice," "fair play," "discrimination," and other less frequently used frames were added as they emerged inductively from the data. In recognition of the fact that multiple frames may be used in the same narrative, in addition to coding for these primary frames, we coded each grievance at every level for possible secondary frames, although not all grievances included a secondary frame.

We used the same procedure for coding staff frames. The initial list of staff frames included "bureaucratic," "policy/procedure," and "legalistic/legal rights." As the full sample was coded, "medical expertise," "needs," "safety/security," and "budgetary constraints" also surfaced, albeit much more rarely. Subsequent to coding, the "policy/procedure" frame was merged with "legalistic/legal rights," because both refer to legal mandates. This merging made it symmetrical with the "legalistic/legal rights" prisoner frame, which included references to policy and official procedures. Similar to the frame coding of inmate grievances, the research team coded staff grievances for primary and possible secondary frames at each of the four levels of review.

Our general definitions of specific prisoner frames were straightforward. "Legalistic/legal rights" frames, for example, included repeated references to constitutional law, statutory law, judicial decisions, the California Code of Regulations/Title 15, or other formal policies. "Needs" frames were characterized by an appellant's emphasis on his physical, mental, or emotional well-being. "Accountability" frames focused on a prisoner's insistence that the CDCR and its employees take responsibility for their actions. Complaints focusing on "procedural justice" emphasized that the procedures themselves were unjust. "Fairness" focused on the principle of equal treatment and playing by the rules. "Discrimination" frames made an explicit claim of biased decision making or official behavior.

Among staff frames, "legalistic/legal rights" was originally applied only to those staff responses that emphasized constitutional law, statutory law, or judicial decisions, while "policy/procedure" was reserved for those that emphasized the California Code of Regulations/Title 15 or other more local policies. The "bureaucratic" frame focused on the decisions of internal administrative committees, classification schemes, and logistical calculations, such as those related to bed space. "Medical expertise" frames emphasized the authority of the medical staff and prioritized their opinions. "Safety/security" frames were characterized by an emphasis on these mission-related imperatives apart from and in addition to other considerations. While it might seem odd that "safety/ security" rarely showed up as a dominant frame in and of itself, this is no doubt because that frame was often eclipsed by an emphasis on policy or bureaucratic processes in which the safety and security rationale was already implicitly embedded.

Our team of four trained research assistants worked diligently to achieve reliability in coding. They first coded a subset of ten grievances each and then compared their results and reasoning. This process was repeated until we were confident that their coding evaluations were comparable, and thereafter they proceeded to code the full sample. In the end, this system yielded a reasonable level of intercoder reliability. Agreement on the frame variable across these four coders, across multiple levels of review, and for staff and inmates, averaged 79.5 percent. Reliability was lowest for prisoners' narratives at the informal level (with percentage agreement on these prisoner frames falling to 60.9 percent) and highest at the first and second formal levels, where percentage agreement on staff frames reached over 91.3 percent. Relatively low intercoder reliability for prisoners' narratives at the informal level is probably in part the result of longer text at that level combined with prisoners' frequent use of multiple frames.

COMPLETE LIST OF PRISONER AND STAFF FRAMES

Prisoner frames	Staff Frames
Legalistic/legal rights	Bureaucratic
Needs	Policy/procedure
Accountability	Legalistic/legal rights
Procedural justice	Medical expertise
Fairness	Safety/security
Discrimination	Needs
Mistake made	Budget
Deservedness	Human mistake
Importance of principle	Overcrowding

Compassion   Logic/reason

Human rights   Other

Safety and security

Other

Cases

Abdul-Akbar v. McKelvie, 239 F.3d 307 (3d Cir. 2001).
Adarand Construction v. Pena, 515 U.S. 200 (1995).
Blackmon v. Garza, No. 11–40316 (5th Cir. 2012). Accessed July 16, 2013,
  http://www.ca5.uscourts.gov/opinions/unpub/11/11–40316.0.wpd.pdf.
Booth v. Churner, 532 U.S. 731 (2001).
Brown v. Board of Education, 347 U.S. 483 (1954).
Brown v. Plata, 583 U.S. __, 131 S. Ct. 1910 (2011).
Campbell v. Chaves, 402 F. Supp. 2d 1101 (D. Ariz. 2005).
City of Memphis v. Greene, 451 U.S. 100 (1981).
City of Richmond v. J.A. Croson Co., 488 U.S. 469 (1989).
Cooper v. Pate, 378 U.S. 546 (1964).
Crawford v. Board of Education, 458 U.S. 527 (1982).
Cruz v. Jordan, 80 F. Supp. 2d 109 (S.D.N.Y. 1999).
Farmer v. Brennan, 511 U.S. 825 (1994).
Gates v. Cook, 376 F.3d 323 (2004).
Gideon v. Wainwright, 372 U.S. 335 (1963).
Gregory v. Chicago, 394 U.S. 111 (1969).
Griswold v. Connecticut, 381 U.S. 479 (1965).
Higgins v. Carpenter, 258 F.3d 797 (8th Cir. 2001).
Hudson v. Palmer, 468 U.S. 517 (1984).
Johnson v. California, U.S. 499 (2004).
Jones v. Bock, 549 U.S. 199 (2007).
Lawrence v. Texas, 539 U.S. 558 (2003).
Lee v. Washington, 390 U.S. 333 (1968).
Luedtke v. Gudmanson, 971 F.Supp. 1263 (E.D. Wis. 1997).
Mapp v. Ohio, 367 U.S. 643 (1961).
McCleskey v. Kemp, 481 U.S. 279 (1987).

McGore v. Wrigglesworth, 114 F.3d 601 (6th Cir. 1997).

Miranda v. Arizona, 384 U.S. 486 (1966).

Neal v. Goord, 267 F.3d 116 (2d. Cir. 2001)

Oses v. Fair, 739 F.Supp. 707 (1990).

Preiser v. Rodriguez, 411 U.S. 475 (1975).

Regents of The University of California v. Bakke, 438 U.S. 265 (1978).

Rhodes v. Chapman, 452 U.S. 337 (1981).

Roe v. Wade, 410 U.S. 113 (1973).

Romer v. Evans, 517 U.S. 620 (1996).

Smith v. Sullivan, 553 F.2d 373 (1977).

Street v. New York, 394 U.S. 576 (1969).

Tinker v. Des Moines, 393 U.S. 503 (1969).

Todd v. Graves, 217 F. Supp. 2d. 958 (S.D. Iowa 2002).

Turner v. Safley, 482 U.S. 78 (1987).

Washington v. Davis, 426 U.S. 229 (1976).

Wilson v. Seiter, 501 U.S. 294 (1991).

Wilson v. Yaklich, 148 F.3d 596 (6th Cir. 1998).

Woodford v. Ngo, 548 U.S. 81 (2006).

Notes

I. INTRODUCTION

1. All prisoners' names used in this book, with the exception of those cited in lawsuits, are pseudonyms, as are those of CDCR officials.

2. Courts have found that subjecting prisoners to intense heat may in some circumstances be a violation of the Eighth Amendment's prohibition of "cruel and unusual punishment" (see, e.g., *Blackmon v. Garza*, No. 11–40316 [5th Cir. 2012]; *Gates v. Cook*, 376 F.3d 323 [2004]; *Smith v. Sullivan*, 553 F.2d 373, 381 [1977]; *Wilson v. Seiter*, 501 U.S. 294, 304 [1991]). Over time, the courts have declared that the Constitution "does not mandate comfortable prisons" (*Rhodes v. Chapman*, 452 U.S. 337, 349 [1981]), but that prison officials "must provide humane conditions of confinement; prison officials must ensure that inmates receive adequate food, clothing, shelter, and medical care, and must 'take reasonable measures to guarantee the safety of the inmates'" (*Farmer v. Brennan*, 511 U.S. 825, 832 [1994], quoting *Hudson v. Palmer*, 468 U.S. 517, 526–27 [1984]).

3. Albiston 1999, 2005; Blackstone, Uggen, and McLaughlin 2009; Earl 2009; Edelman and Cahill 1998; Edelman, Erlanger, and Lande 1993; Edelman, Uggen, and Erlanger 1999; Emerson and Messinger 1977; Engel and Munger 2003; Felstiner, Abel, and Sarat 1980–81; Hendley 2010; Hoffmann 2001, 2003, 2005; Major and Kaiser 2005; Marshall 2003; Morrill et al. 2010; Nielsen 2004; Nielsen and Nelson 2005; Yngvesson 1993.

4. Brief of California Correctional Peace Officers Association and Brief of the Prison Law Office, *Plata v. Schwarzenegger*, 603 F.3d 1088 (9th Cir. 2010); Bureau of Audits and Investigation 2010; Petersilia 2008; Charles Piller, "California Senate Probe Rips Prison Watchdogs." *Sacramento Bee*, December 7, 2010, 1A; Piller, "Guards Accused of Cruelty, Racism." *Sacramento Bee*, May 9, 2010, 1A; Piller, "The Public Eye: Due Process for Prisoner Proceedings Allegedly Violated." *Sacramento Bee*, August 1, 2010, 1A.

5. While we focus here on California prisons, similar conditions have been reported throughout the United States and its territories. Conditions in the Criminal Justice Complex in St. Thomas, the U.S. Virgin Islands, were described during congressional hearings in 1996: "Food preparation areas were infested with roaches, flies, rats and mice. Overflowing toilets caused flooding in prisoner cells, soaking mattresses, bedding and personal belongings kept on the floors of the cells due to overcrowding. Cells were infested with flies, mosquitoes, rats, mice and cockroaches. . . . Asbestos particles were falling from the roofs of cells (Mark I. Soler, president of the Youth Law Center, Hearings on the Prison Litigation Reform Act, quoted in Kuzinski 1997–98, 364). In New York State, an inmate—sentenced for shoplifting and with a long history of mental illness—was found dead in his segregation cell, tied to a concrete "bed." As told by a reporter (Sander 2006, A20): "Shackled to a concrete slab, Timothy Joe Souders spent the final days of his life naked and lying in his own urine, sweating through temperatures higher than 100 degrees in an isolated prison cell. . . . His death led prison officials to revise restraint policies for unruly prisoners, limiting 'top of the bed' restraints to a maximum of six hours." When a federal judge in Michigan ordered a complete ban on such restraints, calling the practice "torture," the response from prison officials was chilling. Such restraints, they said, were "nationally accepted, effective practices in correctional populations" (quoted in Sander 2006, A20).

6. Interesting prison fieldwork has been conducted in other countries, particularly the United Kingdom (see, for example, Bosworth 1999; Carrabine 2005; Crewe 2005; Sparks 1994; Sparks and Bottoms 1995).

7. See Feeley (2007) and Katz (2006, 2007) for incisive portrayals of IRB practices as censorship and their bureaucratic mandates as overzealous, mindless impediments to basic research.

8. As described in detail in the next chapter, the inmate appeals process at the time of our research included four levels of review, beginning with an informal review and ending with a final review done on behalf of the CDCR director of adult institutions in the state capitol. Unfortunately, the CDCR collects systematic data only on the grievances that make it to the third formal level of review.

9. The three prisons have been given pseudonyms.

10. There is an extensive literature on such researcher effects, with much of it focused on the impact of racial differences between researcher and respondent (Davis 1997; Davis and Silver 2003; Davis et al. 2010; Ellison, McFarland, and Krause 2011; McDermott 2011; Reese et al. 1986), and a sparser scholarship on class (Krysan 1988; McDermott 2011) and gender differences (Davis et al. 2010; Huddy et al. 1997; Kane and Macaulay 1993). The findings of these studies are inconclusive. On the whole, they suggest that such interviewer effects are most likely when the topics being discussed relate directly to the interviewer/respondent difference. For example, the racial difference between interviewer and respondent is most likely to affect responses when the topic is explicitly race-related (McDermott 2011). However, comprehensive surveys of this scholarship reveal that the issue is complex, with some scholars suggesting that matching interviewer and respondent by race may introduce its own biases (Davis et al. 2010; Fendrich et al. 1999; Johnson and Parsons 1994; Reese et al.

1986; Rhodes 2004), and that interviewer effects are overlaid with and often mediated by situational and environmental factors (McDermott 2011; Rhodes 1994).

11. Adolfo Flores was the only prisoner who explicitly told us he was nervous. "The nervousness," he explained, "is because I'm not used to bein' around, uh, outside people. I've been in prison almost sixteen years and, uh, so we're used to bein' in with officers and inmates, and when you get close to somebody on the outside, it's kind of awkward." Despite his initial nervousness, Adolfo—who was interviewed in handcuffs and shackled to his chair because he was on "lockdown" status (a condition in which whole prisons, cell blocks, or certain categories of prisoners are confined to their cells)—engaged with us in a conversation that lasted almost two hours and touched on a range of personal and institutional issues.

12. One possible explanation for this respondent's behavior is that the primary interviewer had asked her about the burden of proof when an inmate alleges a violation of policy. Lucinda responded that the burden of proof is always on the one bringing the charges, in this case the prisoner. The interviewer nodded knowingly and expanded in what she thought was affirming agreement: "Just like in a trial, the burden is always on the prosecution." Lucinda's eyes flashed and she retorted angrily, apparently resenting the insinuation that a prisoner could ever be "the prosecutor," even in an analogy: "*No, not like that!* It's *always* about what the *prisoner* did!" This exchange may explain the hostility Lucinda exhibited in the rest of the interview. It is also a testament to the considerable barrier that prisoners confront in presenting themselves as legitimate claimants, a topic discussed in later chapters.

13. Seven of these fully granted grievances could not be found in the Inmate Appeals Branch files. After repeated unsuccessful attempts to locate them, we settled on the final "granted" group of thirty. It is unclear why such a relatively large percentage of granted grievances were missing, especially considering that we readily located all of our original random sample of 292 appeals.

14. *Cooper v. Pate*, 378 U.S. 546 (1964).

15. *Mapp v. Ohio*, 367 U.S. 643 (1961); *Gideon v. Wainright*, 372 U.S. 335 (1963); *Miranda v. Arizona*, 384 U.S. 486 (1966).

16. *Griswold v. Connecticut*, 381 U.S. 479 (1965); *Roe v. Wade*, 410 U.S. 113 (1973).

17. *Gregory v. Chicago*, 394 U.S. 111 (1969); *Tinker v. Des Moines*, 393 U.S. 503 (1969); *Street v. New York*, 394 U.S. 576 (1969).

18. George Wallace, governor of Alabama in the 1960s and notorious opponent of racial integration and civil rights for blacks, ran for governor again in 1983. Apologizing for his previous positions on race, Wallace was re-elected with a heavy infusion of votes from blacks. Senator Robert Byrd apologized multiple times for his opposition to the Civil Rights Act. Among long-term politicians of the period, Senator Strom Thurmond stands out for his refusal to apologize for his voting record on civil rights.

19. See, for example, *Crawford v. Board of Education*, 458 U.S. 527 (1982); *McKleskey v. Kemp*, 481 U.S. 279 (1987); *Washington v. Davis*, 426 U.S. 229 (1976); *City of Memphis v. Greene*, 451 U.S. 100 (1981).

20. See, for example, *Adarand Construction v. Pena*, 515 U.S. 200 (1995); and *City of Richmond v. J.A. Croson Co.*, 488 U.S. 469 (1989).

21. 42 U.S.C. § 12101 et seq.

22. 18 U.S.C. § 3771 et seq.

23. Randall Williams (2010) and others have noted this conjunction of rights movements and repression in a global context, linking the expansion of human rights in authoritarian regimes and the overt and covert violence of U.S. imperialism.

24. *Farmer v. Brennan*, 511 U.S. 825 (1994); *Gates v. Cook*, 376 F.3d 323 (2004); *Hudson v. Palmer*, 468 U.S. 517 (1984); *Rhodes v. Chapman*, 452 U.S. 337 (1981); *Smith v. Sullivan*, 553 F.2d 373 (1977); *Turner v. Safley* 482 U.S. 78 (1987); *Wilson v. Seiter*, 501 U.S. 294 (1991).

25. In 2013, the racially segregated nature of California's prisons for men was showcased in an online public interest news source (Thompson 2013). In this article, the author described a practice in California prisons that includes posting colored signs above the doors of cells, with each color indicating a particular racial or ethnic group (black, white, Hispanic, and other).

26. As of this writing, the most recent court decision relating to racial segregation in prison involved the lockdown practices of California's maximum-security Pelican Bay State Prison (*In re José Morales*, 1st District Court of Appeals of California, filed 1/23/13). In that case, the First District Court of Appeals declared unconstitutional the practice at Pelican Bay of restricting the movement and activities of prisoners based on their race when an incident of violence or threatened violence by race-based gangs occurred. Once again leaving the door open to the discretion of prison managers, the court made an exception for situations deemed by management to be emergencies.

2. "NEEDLES," "HAYSTACKS," AND "DEAD WATCHDOGS"

1. California Inspector General Robert A. Barton (2011, 1) was explicit in linking the threat of riots to the establishment of a grievance system in California: "In the wake of several high-profile inmate riots and takeovers of prisons nationwide during the 1960s and 1970s, reviews of those incidents determined that one of the primary reasons for inmate unrest was inmates' belief that no process existed for them to have their legitimate concerns and grievances addressed by correctional management. As a result, the state determined that it was in the best interests of the inmates, the correctional employees, and the public to create an inmate appeal process. That process, now commonly referred to as the 602 appeal process, commenced in the mid-1970s and has continually evolved since that time."

2. Since the explosion in inmate litigation was a predictable consequence of the skyrocketing number of inmates, Schlanger (2003, 1587) notes with some sarcasm, "It would be equally appropriate to talk about a 'deluge' of inmate requests for food."

3. Judge Newman (1996, 521) reported, "In the 'salad bar' case, forty-three prisoners filed a twenty-seven page complaint alleging major prison deficiencies, including overcrowding, forced confinement of prisoners with contagious dis-

eases, lack of proper ventilation, lack of sufficient food, and food contaminated by rodents. The prisoners' reference to salads was part of an allegation that their basic nutritional needs were not being met. . . . In the 'beige towel' case, the suit was not brought because of a color preference. The prisoner's claim was that the prison had confiscated the towels and a jacket that the prisoner's family had sent him, and then disciplined him with loss of privileges for receipt of the package from his family. . . . In the 'chunky peanut butter' case, the prisoner did not sue because he received the wrong kind of peanut butter. He sued because the prison had incorrectly debited his prison account [for peanut butter purchased and other items]." Newman concluded that such "misleading characterization[s]" (522) of prisoner lawsuits were used to condemn all such litigation as frivolous.

4. The filing fee may be waived if the prisoner is "under imminent danger of serious physical injury" (28 U.S.C. Section 1915[g]).

5. Hearing on H.R. 4109, Prison Abuse Remedies Act of 2007: Testimony before U.S. Congress, House of Representatives Subcommittee on Crime, Terrorism, and Homeland Security, 110th Cong., April 22, 2008, 4–5.

6. The case involved an inmate (Ngo) at San Quentin State Prison in California who, as part of a disciplinary action, was denied access to religious programs such as Bible study sessions. Because Ngo did not initiate his complaint within the fifteen-day period stipulated by California policy, his internal grievance was rejected. Ngo argued that the complaint referred to ongoing treatment and not an isolated incident, and that therefore his appeal was in fact timely. When this argument was rejected by internal reviewers, he turned to the federal courts, where he lost his case because, the judges maintained, he had not met the internal filing deadline and therefore had not properly used the grievance process.

7. In the early 1980s before enactment of the Prison Litigation Reform Act, Brakel (1982) speculated about how a federal exhaustion requirement would work. "An exhaustion requirement," Brakel said, "would no doubt open the grievance procedure to a variety of due process mandates." As we see here, such federal mandates have been conspicuous in their absence.

8. Hearing on H.R. 4109, Prison Abuse Remedies Act of 2007.

9. Brief of Amici Curiae in Support of Petitioners' Writ of Certiorari, Jones v. Bock, No. 05-7058 and Williams v. Overton, No. 05-7142 (filed 2006), 42.

10. Feeley and Swearingen (2004, 472) have likened California inmate grievance procedures to "a Potemkin's village," in that the formal procedures appear to be fair and effective, but they "ward off judicial scrutiny by adopting only the patina of bureaucratic form."

11. Robert Berke and Michael Dillard, Department of Corrections Inmate Grievance and Appeal Procedures: A Report of the Senate Select Committee on Penal Institutions (Sacramento, CA: Senate Select Committee on Penal Institutions, 1973), quoted in Nelson P. Kempsky, "Memo from Deputy Director of Corrections, Nelson Kempsky, to Director of Corrections, R.K. Procunier," April 30, 1973, California State Archives, Department of Corrections, Legal Affairs: 4. Procedural Files, ID#F3717: 973, 1900–1908.

12. D.J. McCarthy, "Memo from Superintendent of California Men's Colony, D.J. McCarthy, to Deputy Director of Corrections, Nelson Kempsky," May

15, 1973, California State Archives, Department of Corrections, Legal Affairs: 4. Procedural Files, ID#F3717: 973, 1900–1908.

13. L.S. Nelson, "Memo from Warden of California State prison, San Quentin, L.S. Nelson, to Deputy Director of Corrections, Walter E. Craven," May 31, 1973, California State Archives, Department of Corrections, Legal Affairs: 4. Procedural Files, ID#F3717: 973, 1900–1908.

14. R.K. Procunier, "Memo from Director of Corrections, R.K. Procunier, to Senator John A. Nejedly, Chair, California Senate Select Committee on Penal Institutions," July 9, 1973, California State Archives, Department of Corrections, Legal Affairs: 4. Procedural Files, ID#F3717: 973, 1900–1908.

15. California State Archives. Department of Corrections. Legal Affairs: 6. Inmate Appeals Quarterly Reports, ID#F3717: 1920–1921.

16. Examiners explained to us that in the past they made more frequent trips to prisons to conduct investigations; however, successive budget cuts, coupled with increased workload, have made prison visits rare.

17. Again, all names of CDCR personnel and prisoners whom we cite are pseudonyms. Because the universe of CDCR personnel is circumscribed, and in some offices (such as the Inmate Appeals Branch) and some positions (such as wardens, deputy wardens, appeals coordinators, etc.) there are so few personnel they might be readily identified, we avoid attaching identifying information (such as race, approximate age, etc.) to their descriptions.

18. Throughout, we leave intact spelling errors, typos, and grammatical mistakes in prisoner grievances and staff responses.

19. Thompkins was an inmate at a prison reception center waiting for transfer to his assigned prison. While the CDCR considers reception centers temporary housing, inmates not infrequently remain there for many months. This inmate expected to be in the reception center for up to six months.

20. The 292 grievances in our random sample average seventeen pages in length, including official responses and attached documentation. The 241 non-disciplinary files are on average fifteen pages, while the 51 disciplinary grievances are on average twenty-eight pages, including the largest file at 101 pages.

21. As we will see in chapter 3, concerns about reprisals for filing grievances—particularly against staff—were widespread, and those concerns were voiced throughout these written appeals.

22. The CDCR allows both individual prisoners and groups of prisoners to file grievances. In our random sample of grievances, 277 (96.5 percent) were submitted by individual prisoners, 10 (3.5 percent) were submitted by groups of prisoners, and 5 were unclear in this regard.

23. A large number of grievances in the sample bypassed the informal level either due to the nature of the complaint or a conflict of interest with the presiding official. Of grievances that do not bypass the informal level, the officials we interviewed were evenly split on whether they thought "they are often granted at the informal level of review." In contrast, the vast majority of prisoners (79.6 percent) said they did not think "they are often granted at the informal level of review."

24. As Milovanovic and Thomas (1989, 55) point out with regard to prisoner litigation, some inmate grievances may result in relief even if they are not

officially granted; however, this informal success rate is impossible to measure empirically.

25. Almost three-quarters (72.7 percent) of these officials also thought they had "partially granted" no more than thirty.

26. It is telling that when we asked prisoners if there were any political groups in prison today working for reform, several told us that if anyone were to do that, they would be sent to "the hole." Ironically, prisoners today may have more formal rights than their predecessors, but their freedom of political speech and association—the political freedoms that facilitated the radical reform movement—have apparently been curtailed in its aftermath. In any case, most of the prisoners we interviewed had little sense of what such a political movement would look like, or even what we were referring to when we asked the question; many initially responded as if we meant racialized gangs. The question resonated only with older African American inmates who said there was no equivalent these days to the Black Panthers and Black Muslims. This is not to say that collective political action by prisoners does not happen, as evidenced by the series of mass hunger strikes in California prisons in 2011 and again in 2013 (Egelko 2013, D5; Medina 2013, A10). The hunger strike of 2013, which at its peak involved thirty thousand prisoners, began as a protest against CDCR practices of solitary confinement and spread to include demands for improved living conditions for all prisoners. Collective pushback is clearly possible even in this environment of official suppression and a depoliticizing culture.

3. NAMING, BLAMING, AND CLAIMING IN AN UNCOMMON PLACE OF LAW

1. See Lawrence Friedman (1971) for an early discussion of "consciousness of right."

2. A ducat is a written form authorizing a prisoner to move around the prison facility for a particular appointment or responsibility, such as a work assignment or medical appointment.

3. These signs are usually posted in areas where only staff may enter and are accompanied by red or yellow lines delineating the exact boundary. In some cases, the signs indicate that an area is out of bounds during certain hours. For example, at one prison there are tables that can be used by prisoners only at certain times of the day, with an "out of bounds" sign posted to that effect and a warning that a 115 will be issued for any violation.

4. Our designations of the race/ethnicity of these prisoners are based on their self-identifications, some of which differ in a number of interesting ways from their official racial classifications. For example, many of those classified by the CDCR as "Hispanic" self-identified as "Mexican," regardless of how many generations they and their families had been U.S. residents or citizens. Conversely, the CDCR sometimes classified men as "Mexican" when they told us they were "Hispanic" or, in one case, "Hispanic/White." Six of the thirty-seven men officially classified as "Black" self-identified as "African American." One man classified by the CDCR as "Black" said he was "Cuban." In the four cases in which

people told us they were of mixed backgrounds—"Indonesian/Mexican," "Mexican and Cuban," "African American/Puerto Rican," and "Korean/ Black"—the CDCR classified them as "Hispanic," "Mexican," "Black," and "Black," respectively. One person who said he was "Native American/Pima" was classified by the CDCR as "Hispanic." Interestingly, the category that remained most consistent across CDCR classification and self-identity was "White." The only (partial) exception to this consistency was Francis Heston. Francis was officially classified as "White" but referred to himself as "European," followed by the statement, "It doesn't matter—whatever they normally do, 'White,' 'Caucasian,' 'European'—it's just my ancestry." Beyond the issue of different classification categories, we are sensitive to the fluid and contingent nature of racial identification, and it must be stressed that these self-descriptors may reflect this moment in time and the prison context. See Saperstein and Penner (2010) for an interesting empirical study of the effect of incarceration on racial identity.

5. Sensitive Needs Yards (SNYs) were established in 1998 as a way to house prisoners who are at risk of violence from other inmates, for example, because they are deactivated gang members or former law enforcement officers, or because of the nature of their crime (e.g., a sex crime, a high-profile crime, etc.). As the *Los Angeles Times* reported in 2005, inmates on SNYs "live with other inmates whose lives, like theirs, would be in danger if they were in the general mix" (Quinones 2005, n.p.).

6. Security Housing Units are a form of indefinite administrative segregation, often used for alleged gang members but also for others whom officials deem too dangerous for other types of housing.

7. Beyond these frequent complaints about living conditions, inadequate medical care, disrespect, and missing property, a number of people talked about the sheer boredom of prison. Martin Pedigrew, who had told us about his skin infection and efforts to get antibiotics, later said, "I'm on my bunk twenty-two hours a day just passing time. . . . It's like if you ever saw the movie *Groundhog Day*. That's what this place is like, over and over. . . . Men like rain because it changes the seasons a little bit." Commenting on the monotony of prison, Orlando Martinez, a Hispanic man who had been in prison over five years on a drug charge, talked movingly about how a group of them had been denied yard time and had just gotten it back. "Believe it or not," he said, "an hour outside, it . . . you know, we can play some handball, we can work out, we can walk the track, you just go out there and sit down, you listen to your headphones or music, and just get lost, and we need that, the yard."

8. In California, prisoners wear blue and correctional officers wear green.

9. There is a statistically significant (at the .01 level) positive correlation between years incarcerated and having filed a grievance. Those who have filed a grievance have spent on average approximately twice as much time in prison as those who have not—9.4 years and 4.1 years, respectively.

10. Jorge Bermudez, who self-identifies as "Mexican," reported filing several grievances. He spontaneously offered, when asked his racial identification, "We're a hush-hush type of people. We don't complain. . . . I mean we complain emotionally, but as far as 'Man, I got a case and I need to fight this case. I'll do

it tomorrow.' It's not gonna happen. And that's the type people we are." When the interviewer asked, "And which group in prison do you think is not the hush-hush people," he responded, "The blacks."

11. The only exception we found to this majority-filing pattern was among the ten people whose interviews were conducted entirely in Spanish. Of these, only four said they had filed a grievance, no doubt explained in part by the added challenge of filing for non-English speakers. Technically, the CDCR is required to "provide the assistance necessary to ensure that inmates who have difficulty communicating in written English have access to the appeal process" (CCR, Title 15 § 3084.1.b); however, there is no indication of any active effort to do so, and no one we spoke with said they had received assistance from the CDCR.

12. While it is possible that some of the grievances these prisoners report were filed at a different facility or custody level, we are confident that current custody level serves as a useful indicator to assess the empirical relationship between custody level and filing.

13. This section of our interview was administered to only eighty-one men from our sample, after an initial run at Desert Valley Center.

14. Prisoners' continued use of the grievance process despite their negative attitudes about it is consistent with Gallagher's (2006) study of legal attitudes and disputing in China.

15. An incident occurred during one interview that was a sharp reminder of how seriously "trouble" is taken in this population. One of the coauthors thought she had developed rapport with Raymond Sterling and happened to joke during the interview that she was "going to get in trouble" for something. Looking straight at her and suddenly serious, Raymond said, "I don't believe that." She asked him what he meant, and he replied derisively, "*You're* not going to get in trouble." The emotional force of this response stunned her, and she apologized, "You are right. I'm sorry." To which Raymond said, quietly but firmly, "So don't say it." Clearly, he knew what getting in trouble was, whatever she was talking about was not it, and she had no right to speak playfully about such serious business.

16. Sarat (1990, 361) describes a similar scenario among the welfare poor in his study of people who sought legal assistance: "They went to legal services without great confidence that their voices would register in that setting or that their speech would matter and doubtful about the efficacy of yet another telling to yet another official 'stranger.'" And much like these prisoners, they appealed to legal services even though they expected retaliation—"to be labeled 'trouble-makers' or 'bad actors'"—if they actually won.

17. Men's Advisory Councils (MACs) are a potential extralegal avenue of redress for some issues. Section 3230 of CCR Title 15 requires the establishment of inmate councils in all California prisons, as vehicles for communication between the inmates and the warden and prison staff. Inmate representatives are elected from each housing unit, with separate representatives for whites, blacks, Hispanics, and—depending on their numbers—other racial groups. As explained in the current "Inmate Orientation Booklet" for reception center inmates at the California Institution for Men, "The express purpose of the MAC

and its representatives is to serve, advise, and communicate with the Warden and other staff those matters of common interest and concern from the general inmate population. The MAC does NOT represent individuals on individual issues. . . . [T]hat is the purpose of the appeals procedure" (2014, 16; emphasis in the original). In short, MACs are confined by law to dealing only with issues that affect the inmate population as a whole and not individual complaints, and this is communicated to inmates when they first enter prison.

18. While the vast majority of these respondents clearly do not file simply to get to court, it is worth noting that any form of legal mobilization on a large scale—whether grievance filing or launching a lawsuit—is inconsistent with the prevailing literature and begs the question of why the prison population is different in this regard.

19. Because our respondents were randomly selected, some came to be interviewed from administrative segregation (Ad Seg). In this case, the officers in the Ad Seg unit brought the respondent out of his cell dressed only in underpants and handcuffs and put him in a single-person cage in a conference room for the interview. Despite these restrictive and oppressive conditions—or maybe because of them—this prisoner seemed eager to talk to us.

20. A prisoner not in our sample told a coauthor in another context, referring to Title 15, "It's the Bible in here."

21. There was remarkably little reference in these interviews to constitutional rights or any other legal documents besides Title 15 and the DOM, which presents a striking contrast to the written grievances, discussed in chapter 7.

22. Michael had a way with words throughout his interview. When the interviewer asked him about a particular grievance, "Were you happy you filed it?" Michael replied, "Am I *happy?* Happiness will be, right now, my first grandchild in my hands and me out there at the lake. . . . No, I'm not gonna say I'm happy."

23. Sarat (1990, 344) describes the legal experiences of the welfare poor: "Law is, for people on welfare, repeatedly encountered in the most ordinary transactions and events of their lives. . . . Law is immediate and powerful because being on welfare means having a significant part of one's life organized by a regime of legal rules invoked by officials." As one of his interviewees put it, for people like him, "the law is all over" (343). Sarat argues that this experience of "immediate and powerful" law shapes the legal consciousness of many of these welfare poor. Law is arguably even more immediate in prison, where virtually all behavior is subject to legal regulation and legal scrutiny is intense, overt, and constant. As with those whom Sarat studied, this environment of law has potentially significant impacts on inmates' legal consciousness.

24. Blackstone, Uggen, and McLaughlin (2009, 664) found that in cases of workplace sexual harassment, the variable most positively correlated with legal mobilization was strong "horizontal worker-to-worker relationships," suggesting that these relationships provide critical support for holding perpetrators accountable. While we have no direct evidence of this in this study, it may be that prisoners' close living quarters, their shared status as prisoners, and the strong horizontal ties among them have an independent effect or may amplify the effect of the legal-institutional context.

25. This roughly parallels our written grievance sample from all prisons, discussed in chapter 2. There, we saw that staff complaints were the fifth-most-common type of grievance, comprising 6.2 percent of the total in the random sample of grievances that reached the final level of review in 2005–2006.

26. In addition to asking about their "most important" grievance, a grievance that was resolved at the informal level (if any), and a grievance that was granted (if any), we asked them to tell us about their most recent grievance. We assumed that the "most recent" grievances would be most representative of grievances in general because they are not selected on any substantive criteria other than least distant in time. Whether we looked at the total set of 217 grievances or only the most recent, fewer than 8 percent of grievances were staff complaints.

27. Interestingly, when we asked CDCR staff what kinds of grievances are easiest to handle, they said it was grievances that involved missing property.

28. The influence of potential retaliation on inmate grievance filing is not unique to our sample of California prisoners. A recent study of the grievance process in the federal prison system reveals that of the inmates who "had a problem but didn't file," the single most common reason was "afraid of staff retribution," with eighteen of fifty-three respondents citing this factor (Bierie 2010).

29. Corentin Durand (2012, 2), quoting French sociologist C. Rostaing, writes of this paradoxical role of law in prison as a form of resistance: "The law has been described by sociologists as a 'hazard to prison peace' because it unsettles the asymmetrical local arrangements on which social order is fragilely based."

4. PRISONERS' COUNTERNARRATIVES

1. When asked his racial self-identification, Roland said it was complicated: "I'm white, but Hispanic in here." He explained that he had grown up around "southern Hispanics," and that is how he is identified in prison. "My race is white," he said, "but [I run with] the southern Hispanics."

2. Notice that while initially only 14.8 percent of these men said they had used the 602 for anything other than what was written on the form, eventually almost 36 percent of them said they had used it to record their story.

3. Almost all of the staff we interviewed believed inmates use the 602 for these purposes (see chapter 5).

4. These agree/disagree statements were administered to only seventy-nine prisoner interviewees, as this section was added to the interview schedule after interviews were completed at California Corrections Facility.

5. Curiously, more than 65 percent agreed or strongly agreed with the very next statement that "most inmates file only for legitimate, serious issues." This mathematical discrepancy may be a methodological effect, as it is conceivable that there is a bias toward agreement. Alternatively, it may be that while some interviewees believe inmates file over "minor issues," at the same time they recognize that issues they consider minor may be "legitimate" to the one who files. This distinction between what the respondent thinks is a minor issue and what

might be legitimate to the filer was something we heard from both inmates and staff.

6. *Pruno* is the colloquial term for an alcoholic drink that prisoners make with fruit juice or anything else that can be fermented.

7. It is thought that the syndrome is a psychological response to, and a method of coping with, the stress of captivity. While it would not be surprising if some prisoners exhibited Stockholm Syndrome symptoms, it cannot by itself explain the pattern we encountered here because prisoners' expressions of empathy and identification often occur in interviews in which the respondents are otherwise highly critical of CDCR practices and prison conditions.

8. While Sarat noted these contrasting views of law among the people he studied, he nonetheless argued that for the most part they had no illusions about law as majestic or impartial. Instead, for them, "law . . . is no better, and no worse, than the social world in which it is embedded" (Sarat, 1990, 378).

5. "NARCISSISTS," "LIARS," PROCESS, AND PAPER

1. Most of the research on prison employees is narrowly psychological in nature and focuses on work stress, job satisfaction, and burnout, with little mention of these workers' relationships to their inmate charges (Garland 2004; Griffin, Hogan, and Lambert 2012; Lambert, Hogan, and Barton 2002; Morgan, Van Haveren, and Pearson 2002). The early work of Jacobs and Kraft (1978) and Jurik (1985), as well as more recent work by Lerman and Page (2012) and Lerman (2013), are among the notable exceptions. However, unlike the present work, their research focuses on the lower-level guards who are in direct contact with inmates but have little policymaking authority. Jurik's work examines the individual attributes of gender, race, and education levels, in conjunction with organizational factors such as the amount of contact with inmates and custody level. Her work is important here because it demonstrates the power of institutional variables in affecting attitudes and related practices. Likewise, Lerman and Page's (2012) recent analysis of original survey data collected on corrections officers in California and Minnesota reveals that California prison officers are significantly more punitive than those in Minnesota, even as officers in both states express similar levels of support for rehabilitation programs. These and other findings lead them to advance an "embedded work role perspective" on prison-officer attitudes, which emphasizes the diverse ways prisons are embedded in larger penal and political environments that have consequences for officers' attitudes. Lerman's recent book, *The Modern Prison Paradox* (2013), based on her extensive survey data, also confirms the effects of various prison environments on both prisoners and those who guard them, with less restrictive/punitive and more rehabilitative institutions associated with a positive impact on prison culture, social networks, and the community at large.

2. In a study of the grievance systems in two Illinois prisons in the early 1980s, Brakel (1982, 130–31) speculated that the reverse could be true: "There is always the possibility that the presence of a grievance mechanism has adverse effects. It raises expectations that in turn may be frustrated by lack of results or the perception of biased decision making. It also increases the general rights

consciousness among inmates and raises the legitimacy of all manner of claims and complaints. These are hardly stabilizing effects." Nonetheless, a variety of reports declare that the value of a grievance system lies in its ability to prevent or reduce violence (Barton 2011), and corrections officials are quick to echo this belief.

3. No prisoner mentioned this function of 602s in our conversations with them, although they did report the practice of dropping "kites" (surreptitious notes) to warn officials of upcoming violence or other issues. Perhaps this use of 602s is rare enough to be outside the experience of the 120 men we spoke with; alternatively, divulging this surreptitious use of the forms might be seen by prisoners as risking a practice whose utility resides in its remaining undercover.

4. Anthropologist Barbara Yngvesson (1993) studied working-class citizens in a Massachusetts county who took their complaints of trouble in their neighborhood to court and the interpretation of this legal mobilization by court clerks. Yngvesson (1993, 6) writes: "Repeated appearances of the same people in court ... contributed to their definition by local officials as 'brainless' and unrestrained, and thus in need of official surveillance. Thus complainants confirmed official assumptions that they were incapable of self-control in the very act of claiming rights as citizens." Just so, while these prison officials acknowledged prisoners' right to file appeals, when they do so they confirm officials' view of them as narcissistic and unable to "abide by the rules."

5. While these officers spoke nostalgically of a prior time when prisoners had fewer rights, as early as the mid-1970s, Jacobs and Kraft (1978, 309) found that the vast majority of guards in their study agreed with the statement "The courts have given inmates so many rights that it is practically impossible to maintain satisfactory discipline."

6. The implication is that while certain amenities or food items (such as specific condiments) might be written into prison regulations and policy, not all deviations from such policies are considered sufficiently significant to be grievable.

7. The tendency to disdain rights claims brought by those already entangled in the criminal justice system is expanded on by Young (2009). Noting that logically it is people who are charged with a crime who typically contest the violation of criminal procedure rights (such as illegal searches), Young observes, "This may color popular perceptions about these kinds of constitutional claims" (72).

8. When we asked prisoners the same question, 85.1 percent said yes.

9. Despite these officials' apparent disdain for frequent filers, when we asked, "Are there particular types of inmates who are most likely to have their appeals denied?" all but three people said no. One of these three hedged: "It depends"; two volunteered that frequent filers might be more likely to be denied (the other one said with a straight face that "liars" are more likely to be denied). Further, when we asked later in the interview, "Does it matter [to the outcome] if the inmate has filed a lot of appeals before?" again only three people said that it did matter. It is difficult to know what to make of this disconnect between these officials' apparent disdain for prisoners who file frequently and their report that this does not affect their decision making. It may be due to their dedication to

the concept of fairness, at least in the abstract (as IAB official Dave Manning said, "To the best of our ability we will be fair, irregardless of what we think of them"). Or it may simply be a concession to the reality that with rare exceptions appeals are denied across the board.

10. This refrain echoes the sentiment of one of the senate's major sponsors of the PLRA, Senator Spencer Abraham. Advocating limiting prisoner lawsuits through the PLRA, Senator Abraham declared: "Convicted criminals, while they must be accorded their constitutional rights, deserve to be punished. I think virtually everybody believes that while these people are in jail they should not be tortured, but they also should not have all the rights and privileges the rest of us enjoy, and that their lives should, on the whole, be describable by the old concept known as hard time" (141 Cong. S. 14316).

11. Indicative of the frequency with which safety and security is cited as officials' reason to deviate from stated policy, after his discussion of daily strip searches, prisoner Min Kim quipped, "They can't use safety and security as a blanket cure-all."

12. Sometimes "operational realities" that were related to budget restraints and other efficiencies (rather than safety and security) were cited as reasons to defer to prison managers. For example, Henry Lopez, an IAB official quoted extensively here, told us that officials at one prison wrote the appeals branch a long memo explaining the budget reasons for replacing hot lunches with sack lunches, and that this had been sufficient to deny inmate grievances on the subject. He noted, "There are dozens of things in the DOM we don't do because of operational realities."

13. Feeley and Swearingen (2004, 435), quoting Jacobs (1980, 430), note that "the prisoners' rights litigation [of the 1970s and 1980s] must be understood as part of a more general movement of 'victimized minorities,' and . . . as 'part of a [broader] mosaic of social change.'" Later Feeley and Swearingen observe, "Prison reform litigation is a lineal descendant of *Brown v. Board of Education* and the rights movement that it spawned." Given this shared etiology, it should not be surprising that prisoners—two-thirds of whom in California are people of color—are subject to the same racialized "special privileges" trope as others who benefited from the broader civil rights movement.

14. In the U.S. legal system, the burden of proof is always on the appellant. Here, this ordinary burden is compounded many times over. In these prisons, an officer's word is believed over an inmate appellant's ("Always. Always. Always"), "even twelve . . . witnesses" are not sufficient to corroborate an inmate's account if the witnesses are inmates, and finding a prisoner's missing money in the pocket of an accused mailroom officer does not qualify even under the relatively lenient standard of "preponderance of evidence" required in civil cases.

15. In her examination of prosecutors' interactions with victims of sexual assault, Frohmann (1998, 395) argues that when prosecutors intend to reject a case, they employ "a rhetorical style that offers a legal rationale for case rejection," which is quite different from the frame they use when they anticipate accepting a case.

16. In his typology of administrative justice, Mashaw (1983) argued that organizational decisions derive their legitimacy from principles of bureaucratic

rationality, professionalism, or moral judgment. According to Mashaw, in the bureaucratic model, decisions are supposed to be based on established rules, and in the professional model correct decisions emanate from the exercise of discretion based on professional experience (e.g., "You have to have worked in a prison" to interpret 602s correctly), whereas in the moral judgment model, decision making requires an interactive process in which competing interests can be heard. While Mashaw's typology was meant to apply primarily to the grounds on which administrative decisions are rendered legitimate to the public, we see here that these are some of the same rationales that CDCR actors rely on to self-legitimate.

17. In his book *The Collapse of American Criminal Justice*, Stuntz (2011) argues that the definition of justice as procedural rather than substantive is in part responsible for the current mass incarceration in the United States. Noting that in contrast to the French Declaration of the Rights of Man, which emphasizes substantive principles, the American Bill of Rights focuses on process, Stuntz posits that this preoccupation with procedure has dramatic implications for imprisonment. *The New Yorker* magazine commentator Adam Gopnik (2012, 73) elaborates Stuntz's argument: "The obsession with due process and the cult of brutal prisons . . . share an essential impersonality. The more professionalized and procedural a system is, the more insulated we become from its effects on real people."

18. The "green sheet" is the page of the 602 form on which the prisoner first describes his complaint.

6. ADMINISTRATIVE CONSISTENCY, DOWNSTREAM CONSEQUENCES, AND "KNUCKLEHEADS"

1. Leanna told us that her 95 percent consistency rate was because "everybody follows the rules. The same rules are followed."

2. In the California prisons, line officers wear green uniforms.

3. The distinction between *inquiry* and *investigation* is also underscored in policy, with the latter requiring more burdensome procedures for how the information gathering unfolds, and potentially entailing more significant consequences for an officer's career.

4. In her book *The Modern Prison Paradox*, Amy Lerman (2013, 125) describes California correctional officers this way, indirectly alluding to this tension between a focus on paramilitary rank and the need to exercise discretion: "For officers, their formal role within the prison is increasingly a paramilitary one, which emphasizes hierarchical ranks (officers, corporals and sergeants, lieutenants and wardens), military-style discipline, and the maintenance of order and security through the use of force when necessary. However, officers are encouraged to use their discretion to resolve issues within the confines of law."

5. Despite the apparent challenges that appeals coordinators face, all of them told us it was "easy" to grant an appeal that had been denied. Even the IAC who said she had to "get thick skin" claimed that it was easy to reverse a prior decision. Whatever the reason for this disconnect between the claim that it is easy to

reverse the decision of another official and the narratives that speak of "exhausting" pushback and "stubborn" egos, it must be seen within a behavioral context in which reversals are exceedingly rare.

6. Appeals coordinator Stacey Taylor told us, "You know, some file all the time. Like the little kid who cries wolf too many times." And as we saw in chapter 5, CDCR officials are often disdainful of frequent filers.

7. Among the minimum requirements to become a California correctional officer is obtaining a high school diploma or equivalency.

8. In the sole exception to this focus on training, Associate Warden Sandra James insisted that the key to doing appeals right is to be "a person of character." "If you have character," she said, "you know what's right. That doesn't take training."

7. GRIEVANCE NARRATIVES AS FRAMES OF MEANING, PROFILES OF POWER

1. Prisons in California vary in terms of the absolute number and the per capita number of grievances they produce in any given year. As described in chapter 1, our random sample was drawn from a complete list of all grievances from all prisons reaching the third level of review. On the high end, one prison contributed twenty-five grievances to our random sample, on the low end another prison contributed only one grievance, and one prison was not represented at all in our sample.

2. Recall that the informal level was only informal in the sense that the grievance was not logged into the system at that point. As mentioned in chapter 2, this informal level has been eliminated by the CDCR.

3. In addition to changing the names of appellants, we have occasionally made small alterations to the text of their grievance narratives to preserve confidentiality. Although we were reluctant to do so because we want to present the prisoners' voices intact, in a few cases it became apparent that providing too many details of an individual's story might reveal his or her identity. Balancing these concerns, we have made sparing and strategic alterations and when we have done so, we put the altered text in brackets. In addition, we have bracketed out the names of all personnel and prisons cited within the grievances.

4. Sarat (2008) has written about clemency petitions in capital cases as "memorializing" stories that record the injustices of the legal system. He suggests (194, quoting Lobel [1995, 1337]) that while they almost always fail in a material sense, these petitions "preserve 'the versions of legal meaning created by groups outside the mainstream of American law.'" Similarly, these prisoners' grievance narratives may preserve their interpretative meaning of events, even as they fail instrumentally.

5. The opposite pattern prevails for staff reviews, with responses becoming longer and more detailed as the grievance works its way up the chain of command. CDCR responses are often longest at the final level in Sacramento, where full-time staff are dedicated to crafting them.

6. "Adverse effect" on a prisoner is the standard used in Section 3084.1 of Title 15, CCR, and policy memos, as the threshold for legitimately filing (and

therefore, the necessary condition for granting) an appeal. In 2011, the threshold was raised from "adverse effect" to the more narrow "*material* adverse effect."

7. It is sometimes difficult to gauge the level of the CDCR's professional composure, as on some rare occasions their responses contained veiled hints of sarcasm. For example, one first-level responder answered an appellant's request to be assigned to a lower custody level, based on his good behavior. In issuing his denial, the respondent quipped, "Although you are to be commended for your disciplinary free period, it is also the expected behavior of all inmates." A similar tone was struck by the warden quoted earlier, who responded to Jimenez's request to be transferred by telling him he could get out of SHU and transfer if he deactivated as a gang member: "The inmate is encouraged to review these options so that he can be housed closer to family." It is difficult to judge the intention of such comments, and in any case the sarcasm they hint at is always implicit and subtextual. In no case in our full sample was there any explicit display of emotion by CDCR responders equivalent to those of the inmates quoted here.

8. The official probably meant to write that the mother did not *sign* it but he had "confirmed" she sent it.

8. CONCLUSION

1. Recall that the famous Stanford prison experiment of 1971, designed to simulate a prison environment to demonstrate "the extraordinary power of institutional environments to influence those who passed through them," had to be ended early due to overly zealous student "guards" and dangerously demoralized student "prisoners" (Haney and Zimbardo 1998, 710).

2. For an excellent overview, see Silbey 2005.

APPENDIX A

1. People were not interviewed unless they gave their informed consent, as required by our Institutional Review Board. Moreover, they were not required to answer any question they chose not to answer and were allowed to discontinue the interview at any time. Recognizing that our interviewees lived in carceral environments, the research design and attendant logistics were organized to ensure that we did not in any way signal to people that they were required to participate, nor did we promise anything in exchange for participating.

References

Abel, Richard L. "Torts." In *The Politics of Law: A Progressive Critique,* edited by David Kairys, 185–200. New York: Pantheon Books, 1982.

Adam, Barry. *The Rise of a Gay and Lesbian Movement.* Boston: Twayne Publishers, 1987.

Adler, Michael. "A Socio-Legal Approach to Administrative Justice." *Law & Policy* 25, no. 4 (2003): 323–52.

Adlerstein, David M. "In Need of Correction: The Iron Triangle of the Prison Litigation Reform Act." *Colum. L. Rev.* 101 (2001): 1681.

Albiston, Catherine. "The Rule of Law and the Litigation Process: The Paradox of Losing by Winning." *Law & Society Review* 33, no. 4 (1999): 869–910.

———. "Bargaining in the Shadow of Social Institutions: Competing Discourses and Social Change in Workplace Mobilization of Civil Rights." *Law & Society Review* 39, no. 1 (2005): 11–49.

Alexander, Michelle. *The New Jim Crow: Mass Incarceration in the Age of Colorblindness.* New York: New Free Press, 2010.

Alexander, Rudolph, Jr., and Jacquelyn C.A. Meshelemiah. "Gender Identity Disorders in Prisons: What Are the Legal Implications for Prison Mental Health Professionals and Administrators?" *Prison Journal* 90, no. 3 (2010): 269–87.

Anderson, Elijah. *Code of the Street: Decency, Violence, and the Moral Life of the Inner City.* New York: W.W. Norton, 1999.

Barton, Robert. *CDCR's Revised Inmate Appeal Process Leaves Key Problems Unaddressed.* Sacramento: California Department of Corrections and Rehabilitation, 2011, www.oig.ca.gov/media/reports/BOA/reports/Special%20 Report%20on%20CDCRs%20Revised%20Inmate%20Appeal%20 Process%20Leaves%20Key%20Problems%20Unaddressed.pdf.

Baumgartner, M. P. "The Myth of Discretion." In *The Uses of Discretion,* edited by Keith Hawkins, 129–62. Oxford: Oxford University Press, 1992.

Beckett, Katherine. *Making Crime Pay: Law and Order in Contemporary American Politics.* New York: Oxford University Press, 1997.

Beckett, Katherine, Kris Nyrop, Lori Pfingst, and Melissa Bowen. "Drug Use, Drug Possession Arrests, and the Question of Race: Lessons from Seattle." *Social Problems* 52, no. 3 (2005): 419–41.

Beetham, David. *The Legitimation of Power.* London: McMillan Education, 1991.

Belbot, Barbara. "Report on the Prison Litigation Reform Act: What Have the Courts Decided So Far?" *Prison Journal* 84 (2004): 290–316.

Bell, Derrick. *And We Are Not Saved: The Elusive Quest for Racial Justice.* New York: Basic Books, 1987.

———. *Faces at the Bottom of the Well: The Permanence of Racism.* New York: Basic Books, 1992.

———. *Silent Covenants: Brown v. Board of Education and the Unfulfilled Hopes for Racial Reform.* Oxford: Oxford University Press, 2004.

Berger, Peter. *Invitation to Sociology: A Humanistic Perspective.* New York: Random House, 1963.

Bierie, David M. "Procedural Justice and Prison Violence: Examining Complaints among Federal Inmates (1994–2009)." Presentation at the Annual Meeting of the American Society of Criminology, San Francisco, November 16, 2010.

Bittner, Egon. "Police Discretion in Emergency Apprehension of Mentally Ill Persons." *Social Problems* 14, no. 3 (1967): 278–92.

Blackstone, Amy, Christopher Uggen, and Heather McLaughlin. "Legal Consciousness and Responses to Sexual Harassment." *Law & Society Review* 43, no. 3 (2009): 631–68.

Blumstein, Alfred, and Jacqueline Cohen. "Theory of Stability of Punishment." *Journal of Criminal Law & Criminology* 64, no. 2 (1973): 198–207.

Bobo, Lawrence, and Ryan A. Smith. "From Jim Crow Racism to Laissez-Faire Racism: The Transformation of Racial Attitudes." In *Beyond Pluralism: The Conception of Groups and Group Identities in America,* edited by Ned Landsman and Andrea Tyree Wendy Katkin, 182–220. Urbana: University of Illinois Press, 1998.

Bordt, Rebecca L., and Michael C. Musheno. "Bureaucratic Cooptation of Informal Disputing Process: Social Control as an Effect of Inmate Grievance Policy." *Journal of Research in Crime and Delinquency* 25 (1988): 7–26.

Bosworth, Mary. *Engendering Resistance: Agency and Power in Women's Prisons.* Aldershot, UK: Ashgate, 1999.

Brakel, Samuel Jan. "Administrative Justice in the Penitentiary: A Report on Inmate Grievance Procedures." *Law & Social Inquiry* 7, no. 1 (1982): 111–40.

Brown, Michael K., Martin Carnoy, Elliott Currie, Troy Duster, David B. Oppenheimer, Marjorie M. Shultz, and David Wellman. *Whitewashing Race: The Myth of a Color-Blind Society.* Berkeley: University of California Press, 2003.

Bumiller, Kristin. "Victims in the Shadow of the Law: A Critique of the Model of Legal Protection." *Signs* 12, no. 3 (1987): 421–39.

———. *The Civil Rights Society: The Social Construction of Victims.* Baltimore, MD: Johns Hopkins University Press, 1988.

Bureau of Audits and Investigations. *Summary and Analysis of the First Seventeen Medical Inspections of California Prisons.* Sacramento: California Inspector General, 2010.

Calhoun, Patrick S., and William P. Smith. "Integrative Bargaining: Does Gender Make a Difference?" *International Journal of Conflict Management* 10, no. 3 (1999): 203–24.

California Department of Corrections and Rehabilitation. "Administrative Interview Process Training." *Administrative Bulletin* 05–03 (2003).

Campbell, Michael C., and Heather Schoenfeld. "The Transformation of America's Penal Order: A Historicized Political Sociology of Punishment." *American Journal of Sociology* 118, no. 5 (2013): 1375–1423.

Carrabine, Eamonn. "Prison Riots, Social Order and the Problem of Legitimacy." *British Journal of Criminology* 45, no. 6 (2005): 896–913.

Chambliss, William J., and Robert B. Seidman. *Law, Order and Power.* Reading: Addison-Wesley, 1971.

Charmaz, Kathy. *Constructing Grounded Theory: A Practical Guide through Qualitative Analysis.* Newbury Park, CA: Pine Forge Press, 2006.

Clemmer, Donald. *The Prison Community.* New York: Rinehart, 1940.

Coates, Dan, and Steven Penrod. "Social-Psychology and the Emergence of Disputes." *Law & Society Review* 15, nos. 3–4 (1980–81): 655–80.

Comfort, Megan. *Doing Time Together.* Berkeley: University of California Press, 2008.

Cover, Robert M. "Foreword: Nomos and Narrative." *Harvard Law Review* 97 (1983): 4–68.

———. "Violence and the Word." *Yale Law Review* 95 (1986a): 1601–29.

———. "The Bonds of Constitutional Interpretation: Of the Word, the Deed, and the Role." *Georgia Law Review* 20 (1986b): 815–33.

Cowan, Dave. "Legal Consciousness: Some Observations." *Modern Law Review* 67, no. 6 (2004): 928–58.

Cressey, Donald R. *The Prison: Studies in Institutional Organization and Change.* New York: Holt, Rinehart & Winston, 1961.

Crewe, Ben. "Prisoner Society in the Era of Hard Drugs." *Punishment & Society* 7, no. 4 (2005): 457–81.

Cuevas, Ofelia O. "Welcome to My Cell: Housing and Race in the Mirror of American Democracy." *American Quarterly* 64, no. 3 (2012): 605–24.

Davis, Darren W. "The Direction of Race of Interviewer Effects among African-Americans: Donning the Black Mask." *American Journal of Political Science* 41, no. 1 (1997): 309–22.

Davis, Darren W., and Brian D. Silver. "Stereotype Threat and Race of Interviewer Effects in a Survey on Political Knowledge." *American Journal of Political Science* 47, no. 1 (2003): 33–45.

Davis, Kenneth Culp. *Discretionary Justice.* Urbana: University of Illinois Press, 1971.

Davis, R. E., et al. "Interviewer Effects in Public Health Surveys." *Health Education Research* 25, no. 1 (2010): 14–26.

Deitch, Michele. "The Need for Independent Prison Oversight in a Post-PLRA World." *Federal Sentencing Reporter* 24, no. 4 (2012): 236–44.

DeLand, Michael. "Basketball in the Key of Law: The Significance of Disputing in Pick Up Basketball." *Law & Society Review* 47, no. 3 (2013): 653–85.

Dudziak, Mary. *Cold War Civil Rights: Race and the Image of American Democracy.* Princeton, NJ: Princeton University Press, 2000.

Durand, Corentin. "Petitions from Beyond the Walls." Presentation at the Annual Meeting of the Law and Society Association, Honolulu, Hawaii, June 7, 2012.

Earl, Jennifer. "When Bad Things Happen: Toward a Sociology of Troubles." *Sociology of Crime, Law, and Deviance* 12 (2009): 231–54.

Edelman, Lauren B., Howard S. Erlanger, and John Lande. "Internal Dispute Resolution—the Transformation of Civil-Rights in the Workplace." *Law & Society Review* 27, no. 3 (1993): 497–534.

Edelman, Lauren B., and Mia Cahill. "How Law Matters in Disputing and Dispute Processing (Or, the Contingency of Legal Matter in Informal Dispute Processes)." In *How Does Law Matter,* edited by Bryan G. Garth and Austin Sarat, 15–44. Chicago: Northwestern University Press, 1998.

Edelman, Lauren B., Christopher Uggen, and Howard S. Erlanger. "The Endogeneity of Legal Regulation: Grievance Procedures as Rational Myth." *American Journal of Sociology* 105, no. 2 (1999): 406–54.

Edwards, Linda H. "Once upon a Time in Law: Myth, Metaphor, and Authority." *Tennessee Law Review* 77 (2010): 883–916.

Edwards, Richard Autour. *Contested Terrain: The Transformation of the Workplace in the Twentieth Century.* New York: Basic Books, 1979.

Egelko, Bob. "Inmate Hunger Strike over Solitary Rules Continues." *San Francisco Chronicle,* July 10, 2013, D5.

Ellison, Christopher G., Michael J. McFarland, and Neil Krause. "Measuring Religiousness among Older African Americans: Exploring Race-of-Interviewer Effects." *Review of Religious Research* 53, no. 1 (2011): 65–84.

Emerson, Robert M. "Case Processing and Interorganizational Knowledge—Detecting the Real Reasons for Referrals." *Social Problems* 38, no. 2 (1991): 198–212.

———. "Responding to Roommate Troubles: Reconsidering Informal Dyadic Control." *Law & Society Review* 42, no. 3 (2008): 483–512.

Emerson, Robert M., and Sheldon L. Messinger. "The Micro-Politics of Trouble." *Social Problems* 25 (1977): 121–34.

Emerson, Robert M., and Blair Paley. "Organizational Horizons and Complaint-Filing." In *The Uses of Discretion,* edited by Keith Hawkins, 231–47. Oxford: Oxford University Press, 1992.

Engel, David M., and Frank W. Munger. *Rights of Inclusion: Law and Identity in the Life Stories of Americans with Disabilities.* Chicago: University of Chicago Press, 2003.

Ewick, Patricia, and Susan S. Silbey. *The Common Place of Law: Stories from Everyday Life.* Chicago: University of Chicago Press, 1998.

Farrington, Keith. "Modern Prison as Total Institution? Public Perception Versus Objective Reality," *Crime and Delinquency* 38, no. 1 (1992): 6–26.

Feeley, Malcolm M. "Legality, Social Research, and the Challenge of Institutional Review Boards." *Law & Society Review* 41, no. 4 (2007): 757–76.

Feeley, Malcolm M., and Edward L. Rubin. *Judicial Policy Making and the Modern State: How the Courts Reformed America's Prisons.* Cambridge: Cambridge University Press, 1998.

Feeley, Malcolm M., and Van Swearingen. "The Prison Conditions Cases and the Bureaucratization of American Corrections: Influences, Impacts and Implications." *Pace Law Review* 24 (2004): 433–75.

———. "Reducing Litigation Exposure: An Evaluation of Structural Problems within the California Department of Corrections and Rehabilitation." Unpublished report submitted in fulfillment of Grant #2006-1740 (2008), Sponsored Projects Office, University of California Berkeley, 021365-003.

Felstiner, William L.F., Richard L. Abel, and Austin Sarat. "The Emergence and Transformation of Disputes: Naming, Blaming, and Claiming." *Law & Society Review* 15, nos. 3–4 (1980–81): 631–54.

Fendrich, Michael, et al. "Validity of Drug Use Reporting in a High-Risk Community Sample: A Comparison of Cocaine and Heroin Survey Reports with Hair Tests." *American Journal of Epidemiology* 149, no. 10 (1999): 955–62.

Ferree, Myra Marx, and Beth B. Hess. *Controversy and Coalition: The New Feminist Movement.* Boston: Twayne, 1985.

Fitzpatrick, Peter. *The Mythology of Modern Law.* New York: Routledge, 1992.

Fleisher, Mark S., and Jessie L. Krienert. *The Myth of Prison Rape : Sexual Culture in American Prisons.* Lanham: Rowman & Littlefield, 2009.

Fletcher, Joyce K. *Disappearing Acts: Gender, Power and Relational Practice at Work.* Cambridge: MIT Press, 1999.

Foucault, Michel. *Discipline and Punish: The Birth of the Prison.* New York: Pantheon Books, 1977.

Freeman, Alan D. "Antidiscrimination Law from 1954 to 1989: Uncertainty, Contradiction, Rationalization, Denial." In *The Politics of Law: A Progressive Critique,* edited by David Kairys, 285–311. New York: Pantheon Books, 1982.

Friedman, Lawrence M. "The Idea of Right as a Social and Legal Concept." *Journal of Social Issues* 27, no. 2 (1971): 189–98.

Frohmann, Lisa. "Constituting Power in Sexual Assault Cases: Prosecutorial Strategies for Victim Management." *Social Problems* 45, no. 3 (1998): 393.

Gaes, Gerald G., Scott D. Camp, Julianne B. Nelson, and William G. Saylor. *Measuring Prison Performance: Government Privatization and Accountability.* Walnut Creek, CA: AltaMira Press, 2004.

Gallagher, Mary E. "Mobilizing the Law in China: 'Informed Disenchantment' and the Development of Legal Consciousness." *Law & Society Review* 40, no. 4 (2006): 783–816.

Garland, David. *The Culture of Control: Crime and Social Order in Contemporary Society.* Chicago: University of Chicago Press, 2001.

———. "Beyond the Culture of Control." *Critical Review of International Social and Political Philosophy* 7, no. 2 (2004): 160–89.

———. "Penality and the Penal State." *Criminology* 51 (2013): 475–517.

Gilliom, John. *Overseers of the Poor: Surveillance, Resistance, and the Limits of Privacy.* Chicago: University of Chicago Press, 2001.

Gilmore, Ruth Wilson. *Golden Gulag: Prisons, Surplus, Crisis, and Opposition in Globalizing California.* Berkeley: University of California Press, 2007.

Gitlin, Todd. *The Whole World Is Watching: Mass Media in the Making and Unmaking of the New Left.* Berkeley: University of California Press, 1980.

Glaze, Lauren E. "Correctional Populations in the United States, 2009." *Bureau of Justice Statistics Bulletin* (2010).

Goffman, Alice. *On the Run: Fugitive Life in an American City.* Chicago: University of Chicago Press, 2014.

Goffman, Erving. *Asylums: Essays on the Social Situation of Mental Patients and Other Inmates.* Garden City: Doubleday, 1961.

———. *Frame Analysis: An Essay on the Organization of Experience.* Boston: Northeastern University Press, 1974.

Goldberg, Robert A. *Grassroots Resistance: Social Movements in the Twentieth Century.* Belmont, CA: Wadsworth, 1991.

Goodman, Phillip. "It's Just Black, White, or Hispanic: An Observational Study of Racializing Moves in California's Segregated Prison Reception Centers." *Law & Society Review* 42, no. 4 (2008): 735–70.

Gopnik, Adam. "The Caging of America." *New Yorker,* January 30, 2012, www.newyorker.com/arts/critics/atlarge/2012/01/30/120130crat_atlarge_gopnik.

Gossett, Thomas F. *Race: The History of an Idea in America.* Oxford: Oxford University Press, 1997.

Griffin, Marie L., Nancy L. Hogan, and Eric G. Lambert. "Doing 'People Work' in the Prison Setting: An Examination of the Job Characteristics Model and Correctional Staff Burnout." *Criminal Justice and Behavior* 39, no. 9 (2012): 1131–47.

Gwartney-Gibbs, Patricia A., and Denise H. Lach. "Sociological Explanations for Failure to Seek Sexual Harassment Remedies." *Conflict Resolution Quarterly* 9, no. 4 (1992): 365–74.

———. "Gender and Workplace Dispute Resolution: A Conceptual and Theoretical Model." *Law & Society Review* 28, no. 2 (1994): 265–96.

Hagan, John. *Who Are the Criminals? The Politics of Crime Policy from the Age of Roosevelt to the Age of Reagan.* Princeton, NJ: Princeton University Press, 2010.

Haltom, William, and Michael McCann. *Distorting the Law: Politics, Media, and the Litigation Crisis.* Chicago: University of Chicago Press, 2009.

Haney, Craig, and Philip Zimbardo. "The Past and Future of U.S. Prison Policy: Twenty-Five Years after the Stanford Prison Experiment." *American Psychologist* 53, no. 7 (1998): 709.

Harding, David J. "Cultural Context, Sexual Behavior, and Romantic Relationships in Disadvantaged Neighborhoods." *American Sociological Review* 72, no. 3 (2007): 341–64.

Hawkins, Keith, ed. *The Uses of Discretion.* Oxford: Oxford University Press, 1992.

Hendley, K. "Mobilizing Law in Contemporary Russia: The Evolution of Disputes over Home Repair Projects." *American Journal of Comparative Law* 58, no. 3 (2010): 631–78.

Hoffmann, Elizabeth A. "Confrontations and Compromise: Dispute Resolution at a Worker Cooperative Coal Mine." *Law & Social Inquiry* 26, no. 3 (2001): 555–96.

———. "Legal Consciousness and Dispute Resolution: Different Disputing Behavior at Two Similar Taxicab Companies." *Law and Social Inquiry: Journal of the American Bar Foundation* 28, no. 3 (2003): 691–716.

———. "Dispute Resolution in a Worker Cooperative: Formal Procedures and Procedural Justice." *Law & Society Review* 39, no. 1 (2005): 51–82.

Huddy, Leonie, et al. "The Effect of Interviewer Gender on the Survey Response." *Political Behavior* 19, no. 3 (1997): 197–220.

Human Rights Watch. *No Equal Justice: The Prison Litigation Reform Act in the United States.* New York: Human Rights Watch, 2001.

Hunt, Geoffrey, Stephanie Riegel, Tomas Morales, and Dan Waldrof. "Changes in Prison Culture: Prison Gangs and the Case of the 'Pepsi Generation.'" *Social Problems* 40 (1993): 398–409.

Inciardi, James A. *Criminal Justice.* San Diego, CA: Harcourt Brace, 1990.

Irwin, John. *The Warehouse Prison: Disposal of the New Dangerous Class.* Los Angeles: Roxbury, 2005.

Jackson, Jonathan, Tom R. Tyler, Ben Bradford, Dominic Taylor, and Mike Shiner. "Legitimacy and Procecudural Justice in Prisons." *Prison Service Journal* 191 (2010): 1–10.

Jacobs, James B. "The Prisoners' Rights Movement and Its Impacts, 1960–1980." *Crime and Justice* 2 (1980): 429–70.

Jacobs, James B., and Lawrence J. Kraft. "Integrating the Keepers: A Comparison of Black and White Prison Guards in Illinois." *Social Problems* (1978): 304–18.

Jenness, Valerie. "From Policy to Prisoners to People: A 'Soft Mixed Methods' Approach to Studying Transgender Prisoners." *Journal of Contemporary Ethnography* 39, no. 5 (2010): 517–53.

Jenness, Valerie, and Ryken Grattet. *Making Hate a Crime: From Social Movement to Law Enforcement.* New York: Russell Sage, 2001.

Jenness, Valerie, et al. "Accomplishing the Difficult, but Not Impossible: Collecting Self-Report Data on Inmate-on-Inmate Sexual Assault in Prison." *Criminal Justice Policy Review* 21 (2010): 3–30.

Johnson, Robert. *Death Work: A Study of the Modern Execution Process.* Los Angeles: Wadsworth, 1998.

Johnson, Timothy P., and Jennifer A. Parsons. "Interviewer Effects on Self-Reported Substance Use among Homeless Persons." *Addictive Behaviors* 19, no. 1 (1994): 83–93.

Jurik, Nancy C. "Individual and Organizational Determinants of Correctional Officer Attitudes toward Inmates." *Criminology* 23, no. 3 (1985): 523–40.

Kaiser, Cheryl R., and Carol T. Miller. "Stop Complaining! The Social Costs of Making Attributions to Discrimination." *Personality and Social Psychology Bulletin* 27, no. 2 (2001): 254–63.

Kaminski, Marek M. "Games Prisoners Play: Allocation of Social Roles in a Total Institution." *Rationality and Society* 15, no. 2 (2003): 188–217.

Kane, Emily W., and Laura J. Macaulay. "Interviewer Gender and Gender Attitudes." *Public Opinion Quarterly* 57, no. 1 (1993): 1–28.

Kanter, Rosabeth Moss. "Differential Access to Opportunity and Power." In *Discrimination in Organizations,* edited by Rodolfo Alvarez, Kenneth G. Lutterman, and associates, 52–68. San Francisco: Jossey-Bass, 1979.

Katz, Jack. "Ethical Escape Routes for Underground Ethnographers." *American Ethnologist* 33, no. 4 (2006): 499–506.

———. "Toward a Natural History of Ethical Censorship." *Law & Society Review* 41, no. 4 (2007): 797–810.

Katzenstein, Mary Fainsod. "Rights without Citizenship: Activist Politics and Prison Reform in the United States." In *Routing the Opposition: Social Movements, Public Policy, and Democracy,* edited by David S. Meyer, Valerie Jenness, and Helen Ingram, 236–58. Minneapolis: University of Minnesota Press, 2005.

Kennedy, Randall. *Race, Crime, and the Law.* New York: Vintage Books, 1998.

Kirkland, Anna. "Think of the Hippopotamus: Rights Consciousness in the Fat Acceptance Movement." *Law & Society Review* 42, no. 2 (2008): 397–432.

Kruttschnitt, Candace, and Rosemary Gartner. *Marking Time in the Golden State : Women's Imprisonment in California.* Cambridge: Cambridge University Press, 2005.

Kruttschnitt, Candace, and Jeanette Hussemann. "Micropolitics of Race and Ethnicity in Women's Prisons in Two Political Contexts." *British Journal of Sociology* 59 (2008): 709–28.

Krysan, Maria. "Privacy and the Expression of White Racial Attitudes: A Comparison across Three Contexts." *Public Opinion Quarterly* 62, no. 4 (1988): 506–44.

Kuzinski, Eugene J. "The End of the Prison Law Firm? Frivolous Inmate Litigation, Judicial Oversight, and the Prison Litigation Reform Act of 1995." *Rutgers Law Journal* 29 (1997–98): 361–400.

Lambert, Eric G., Nancy Lynne Hogan, and Shannon M. Barton. "Satisfied Correctional Staff: A Review of the Literature on the Correlates of Correctional Staff Job Satisfaction." *Criminal Justice and Behavior* 29, no. 2 (2002): 115–43.

Larson, Doran. "Why Scandinavian Prisons Are Superior." *Atlantic Monthly,* September 24, 2013, www.theatlantic.com/international/archive/2013/09/why-scandinavian-prisons-are-superior/279949/.

Lazarus-Black, Mindie, and Susan F. Hirsch. *Contested States: Law, Hegemony, and Resistance.* New York: Routledge, 1994.

Lempert, Richard. "Discretion in a Behavioral Perspective: The Case of a Public Housing Eviction Board." In *The Uses of Discretion,* edited by Keith Hawkins, 185–230. Oxford: Oxford University Press, 1992.

Lempert, Richard, and Joseph Sanders. *An Invitation to Law and Social Science.* Philadelphia: University of Pennsylvania Press, 1986.

Lerman, Amy E. *The Modern Prison Paradox: Politics, Punishment, and Social Community.* Cambridge: Cambridge University Press, 2013.

Lerman, Amy E., and Joshua Page. "The State of the Job: An Embedded Work Role Perspective on Prison Officer Attitudes." *Punishment & Society* 14, no. 5 (2012): 503–29.

Levine, Harry G., and Deborah Peterson Small. *Marijuana Arrest Crusade: Racial Bias and Police Policy in New York City, 1997–2007.* New York Civil Liberties Union, 2008, www.nyclu.org/files/MARIJUANA-ARREST-CRU-SADE_Final.pdf.

Lind, E. Allen, Yuen J. Huo, and Tom R. Tyler. "And Justice for All: Ethnicity, Gender, and Preferences for Dispute Resolution Procedures." *Law and Human Behavior* 18, no. 3 (1994): 269–90.

Lipsky, Michael. *Street-Level Bureaucracy: Dilemmas of the Individual in Public Services.* New York: Russell Sage Foundation, 1980.

Lobel, Jules. "Losers, Fools & Prophets: Justice as Struggle." *Cornell Law Review* 80 (1995): 1331–42.

Loury, Glenn C. "Why Are So Many Americans in Prison? Race and the Transformation of Criminal Justice." *Boston Review* (2007): 7–10.

Lovell, George I. "Justice Excused: The Deployment of Law in Everyday Political Encounters." *Law & Society Review* 40, no. 2 (2006): 283–324.

———. *This Is Not Civil Rights: Discovering Rights Talk in 1939 America.* Chicago: University of Chicago Press, 2012.

Lowry, Lance. "In Texas, Inmates and Officers Swelter," *New York Times,* November 22, 2013, A29.

Major, Brenda, and Cheryl Kaiser. "Perceiving and Claiming Discrimination." In *Handbook of Employment Discrimination Research: Rights and Realities,* edited by Laura Beth Nielsen and Robert L. Nelson, 285–301. Dordrecht, The Netherlands: Springer, 2005.

Manza, Jeff, and Christopher Uggen. 2006. *Locked Out: Felon Disenfranchisement and American Democracy.* New York: Oxford University Press, 2006.

Maroney, Terry A. "The Struggle against Hate Crime: Movement at a Crossroads." *New York University Law Review* 73 (1998): 564–620.

Marshall, Anna-Maria. "Injustice Frames, Legality, and the Everyday Construction of Sexual Harassment." *Law & Social Inquiry* 28, no. 3 (2003): 659–89.

Mashaw, Jerry L. *Bureaucratic Justice : Managing Social Security Disability Claims.* New Haven, CT: Yale University Press, 1983.

Matsuda, Mari. "Looking to the Bottom: Critical Legal Studies and Reparation." *Harvard Civil Rights-Civil Liberties Law Review* 22 (1987): 323–400.

McCann, Michael W. *Rights at Work: Pay Equity Reform and the Politics of Legal Mobilization.* Chicago: University of Chicago Press, 1994.

McDermott, Monica. "Racial Attitudes in City, Neighborhood, and Situational Contexts." *Annals of the American Academy of Political and Social Science* 634 (2011): 153–73.

Medina, Jennifer. "Hunger Strike by California Inmates, Already Large, Is Expected to Be a Long One." *New York Times,* July 11, 2013, A10.

Merry, Sally Engle. "Going to Court: Strategies of Dispute Management in an American Urban Neighborhood." *Law & Society Review* 13, no. 4 (1979): 891–925.

————. *Getting Justice and Getting Even: Legal Consciousness among Work-ing-Class Americans.* Chicago: University of Chicago Press, 1990.

Meyer, John W., and Brian Rowan. "Institutionalized Organizations: Formal Structure as Myth and Ceremony." *American Journal of Sociology* (1977): 340–63.

Michelson, Ethan. "Climbing the Dispute Pagoda: Grievances and Appeals to the Official Justice System in Rural China." *American Sociological Review* 72, no. 3 (2007): 459–85.

Miller, Richard E., and Austin Sarat. "Grievances, Claims, and Disputes: Assess-ing the Adversary Culture." *Law & Society Review* 15, nos. 3–4 (1981): 525–66.

Milner, Neal. "The Denigration of Rights and the Persistence of Rights Talk: A Cultural Portrait." *Law & Social Inquiry* 14, no. 4 (1989): 631–75.

Milovanovic, Dragan, and Jim Thomas. "Overcoming the Absurd: Prisoner Litigation as Primitive Rebellion." *Social Problems* 36, no. 1 (1989): 48–60.

Minow, Martha. "Interpreting Rights: An Essay for Robert Cover." *Yale Law Journal* 96 (1987): 1860–1915.

Morgan, Robert D., Richard A. Van Haveren, and Christy A. Pearson. "Correc-tional Officer Burnout: Further Analyses." *Criminal Justice and Behavior* 29, no. 2 (2002): 144–60.

Morrill, Calvin, et al. "Legal Mobilization in Schools: The Paradox of Rights and Race among Youth." *Law & Society Review* 44, nos. 3–4 (2010): 651–93.

Morris, Aldon D. *The Origins of the Civil Rights Movement: Black Communi-ties Organizing for Change.* New York: Free Press, 1984.

Moynihan, Donald P. "The Impact of Managing for Results Mandates in Cor-rections: Lessons from Three States." *Criminal Justice Policy Review* 16, no. 1 (2005): 18–37.

Murakawa, Naomi. "The Racial Antecedents to Federal Sentencing Guidelines." *Roger Williams University Law Review* 11 (2006): 473–94.

Nathan, Vincent M. *Evaluation of the Inmate Grievance System: Ohio Depart-ment of Rehabilitation & Correction.* Ohio Department of Rehabilitation and Correction, 2001, www.law.yale.edu/documents/pdf/Nathan_Evalua-tion_of_the_Ohio_Grievance_System.pdf.

National Council on Crime and Delinquency. *And Justice for Some: Differential Treatment of Youth of Color in the Justice System.* Oakland: National Coun-cil on Crime and Delinquency, 2007.

Newman, Jon O. "Pro Se Prisoner Litigation: Looking for Needles in Hay-stacks." *Brooklyn Law Review* 62 (1996): 519.

Nielsen, Laura Beth. *License to Harass: Law, Hierarchy, and Offensive Public Speech.* Princeton, NJ: Princeton University Press, 2004.

Nielsen, Laura Beth, and Robert L. Nelson. "Scaling the Pyramid: A Sociolegal Model of Employment Discrimination Litigation." In *Handbook of Employ-ment Discrimination Research: Rights and Realities,* edited by Laura Beth Nielsen and Robert L. Nelson, 3–35. Dordrecht, The Netherlands: Springer, 2005.

Pager, Devah. *Marked: Race, Crime, and Finding Work in an Era of Mass Incar-ceration.* Chicago: University of Chicago Press, 2007.

Pastore, Ann L., and Kathleen Maguire, eds. *Sourcebook of Criminal Justice Statistics, 2001*. Washington, DC: U.S. Department of Justice, 2002.

Petersilia, Joan. "California's Correctional Paradox of Excess and Deprivation." In *Crime and Justice: A Review of Research*, edited by Michael Tonry, 37:207–78. Chicago: University of Chicago Press, 2008.

Pettit, Becky, and Bruce Western. "Mass Imprisonment and the Life Course: Race and Class Inequality in US Incarceration." *American Sociological Review* 69, no. 2 (2004): 151–69.

Polletta, Francesca. "The Structural Context of Novel Rights Claims: Southern Civil Rights Organizing, 1961–1966." *Law & Society Review* 34, no. 2 (2000): 367–406.

Pratt, John. "Scandinavian Exceptionalism in an Era of Penal Excess." *British Journal of Criminology* 48 (2008): 119–37.

Provine, Doris Marie. *Unequal under Law: Race in the War on Drugs*. Chicago: University of Chicago Press, 2007.

Quinones, Sam. "Easing the Hard Time." *Los Angeles Times*, September 16, 2005, http://articles.latimes.com/print/2005/sep/16/local/me-prison16.

Rafter, Nicole H. *Creating Born Criminals*. Champaign: University of Illinois Press, 1997.

———. *The Criminal Brain: Understanding Biological Theories of Crime*. New York: New York University Press, 2008.

Reiman, Jeffrey. *The Rich Get Richer and the Poor Get Prison*. New York: John Wiley and Sons, 1979.

Reese, Stephen D., et al. "Ethnicity-of-Interviewer Effects among Mexican-Americans and Anglos." *Public Opinion Quarterly* 50, no. 4 (1986): 563–72.

Rhodes, Lorna A. *Total Confinement: Madness and Reason in the Maximum Security Prison*. Berkeley: University of California Press, 2004.

Rhodes, P. J. "Race-of-Interviewer Effects: A Brief Comment." *Sociology* 28, no. 2 (1994): 547–58.

Rideau, Wilbert. "Why Prisoners Protest." *New York Times*, July 17, 2013, A21.

Robinson, Brandon N. "*Johnson v. California*: A Grayer Shade of *Brown*." *Duke Law Journal* 56 (2006): 343–75.

Rosenberg, Gerald N. *The Hollow Hope: Can Courts Bring About Social Change?* Chicago: University of Chicago Press, 1991.

Sainsbury, Roy. "Administrative Justice, Discretion and the 'Welfare to Work' Project." *Journal of Welfare & Family Law* 30 (2008): 323–38.

Sandefur, Rebecca. "Access to Civil Justice and Race, Class, and Gender Inequality." *Annual Review of Sociology* 34 (2008).

Sander, Libby. "Inmate's Death in Solitary Cell Prompts Judge to Ban Restraints." *New York Times*, November 15, 2006, www.nytimes.com/2006/11/15/us/15prison.html.

Saperstein, Aliya, and Andrew M. Penner. "The Race of a Criminal Record: How Incarceration Colors Racial Perceptions." *Social Problems* 57, no. 1 (2010): 92–113.

Sarat, Austin. "'The Law Is All Over': Power, Resistance and the Legal Consciousness of the Welfare Poor." *Yale Journal of Law and the Humanities* 2, no. 2 (1990): 343–79.

―――. "Memorializing Miscarriages of Justice: Clemency Petitions in the Killing State." *Law & Society Review* 42 (2008): 183–224.

Sarat, Austin, and William L.F. Felstiner. *Divorce Lawyers and Their Clients: Power and Meaning in the Legal Process.* New York: Oxford University Press, 1995.

Scheingold, Stuart. *The Politics of Rights: Lawyers, Public Policy and Political Change.* New Haven, CT: Yale University Press, 1974.

Schlanger, Margo. "Inmate Litigation." *Harvard Law Review* 116, no. 6 (2003): 1555–1706.

Schlanger, Margo, and Giovanna E. Shay. "Preserving the Rule of Law in America's Jails and Prisons: The Case for Amending the Prison Litigation Reform Act." *Journal of Constitutional Law* 11 (2008): 139–54.

Schneider, Elizabeth M. "Dialectic of Rights and Politics: Perspectives from the Women's Movement." *New York University Law Review* 61 (1986): 589.

Scotch, Richard K. *From Good Will to Civil Rights: Transforming Federal Disability Policy.* Philadelphia, PA: Temple University Press, 1984.

Scott, James C. *Weapons of the Weak: Everyday Forms of Peasant Resistance.* New Haven, CT: Yale University Press, 1985.

Shapiro, Joseph P. *No Pity: People with Disabilities Forging a New Civil Rights Movement.* New York: Random House, 1993.

Silbey, Susan S. "After Legal Consciousness." *Annual Review Law Social Science* 1 (2005): 323–68.

Sillen, Robert. "Cruel and Unusual Health Care." *Sacramento Bee*, October 8, 2006, E5.

Simon, Jonathan. "The 'Society of Captives' in the Era of Hyper-Incarceration." *Theoretical Criminology* 4, no. 3 (2000): 285–308.

―――. *Governing through Crime: How the War on Crime Transformed American Democracy and Created a Culture of Fear.* Oxford: Oxford University Press, 2007.

Smart, Carol. *Feminism and the Power of Law.* London: Routledge, 1989.

Smith, Sarah. "Grievous or Gratifying? Inmate Grievance Processes and Justice in a California Women's Prison." PhD diss., Department of Criminology, Law and Society, University of California, Irvine, 2012.

Sparks, J.R., and A.E. Bottoms. "Legitimacy and Order in Prisons." *British Journal of Sociology* 46, no. 1 (1995): 45–62.

Sparks, Richard. "Can Prisons Be Legitimate? Penal Politics, Privatization, and the Timeliness of an Old Idea." *British Journal of Criminology* 34 (1994): 14–28.

Sparks, Richard, Anthony E. Bottoms, and Will Hay. *Prisons and the Problem of Order.* Oxford: Clarendon Press, 1996.

Steffensmeier, Darrell, Jeffrey Ulmer, and John Kramer. "The Interaction of Race, Gender, and Age in Criminal Sentencing: The Punishment Cost of Being Young, Black, and Male." *Criminology* 36, no. 4 (1998): 763–97.

St. John, Paige. "Health Order Targets New Prison," *Los Angeles Times*, February 5, 2014, AA1, AA6.

Stuntz, William J. *The Collapse of American Criminal Justice.* Cambridge, MA: Harvard University Press, 2011.

Swidler, Ann. "Culture in Action: Symbols and Strategies." *American Sociological Review* 51, no. 2 (1986): 273–86.

Sykes, Gresham M. *The Society of Captives: A Study of a Maximum Security Prison.* Princeton, NJ: Princeton University Press, 1958.

Thompson, Christie. "Are California Prisons Punishing Based on Race?" *ProPublica*, April 12, 2013, www.propublica.org/article/are-california-prisons-punishing-inmates-based-on-race.

Useem, Bert, and Peter Kimball. *States of Siege: US Prison Riots, 1971–1986..* New York: Oxford University Press, 1989.

Vaid, Urvashi. *Virtual Equality: The Mainstreaming of Gay & Lesbian Liberation.* New York: Anchor Books, 1995.

Wacquant, Loïc. "Deadly Symbiosis: When Ghetto and Prison Meet and Mesh." *Punishment & Society* 3, no. 1 (2001): 95–133.

———. "The Curious Eclipse of Prison Ethnography in the Age of Mass Incarceration." *Ethnography* 3 (2002): 371–98.

———. "Class, Race & Hyperincarceration in Revanchist America." *Daedalus* 139, no. 3 (2010): 74–90.

Wakefield, Sara, and Christopher Uggen. "Incarceration and Stratification." *Annual Review of Sociology* 36 (2010): 387–406.

Ward, Geoff. *The Black Child-Savers: Racial Democracy and American Juvenile Justice.* Chicago: University of Chicago Press, 2012.

Weaver, Vesla M. "Frontlash: Race and the Development of Punitive Crime Policy." *Studies in American Political Development* 21 (2007): 230–65.

Weed, Frank. *Certainty of Justice: Reform in the Crime Victim Movement.* New York: Aldine, 1995.

Weinreb, Alexander A. "The Limitations of Stranger-Interviews in Rural Kenya." *American Sociological Review* 71, no. 6 (2006): 1014–39.

Western, Bruce. *Punishment and Inequality in America.* New York: Russell Sage Foundation, 2006.

White, Lucie E. "Subordination, Rhetorical Survivor Skills, and Sunday Shoes: Notes on the Hearing of Mrs. G." *Buffalo Law Review* 38, no. 1 (1990): 1–58.

Williams, Patricia. *The Alchemy of Race and Rights: Diary of a Law Professor.* Cambridge, MA: Harvard University Press, 1991.

Williams, Randall. *The Divided World: Human Rights and Its Violence.* Minneapolis: University of Minnesota Press, 2010.

Wilson, William Julius. *The Bridge over the Racial Divide: Rising Inequality and Coalition Politics.* Berkeley: University of California Press, 1999.

Yngvesson, Barbara. *Virtuous Citizens, Disruptive Subjects: Order and Complaint in a New England Court.* New York: Routledge, 1993.

Young, Alford A., Jr. *The Minds of Marginalized Black Men: Making Sense of Mobility, Opportunity, and Life Chances.* Princeton, NJ: Princeton University Press, 2004.

Young, Kathryne M. "Rights Consciousness in Criminal Procedure: A Theoretical and Empirical Inquiry." *Sociology of Crime Law and Deviance* 12 (2009): 67–95.

Index

prison *(continued)*
nature of, 17–18, 112, 189–91; reception centers at, 40, 210n19; reform groups in, 211n26; rights consciousness in, 55; safety/security as goal of, 113–15, 185, 218n11; as site of law, 55, 71–75, 77–79, 182–83; as site of punishment, 218n10; as "total institution," 55, 73–74, 151
prison conditions: deplorable nature of, 188–89, 191, 192, 206n5; Eighth Amendment as applicable to, 6, 205n2; hunger strikes for improvements in, 211n26; overcrowding, 170; PLRA and, 28
prison conditions grievances, 38, 43, 56–58, 77, 120–21, 170
prisoner lawsuits, 25–28, 46, 47, 171, 208–9n3, 209n4, 218n10
prisoners' rights movement, 13, 24–25, 46, 218n13
prison fieldwork, 7, 188, 206nn6–7
prison grievance system/process: conflicting logics in, 3–5; legal mandate for, 4; prisoner view of, 2; staff view of, 2–3. *See also* 602 process (CDCR grievance process)
Prison Litigation Reform Act (PLRA; 1996): congressional hearings on, 206n5; consequences of, 28; court upholding of, 29–30; criticisms of, 28–29; exhaustion requirement of, 29–31, 70, 209n7; "frivolous" prisoner lawsuits and, 26–28, 30–31, 46, 208–9n3; inmate grievance filings following, 19, 47, 79; internal dispute resolution and, 46–47; passage of, 6, 25–26, 46; prison grievance system established by, 3, 31–37; provisions of, 27–28, 29; punishment focus following passage of, 218n10; rights consciousness and, 47–48, 79
prison riots, 94, 95, 101–2, 208n1
prison staff, research studies on, 98, 216n1
procedural justice frames, 152, 173
Procunier, R.K., 33
programmatic grievances, 38, 41–42, 56, 77
property grievances, 2, 36–37, 38, 40–41, 50, 56, 59–60, 62, 68–69, 77, 82–83, 120–21, 123, 126, 141–42, 151, 164, 175, 215n27
Provine, Doris Marie, 15, 132
pruno, 216n6

Quinones, Sam, 212n5

race: in California prisons, 18, 112, 208nn25–26; grievance filing rates and, 64, 212–13n10; interviewer effects and, 206–7n10; in legal encounters, 132; prisoners and, 190, 211–12n4; prison "operational realities" and, 112; prison staff and, 105, 128
racial economic justice, 78
racism, 114–15, 124, 190
Rafter, Nicole H., 114
Ramirez, Luis, 72, 74, 78
Reese, Stephen D., 206–7n10
Regents of The University of California v. Bakke, 14
Rehnquist, William, 26, 28
Reiman, Jeffrey, 132
release dates, 69, 120–21, 123, 143–44
religious rights, 109, 112–13, 152, 160, 174, 190, 209n6
repeat offender laws, 82
Republican Party, 25
researcher effects, 206–7n10
restraint policies, 206n5
retaliation, 31, 35–36, 52
Reyes, Sandy, 36, 117
Rhodes, Lorna A., 7, 9–10, 62, 98, 207n10
Rhodes v. Chapman, 205n2
Rideau, Wilbert, 67
"Rights and Responsibility" form, 35–36
rights consciousness: carceral logic and, 22, 74–75, 146, 181, 184–85, 187; grievance filing as, 4, 77–79; law in prison and, 55; mass incarceration and, 3; PLRA and, 47–48, 79; prison grievance systems and, 216–17n2; research studies on, 52–53; 602 process and, 178–79
Rivera, Ronaldo, 154–55, 162
Roberts, John, 30
Robinson, Brandon, 18
Romer v. Evans, 14
Rosenberg, Gerald N., 12, 13, 14, 78
Rostaing, C., 215n29
Rowan, Brian, 116
Rubin, Edward L., 25
Rubio, José, 156–57, 160, 162
Rules of Appellate Procedure, 28
Russell, Richard, 13

safety, 4–5, 113–15
Sainsbury, Roy, 21
same-sex marriages, 14
Sanchez, Anthony, 101, 102–3, 122, 133
Sanchez, Daniel, 90, 92–93